Fauquier County, Virginia

Minute Book Abstracts

1767–1769

Ruth and Sam Sparacio

HERITAGE BOOKS
2020

HERITAGE BOOKS
AN IMPRINT OF HERITAGE BOOKS, INC.

Books, CDs, and more—Worldwide

For our listing of thousands of titles see our website
at
www.HeritageBooks.com

Published 2019 by
HERITAGE BOOKS, INC.
Publishing Division
5810 Ruatan Street
Berwyn Heights, Md. 20740

International Standard Book Number
Paperbound: 978-1-68034-487-5

FAUQUIER COUNTY, VIRGINIA
MINUTE BOOK
1764-1768

p. 339 - At a Court continued and held for Fauquier County the 24th day of November 1767

Present JOSEPH BLACKWELL, WILLIAM BLACKWELL, ARMISTEAD CHURCHHILL, JEREMIAH DARNALL and JOSEPH HUDNALL Gent.

- DANIEL FLOWREE, Plt. agt. VALENTINE FLYNN, Feft. In Case

The persons appointed to settle all matters in difference between the parties relating to this Cause, returned their report in these words, "To all to whom these presents may come, we JOHN BELL and WILLIAM EDMONDS being appointed by Fauquier County Court to settle and determine a certain matter in dispute depending between DANIEL FLOWREE Plt. and VALENTINE FLYNN, Deft., having deliberately heard and understood their allegations and proofs of both the said parties, do arbitrate decree and judge that the said VALENTINE FLYNN pay unto the said DANIEL FLOWREE his heirs Exors &c., the sum of five pounds current money of Virginia and the costs of suit in this behalf expended; Witness our hands and seals this 27th day of October 1767. JOHN BELL S. S. WILLIAM EDMONDS, S. S." Wherefore it is considered by the Court that the Plt. recover against the said Deft. the said five pounds and his costs by him in this behalf expended & the said Deft. in mercy, &c.

- CHARLES DICK, Plt. agt. JOHN CRUMP, Deft. In Case

This day came the Plt. by his Attorney and came also WILLIAM BLACKWELL, Gent. who became Special Bail and Pledge for the Defendant in this case, and the said Deft. by CUTHBERT BULLITT, his Attorney, pray and has leave to imparl specially to the Plts. Declaration untill the next Court & then to plead

- Present. WILLIAM EUSTACE, Gent.

- On the motion of JOSEPH HUDNALL, Gent., leave is granted him to clear a bridle way from his House to the Courthouse

- MARTIN HARDIN, Plt. agt. JOHN ARISS, Deft. In Debt

This suit abates, the Sherif having returned that the Deft. is no Inhabitant of this County

p. 340 Fauquier County Court 24th of November 1767

- DAVID DALYELL, GEORGE OSWALLD & COMPY, Plts. agt. MARY ISHAM KIRK, Deft. In Debt

This day came the Plts. by their Attorney & came also THOMAS KEITH and became Special Bail and Pledge for the Defendant in this suit, and the said Deft. by CUTHBERT BULLITT, her Attorney, prays Oyer of the Writing in the Declaration mentioned and to her it is granted &c.

- JOHN ROUSSAU, Plt. agt. JAMES WINN, Deft. In Case

This day came the Plt. by his Attorney and came allso MINOR WINN who became Special Bail and Pledge for the Deft. in this suit, and the said Deft. by his Attorney prays and has leave to imparl specially to the Plts. Declaration untill the next Court and then to plead

- WILLIAM ELLZEY, Plt. agt. JOHN REDMAN, Deft. In Debt

This day came the Plt. in his proper person and the said Defendant altho solemnly called came not but made default, Therefore it is considered by the Cour that the Order of the last Court against the said Defendant be confirmed and that the Plt. recover against the said Deft. six pounds, twelve shillings and four pence, the Debt in the Declaration mentioned & his costs by him in this behalf expended & the said Deft. in mercy &c., But this Judgment is to be discharged by the paiment of three pounds six shillings and two pence with Interest thereon to be computed after the rate of five per centum per annum from the twenty sixth day of June 1765 till paid and the costs

- GEORGE WILLSON, Plt. agt. JAMES WINN, Deft. In Debt

This day came the Plt. by his Attorney and came also MINOR WINN and became Special Bail and Pledge for the Deft. in this suit, and the said Defendant by his Attorney prays Oyer of the Writing in the Declaration mentioned & to him it is granted &c.

- Ordered that JOHN RECTOR, JACOB RECTOR, CHARLES TAYLOR and HENRY RECTOR be summoned to appear at the next Court to shew cause why they have not returned their report on the Road they were appointed to view

p. Fauquier County Court 24th of November 1767

341 - The persons appointed to view a way from YOUNGs Old Field into the Old County Road by WILLIAM ROUSSAUs returned their report in these words, "In Obedience to an Order of Fauquier Court bearing date September 1767, We JOHN CATLETT, GEORGE TURBEFIELD KENNER & GEORGE CROSBY have viewed the way purposed by ORIGINALL YOUNG and others and we find it a very convenient way for the upper Inhabitants to AQUIA WHAREHOUSE and the people of the lower part of Fauquier County to ELK RUN CHURCH, and to Fauquier Courthouse, that is to say, from YOUNGs Old Field to said EDWARD LARRANCEs Cornfield Fence on TOWN RUN, thence over the said Run up the side of the said LARRANCEs Pasture Fence, thence in a Lane between ROBERT and RICHARD LUTTRILLs, thence from the Lane a strait course to a Branch beyond RICHARD LUTTRILLs where the present Path now crosses is partly on the present Path goes into the Old County Road. WILLIAM ROUSSAU, JOHN CATLETT, GEO. TURB: KENNER, GEORGE CROSBY." It is ordered that the said Road be established according to the said Report

- RICHARD TUTT, JUNR., Plt. agt. JOHN JETT, Deft. In Case

This day came as well the Plt. by his Attorney as the Deft. in his proper person and the said Defendant acknowledged the Plts. action against him for twelve pounds, two shillings and three pence. Therefore it is considered by the Court that the Plt. recover against the said Deft. the said twelve pounds, two shillings and three pence & his costs by him in this behalf expended, and the said Defendant in mercy, &c.

- CUMBERLAND WILLSON, Plt. agt. JOHN HAMMITT, Deft. In Case

This suit abates, the Sherif haveing returned that the Deft. is no Inhabitant of this County

- Present. WILLIAM EDMONDS)
- Absent. WILLIAM EUSTACE) Gent.

- Ordered that the Church Wardens of Hamilton Parish bind WILLIAM MULLRONY to ALEXANDER JAMESON who is to learn him the Trade of a Carpenter

- ORIGINALL YOUNG, Plt. agt. AARON HARDWHICH, Deft. On a Petition

Judgment is granted the Plt. against the said Deft. for thirty nine pounds of tobacco and one pound two shillings and his costs by him in this behalf expended

p. Fauquier County Court 24th of November 1767

342 - EDWARD ONEAL, Plt. agt. RAWLEIGH CHINN, Deft., On a Petition

Discontinued

- ALEXANDER WOODSIDES, Plt. agt. THOMAS GRUBBS, Deft. On a Petition
Judgment is granted the Plt. against the said Deft. for five pounds and his costs by him in this behalf expended

- PETER KAMPER, Plt. agt. WILLIAM McCLANAHAM, Deft. In Trespass, Assault & Battery
Discontinued being agreed by the parties

- PHILIP WATERFIELD, Plt. agt. THOMAS GRUBBS, Deft. On a Petition
Judgment is granted the Plt. against the said Deft. for two pounds, five shillings and fifty two pounds of tobacco and his costs by him in this behalf expended

- WILLIAM POWELL, Plt. agt. ALEXANDER PARKER, Deft. In Case
This day came the parties by their Attorneies and thereupon came also a Jury, to wit, JOHN BAILY, DAVID STIGLER, GEORGE SETTLE, WILLIAM RUSSELL, ISAAC SETTLES, JAMES FRAZER, HENRY KAMPER, WILLIAM DULING, PETER KAMPER, THOMAS POPE, JOHN HATHAWAY & WILLIAM MORGAN, who being elected tried and sworn the truth to speak upon the issue joined, upon their Oaths do say that the Defendant did assume upon himself in manner and form as the Plt. against him hath declared and they do assess the Plts. damages by means of the Defts. breach of that assumption to eight pounds, ten shillings and six pence besides his costs. Therefore it is considered by the Court that the Plt. recover against the said Deft. his damages aforesaid in form aforesaid assessed and his costs by him in this behalf expended; And the said Deft. in mercy, &c.

- ALEXANDER WODROW & JOHN NEILSON, Plts. agt. JOSHUA WELCH & THOMAS WITHERS, Defts. On a Writ of Scire Facias

p. <u>Fauquier County Court 24th of November 1767</u>
343 to revive a Judgment obtained by the Plts. against the said Defts. for five pounds six shillings and nine pence and one hundred and eighty six pounds and fifteen shillings &c.

This day came the parties by their Attorneys and thereupon came also a Jury, to wit, JOHN BAILY, DAVID STIGLER, GEORGE SETTLE, WILLIAM RUSSELL, ISAAC SETTLES, JAMES FRAZER, HENRY KAMPER, WILLIAM DULING, PETER KAMPER, THOMAS POPE JOHN HATHAWAY and WILLIAM MORGAN, who being elected tried and sworn the truth to speak upon the issue joined, upon their Oaths do say that the Defts. have not paid the said five pounds, six shillings and nine pence and one hundred and eighty six pounds of tobacco as by replying the Plts. have alledged; Therefore it is considered by the Court that the Plts. may have their execution against the said Defendants for the said five pounds, <u>one shilling</u> and nine pence & their costs by them in this behalf expended and the said Defts. in mercy, &c.

- GLASSFORD and HENDERSON, Merchants in Glasgow, Plts. agt. STEPHEN NOLAND, Deft. On an Attachment
It is considered by the Court that the Plts. recover against the said Deft. fifteen pounds, nine shillings and eleven pence three farthings and their costs by them in this behalf expended and the said Deft. in mercy, &c. And it is ordered that the residue of the money in the hands of the Sherif after satisfying a Judgment obtained by ALEXANDER FARROW against the Deft., be condemned towarded satisfying this Judgment

- The Attachment obtained by JOHN ANDERSON against the Estate of GEORGE TURNER is dismissed

- The Attachment obtained by MARTIN PICKETT against the Estate of JOHN GARNER is dismissed

- The Attachment obtained by WILLIAM CARR, Gent. against the Estate of ALEXANDER FARROW is dismissed

- THOMAS LORD FAIRFAX, Plt. agt. WILLIAM WRIGHT, Deft. On an Attachment
This day came the Plt. by his Attorney and came also JOHN WHEATLEY, the Garnishee, who being sworn declared he had not effects of the Defts. in his hands & the Attachment is continued till the next Court

- JOHN NEAVILL, Plt. agt. JOSEPH NEALE, Deft. On an Attachment
This day came the Plt. by his Attorney and came also WILLIAM ELLZEY

p. Fauquier County Court 24th of November 1767

344 and became Special Bail and Pledge for the Deft. in the Attachment, And it is ordered that the same be dismissed and that the Plt. pay to the Deft. his costs by him in this behalf expended

- SIMON MILLER, Plt. agt. JOHN MILLER, Deft. On an Attachment
This day came the Plt. by his Attorney and the Sherif haveing returned that he had attached a parcell of tobacco & one hogshead and the Deft. failing to appear and replevy the same, altho called, It is considered by the Court that the Plt. recover against the said Deft. seventeen pounds, sixteen shillings and seven pence and his costs by him in this behalf expended and the said Deft. in mercy, &., And it is ordered that the Sherif sell the attached effects and return an Account of the Sales to the Court

- The Attachment obtained by WILLIAM FIELD against the Estate of REUBIN PAYNE is dismissed

- The Attachment obtained by SIMON TRIPLETT against the Estate of THOAMS BROWN is dismissed

- The Attachment obtained by THOMAS BLACKBURN against the Estate of FRANCIS MOORE is dismissed

- THOMAS LORD FAIRFAX, Plt. agt. JOHN STONE, Deft. On an Attachment
JOHN BLACKWELL, Garnishee, being sworn declares he had three hundred and fifty four pounds of tobacco of the Defts. Estate in his hands and the Attachment is continued till the next Court

- JAMES FOLEY, Plt. agt. ALEXANDER FARROW, Deft. On an Attachment
It appearing to the Court that the Attachment and Bond are not agreeable to the Act of Assembly. It is ordered that the Attachment be dismissed, which the Plts. Attorney objected to as the Deft. nor any Attorney for him appeared to make the Exception

- Ordered that RICHARD HEALYs two Tithes and five hundred acres of Land be added to the List

p. Fauquier County Court 24th of November 1767

345 - EDWARD DOUGLASS, Plt. agt. JOHN HALEY & JOHN REED, Defts. In Debt
This day came the Plt. by his Attorney and the said Defts. not appearing tho solemnly called, It is considered by the Court that the Order of the last Court against the said Deft. and EDWARD GODFREY and ANTHONY GARRARD, their Securities, be confirmed and that the Plt. recover against the said Defts. & their said Securities six pounds current money of Virginia, the Debt in the Declaration mentioned & his costs by him in this behalf expended, & the said Defts. in mercy, &c.

- Ordered that the Court be adjourned til tomorrow morning ten of the Clock

" JOSEPH BLACKWELL "

- At a Court continued and held for Fauquier County the 25th day of November 1767

Present	JOSEPH BLACKWELL	ARMISTEAD CHURCHHILL	
	WILLIAM EDMONDS	JOSEPH HUDNALL	Gent.

- The Attachment obtained by THOMAS RENOE against the Estate of THOMAS GARNER JUNR., is dismissed

- JOHN STACY, Plt. agt. FRANCIS MOORE, Deft. On an Attachment

This Attachment is dismissed and it is ordered that the Plt. pay to the Deft. his costs by him in this behalf expended

- SIMON MILLER, agt. JOHN MILLER, Deft. On an Attachment

The Attachment obtained by the Plt. against the Estate of the said Deft. is dismissed

- DANIEL BRADFORD is appointed Surveyor of the Road from MARRS BRIDGE to COVINGTONs and it is ordered that he with the Tithes belonging to the said Road do clear and keep the same in repair according to Law

- The Attachment obtained by THOMAS STONE, JUNR., against the Estate of WILLIAM REDING is dismissed

- Messrs. ANDREW COCKRANE, WM. CUNNINGHAME & CO., Plts. agt.
THOMAS CHINN, Deft. On an Attachment

This day came the Plts. by their Attorney and the Sherif haveing returned

p. Fauquier County Court 25th of November 1767

346 that he had attached one Negro named Ned of the Defts. Estate and the Deft. failing to appear and replevy the same, altho called, it is considered by the Court that the Plts. recover against the said Deft. one hundred and fifty one pounds, twelve shillings and five pence and their costs by them in this behalf expended; And the said Deft. in mercy, &c., And it is ordered that the Sherif sell the attached effects and return an Account of the Sales to the Court

- MARTIN PICKETT & COMPANY, Plts. agt. VINCENT GARNER, Deft. In Case

By consent of the Plts. the Writ of Enquiry against the Deft. in this suit is set aside and the Deft. acknowledged the Plts. action against him for eleven pounds, thirteen shillings and six pence with Interest thereon to be computed after the rate of five per centum per annum from the eighteenth day of June 1765 till paid. Therefore it is considered by the Court that the Plts. recover against the said Deft. the said eleven pounds, thirteen shillings and six pence with Interest thereon as aforesaid & their costs by them in this behalf expended, & the said Deft. in mercy, &c.

- The Grand Jury returned into Court and made their Presentments as follows, to wit. "We the Jurors of our Sovereign Lord the King for the Count aforesaid upon our Oath present JAMES CRAIG, Clerk, JOHN CRUMP, JOSEPH BULLETT, GILLSON FOOTE and HANNAH his Wife, WILLIAM KESTERSON, THOMAS KEITH, JOHN WRIGHT, SENR., ELIZABETH PAGE, EDWARD WILLBURN, PAUL WILLIAMS, THOMAS CHINN, JOHN ANDERSON, THOMAS CONWAY, SENR., MARTIN PICKETT, JOHN HEADLY and THOMAS ALLAN of the Parish of Hamilton and County of Fauquier & LANDON CARTER of RICHMOND County and CHARLES CARTER of LANCASTER County, Executors of CHARLES CARTER, deceased, THOMAS LORD FAIRFAX of FREDERICK County, JOHN FITZHUGH of the County of STAFFORD, FRANCIS THORNTON of the County of KING GEORGE, JOHN MERCER of the County of STAFFORD and WILLIAM BERNARD of the County of WESTMORELAND and BURGES SMITH of LANCASTER County for that they did not on the tenth day of June last past or at any time before or since enter their Lands situate and lying in the County of Fauquier aforesaid, to wit, the said JAMES CRAIG two hundred acres, JOHN CRUMP, six hundred acres; JOSEPH BULLITT two hundred and seventy acres, GILLSON FOOTE and HANNAH his Wife four hundred acres belonging to their Ward, JOHN HEDGMAN, WILLIAM KESTERSON seventy acres; THOS: KEITH five hundred acres, JOHN WRIGHT, SENR. two hundred and thirty six acres, ELIZABETH PAGE one hundred acres, EDWARD MILLBURN one

p. Fauquier County Court 25th of November 1767
347 hundred acres, PAUL WILLIAMS three hundred acres; THOMAS CHINN eight hundred acres, JOHN ANDERSON five hundred and eighty five acres, THOMAS CONWAY, SENR. one hundred acres, MARTIN PICKETT one hundred acres, JOHN HEADLEY seventy acres, LANDON CARTER and CHARLES CARTER ten thousand acres belonging to the Estate of CHARLES CHARTER, deceased, THOMAS LORD FAIRFAX thirty thousand acres, JOHN FITZHUGH of the County of STAFFORD one thousand acres, FRANCIS THORNTON four hundred acres, JOHN MERCER ten thousand acres & WILLIAM BERNARD four hundred acres & BURGESS SMITH two thousand six hundred acres with one or eihter of the Justices appointed to take the Lists of Tithables in the County aforesaid for this present year according to the Act of Assembly in that case made and provided by the knowledge of two of us;

We present JAMES CRAIG, Clerk, of the Parish of Hamilton and County of Fauquier, WILLIAM SUTTON, JAMES DAVIS, SAMUEL HADDOX, WILLIAM PICKETT, THOMAS PARKER, GEORGE BERRY, SARAH YOUNG, JOHN McNEIL, JOHN WRIGHT, SENR. JOHN CATLETT, JUNIOR, JAMES KEY, JOHN MARSHALL all of the Parish and County last mentioned for that they did not on the tenth day of June last past or at any time before or since enter their Tithables to wit, JAMES CRAIG one tithable, WILLIAM SUTTON one, JAMES DAVIS two, SAMUEL HADDOX one, WILLIAM PICKETT five, THOMAS PARKER one, GEORGE BERRY one, SARAH YOUNG six, JOHN McNEIL one, JOHN WRIGHT, SENR. five, JOHN CATLETT JUNIOR one, JAMES KEY two, JOHN MARSHALL two, JOHN MARKHAM four, with one or either of the Justices appointed to take the List thereof in the County aforesaid for the present year according to Act of Assembly in that case made and provided; by the knowledge of two of us;

We present JOHN BARTON of the Parish of Hamilton and County of Fauquier for retailing spiritous Liquors at the Parish and County mentioned without Licence and contrary to Act of Assembly within six months last past by the knowledge of two of us;

We present JOHN WHEATLEY for profane swearing at the Parish of Hamilton in the County of Fauquier within one month last past by the knowledge of two of us;

We present WILLIAM SANDERS for being drunk and profane swearing at the Parish and County last mentioned within one month last past by the knowledge of two of us;

We present BAILY JOHNSON for profane swearing at the Parish and County last mentioend within one month last past by the knowledge of two of us;

We present BRYAN OBANNON and THOMAS ELLIOTT for getting Drunk and profain swearing at the Parish and County last mentioned whitn one month last past by the knowledge of two of us;

p. Fauquier County Court 25th of November 1767
348 We present JOSHUA WELCH and FRANCIS HATTER for playing at an unlawfull game at Card in a Publick House at the Parish and County last mentioned within six months last past by the knowledge of two of us;

We present MINOR WINN for suffering unlawfull gameing, to wit, Cards in this Publick House at the Parish and County last mentioned within six months last past by the knowledge of two of us;

We present STEPHEN PRICHARD for marrying and cohabitiang with MARGARET KENNER alias PRITCHARD, Sister to his former Wife, contrary to Act of Assembly by the knowledge of two of us;

We present RICHARD HENRY LEE of WESTMORELAND County, JAMES EWELL of LANCASTER County, JAMES BALL, Guardian of BURGESS BALL, of LANCASTER County and RICHARD PAYNE of WESTMORELAND County for that they did not on the tenth day of

June last past or at any time before or since enter their Lands situate lying and being in the said County of Fauquier, to wit, RICHARD HENRY LEE twelve hundred acres, JAMES EWELL two thousand acres, JAMES BALL for BURGESS BALL's Land, his Ward, six thousand two hundred acres, RICHARD PAYNE eight hundred acres with one or either of the Justices appointed to take the List of Tithables in the County aforesaid for this present year according to the Act of Assembly in that case made and provided by the knowledge of two of us;

We present ISAAC ROBERTS, JAMES WOOD, JOHN NELSON, JUNIOR for playing at an unlawfull game at Card, to wit, in a Publick House at the Parish of Hamilton and County of Fauquier within six months last past by the knowledge of two of us;

We present the Surveyor of the Road from ELIAS EDMONDS to WILLIAM UNDER WOODs for not keeping the same in repair within six month last past by the knowledge of two of us

HENRY PEYTON, Foreman

- Ordered that the several persons presented by the Grand Jury be summoned to appear at the next Court to answer the same respectively

- Ordered that the Court be adjourned til the Court in Course

" JOSEPH BLACKWELL,"

p. 349 - At a Court held for Fauquier County the 28th day of February 1768

Present ARMISTEAD CHURCHHILL, WILLIAM EDMONDS
JOSEPH HUDNALL & JAMES SCOTT Gent.

- JOHN ROUSSAU made Oath to a Book of Accounts kept by him for CUTHBERT HARRISON which was ordered to be certified

- On the motion of GEORGE NEAVILL setting forth that he has Land on one side of CEDAR RUN and that he intends to build a Water Mill and praying that an acre of Land on the opposite side made be laid of for such use, It is ordered that the Sherif summon a Jury of twelve Freeholders of the Vicinage to meet upon the Land motioned for who having met and duly sworn before a Majistrate or the Sheriff shall diligently view and examine the said Land and Lands adjacent thereto on both sides the said Run which may be effected or laid under water by building such Mill, together with the Timber and other conveniences thereon and upon the same with the true value of such acre and of the damages to the party holding the same or to any other person or persons under their hands and seals to the Court

- Ordered that the Court be adjourned till the Court in Course

" ARMISTEAD CHURCHHILL "

- At a Court held for Fauquier County the Twenty fifth day of April 1768

Present THOMAS HARRISON, WILLIAM BLACKWELL
ARMISTEAD CHURCHHILL & JOSEPH HUDNALL Gent.

- WILLIAM ASBURY is appointed Surveyor of the Road from BROAD RUN to BARTONs Tract and it is ordered that he with the Tithes belonging to the said Road do clear and keep the same in repair according to Law

- ROBERT HINSON is appointed Surveyor of the Road in the room of PETER PEARCE and it is ordered that he with the Tithes belonging to the said Road and those belonging to JOHN ALEXANDER, do clear and keep the same in repair according to Law

- Ordered that the Sherif summon a competent number of Freeholders quallified according to Law to be impannelled and sworn a Grand Jury of Inquest for teh body of this County at the next Court

p. Fauquier County Court 25th of April 1768

350 - An Indenture of Bargain and Sale between JESSE EWELL and CHARLOTTE his Wife and JAMES EWELL and MARY his Wife of one part and ROBERT SCOTT of the other part & a Receit thereon endorsed were proved by the Oath of WILLIAM CARR a witness thereto

- The Last Will and Testament of JOHN NEAVILL, deced., was proved by the Oaths of JAMES YOUNG and ALEXANDER PARKER, witnesses thereto and ordered to be recorded; And on the motion of WILLIAM CARR, who made Oath and acknowledged a Bond as the Law directs, Certificate is granted him for obtaining Letters of Administration with the said Will annexed, the Exors. therein named haveing refused to take upon the Execution thereof

- Ordered that JOHN THORNBERRY, ALEXANDER PARKER, JAMES YOUNG and EDWARD DICKENSON or any three of them being first sworn do appraise the Estate of JOHN NEAVILL, deced., and return the appraisment to the Court

- Indentures of Lease and Release between GEORGE LAMKIN and SARAH his Wife of the one part and DANIEL JENIFER of the other part and a Receit on the said Release endorsed were acknowledged by the said GEORGE tob e his act and deed & ordered to be recorded

- An Indenture of Bargain & Sale between GAVIN LAWSON of the one part and REUBIN BRAMLETT of the other part was acknowledged by the said GAVIN to be his act and deed & ordered to be recorded

- JAMES ARNOLD is appointed Surveyor of the Road in the room of PAUL WILLIAMS and it is ordered that he with the Tithes belonging to the said Road do clear and keep the same in repair according to Law

- NEIL JAMESON & COMPANY, Plts. agt. WILLIAM TRIPLETT, Deft. In Case

This day came the Plts. by their Attorney and by their consent the Judgment and Writ of Enquiry against the said Deft. is set aside and the Deft. acknowledged the Plts. action against him for twenty two pounds, five shillings and four pence farthing. Therefore it is considered by the Court that the Plt. recover against the said Deft. the said twenty two pounds, five shillings and four pence farthing & their costs by them in this behalf expended & the said Deft. in mercy, &c., Execution stayed nine months

p. Fauquier County Court 25th of April 1768

351 - DAVID CHEVIS, Plt. agt. WILLIAM TRIPLETT, Deft. In Case

This day came the Plt. by his Attorney and by his consent the Judgment and Writ of Enquiry against the said Deft. is set aside and the said Deft. acknowledged the Plts. action against him for twenty pounds, six shillings and ten pence half penny with Interest thereon to be computed from the eighteenth day of May 1764 till paid. Therefore it is considered by the Court that the Plt. recover against the said deft. the said twenty pounds, six shillings and ten pence half penny with Interest thereon as aforesaid & his costs by him in this behalf expended & the said Deft. in mercy &c. Execution stayed twelve months

- JOHN CASEY, Assee. of WILLIAM BLACKWELL, Sherif of Fauquier County, Plt. agt. WILLIAM TRIPLETT & JOHN JETT, Defts. In Debt

This day came as well the Plt. by his Attorney as the Defts. in their proper persons and the said Defts. acknowledge the Plts. action against them. Therefore it is considered by the Court that the Plt. recover against the said Defts. one pound, thirteen shillings and two pence current money and fourteen hundred and fifty six pounds of tobacco, the Debt in the Declaration mentioned & his costs by him in this behalf expended, And the said Deft. in mercy, &c., But this Judgment is to be discharged by the paiment of sixteen shillings and seven pence and seven hundred and twenty eight pounds of tobacco with Interest to be computed after the rate of five per centum per annum from the first day of September 1767 til paid and the costs. Execution stayed twelve months

- WILLIAM CRAIGHILL, Plt. agt. JOHN JETT, Deft. On a Petition

Judgment isgratned the Plt. against the said Deft. for one thousand pounds Crop tobacco and his costs by him in this behalf expended.

- An Inventory and Appraisment of the Estate of MARY TYLER, deced., was returend and ordered to be recorded

- JAMES SHACKLEFORD is appointed Surveyor of the Road from SAMUEL THORNBERRYs to the County Line and it is ordered that he with the Tithes that shall be appointed by GILSON FOOTE, Gent., do clear and keep the same in repair according to Law

- HURIAH HULIT is appointed Surveyor of the Road from the MALL BRANCH

p. Fauquier County Court 25th of April 1768

352 to SAMUEL THORNBERRYs and it is ordered that he with the Tithes that shall be appointed by GILSON FOOTE, Gent., do clear and keep the same in repair according to Law

- On the motion of HENRY HAYNES, it is ordered that DANIEL JENIFER pay him seventy nine pounds of tobaco for one days attendance, comeing eighteen miles and returning, as a witness to prove Deeds from GEORGE LAMKIN and SARAH his Wife to the said JENIFER

- On the motion of WILLIAM WILLSON, it is ordered that DANIEL JENIFER pay him seventy nine pounds of tobacco for one days attendance, comeing eighteen miles and returning as a Witness to proved Deeds from GEORGE LAMKIN and SARAH his Wife to the said JENIFER

- An Inventory and Appraisment of the Estate of MARY TYLER, deced., was returned and ordered to be recorded

- JOHN RALLS, Plt. agt. JOHN CUMMINS, Deft. On an Attachment

This day came the Plt. by his Attorney and it appearing to the Court that there had been a Cow and Calf of the value of fifty shillings in the hands of SIMON CUMMINS, the Garnishee, which was imbezelled, It is considered by the Court that the Plt. recover against the said Deft. ten pounds, sixteen shillings and a penny half penny & his costs by him in this behalf expended; & the said Deft. in mercy, &c. And it is ordered that the value of the said Cow and Calf be condemned in the hands of the said Garnishee towards satisfying this Judgment

- Absent. ARMISTEAD CHURCHHILL)
- Present WILLIAM EDMONDS & GILSON FOOTE) Gent.

- A Lease from RICHARD HENRY LEE to MARTIN PICKETT was proved by the Oaths of JAMES CRAIG, JOSEPH BLACKWELL and FRANCIS ATWELL, witnesses thereto, and ordered to be recorded

- A Commission for takeing the acknowledgment and privy examination of ALICE, the Wife of BURGES SMITH, on a certain Deed made by the said BURGES SMITH and ALICE his Wife to JAMES BALL and a Certificate of the

p. Fauquier County Court 25th of April 1768

353 Execution thereof was returned and ordered to be recorded

- A Commission for taking the acknowledgment and privy examination of ALICE the Wife of BURGES SMITH in a certain Deed made between the said BURGES SMITH and

ALICE his Wife to JOHN RECTOR and a Certificate of the Execution thereof was returned and ordered to be recorded

- A Lease from RICHARD HENRY LEE to MARTIN PICKETT was proved by the Oaths of JOSEPH BLACKWELL and JOSEPH WILLIAMS, witnesses thereto, and ordered to be recorded

- On the motion of HENRY TYLER against JOHN WRIGHT, late Sherif of PRINCE WILLIAM County, for fees put into his Under Sherifs hands to collect, it is ordered that the same be dismist with costs and a Lawyers fee

- JOHN COMBS, JUNR. is appointed a Constable in this County in the room of JOSHUA TULLOS and it is ordered that he take the Oaths prescribed by Law before a Justice of this County

- EUPHIMA DAVIS, Plt. agt. PHILIP DAVIS, Deft. In Chancery
Discontinued, being agreed by the parties

- Messieurs WILLIAM CHILE & JAMES CRAP, Plts. agt. JOHN ALLAN, Deft.
Upon a Writ of Scire Facias to revive a Judgment obtained by the Plts. against the said Deft. for two pounds, one shillling and six pence half penny with Interest thereon to be computed after the rate of five per centum per annum from the first day of July 1763 till paid for Debt, and also one hundred and eighty two pounds of tobacco and fifteen shillings or one hundred and fifty pounds of tobacco
It is considered by the Court that the Plts. may have their Execution against the said Deft. for the Debt and Costs aforesaid according to the force form and effect of the recovery aforesaid and that they recover against the said Deft. their costs by them in this behalf expended and the said Deft. in mercy, &c.

- ALEXANDER WOODSIDES, Plt. agt. ALEXANDER BRADFORD, Deft.
In Trespass, Assault and Battery
Agreed, the Deft. paying costs

p. Fauquier County Court 25th of April 1768

354 - MARTIN PICKETT and COMPANY, Plts. agt. REUBIN BRAGG, Deft. In Case
Agreed, the Defendant paying costs

- CHARLES COLVIN, Plt. agt. RICHARD LUTTRILL, Deft.
In Trespass, Assault and Battery
Discontinued being agreed by the parties

- MARTIN PICKETT, Plt. agt. GEORGE BOSWELL, Deft. In Debt
This day came the Plt. by his Attorney and came also WILLIAM BOSWELL and became Special Bail and Pledge for the Deft. in this suit, and the said Deft. prays Oyer of the Writing Obligatory in the Declaration mentioned and to him it is granted &c.

- PHILIP JACOB IRION, Plt. agt. JOHN HEIRMANS, Deft. In Debt
This day came the Plt. by his Attorney and came also WILLIAM HUTCHINSON and became Special Bail and Pledge for the Deft. in this suit and the said Deft. acknowledged the action of the Plt. against him. Therefore it is considered by the Court that the Plt. recover against the said Deft. thirty six pounds, eight shillings, the Debt in the Declaration mentioned, and his costs by him in this behalf expended, And the said Deft. in mercy, &c., But this Judgment is to be discharged by the paiment of eighteen pounds, four shillings current money of Virginia with Interest thereon to be computed after the rate of five per centum per annum from the first day of December 1766 till paid and the costs. Execution stayed six months

- FRANCIS HACKLEY, Plt. agt. PETER GRANT, Deft. In Case
Discontinued, being agreed by the parties

- FRANCIS HACKLEY, Plt. agt. JAMES BROWN, Deft. On a Petition
Discontinued, being agreed by the parties
- Ordered that THOMAS HARRISON pay WILLIAM PICKETT

p. Fauquier County Court 25th of April 1768
355 seventeen pounds, ten shillings, it being in full for building a PRISON for this County
- Ordered that the Church Wardens of Hamilton Parish bind WILLIAM GRAVES to JOHN HATHAWAY who is to learn him the Trade of a Carpenter and House Joiner
- Messrs. ANDREW COCKRANE, WILLIAM CUNNINGHAME, and COMPANY, Plts. agt. JOHN HEADLY, Defts. In Case
This day came the Plts. by their Attorney and came also THOMAS HATHAWAY and became Special Bail and Pledge for the Deft. in this suit, and the said Deft. prays and has leave to imparl specially to the Plts. Declaration untill the next Court and then to plead
- JOHN RALLS, Plt. agt. ALEXANDER CUMMINS, Deft. On a Petition
Judgment is granted the Plt. against the said Deft. for two pounds, five shillings and his costs by him in this behalf expended
- The Same, Plt. agt. PETER CUMMINS, Deft. On a Petition
Judgment is granted the Plt. against the said Deft. for his costs by him in this behalf expended
- The Same, Plt. agt. CHARLES COLVILL, Deft. On a Petition
Judgment is granted the Plt. against the said Deft. for one pound, two pence and his costs by him in this behalf expended
- The Same, Plt. agt. WILLIAM FOOTE, Deft. On a Petition
Judgment is granted the Plt. against the said Deft. for three pounds, one shilling and eight pence and his costs by him in this behalf expended
- The Same, Plt. agt. THOMAS BRIDEWELL, Deft. On a Petition
Judgment is granted the Plt. against the said Deft. for two pounds, five shillings and one penny half penny with Interest thereon to be computed after the rate of five per centum per annum from the twelvth

p. Fauquier County Court 25th of April 1768
356 day of December 1767 till paid and his costs by him in this behalf expended
- Ordered that the Court be adjourned till the Court in Course
" WILLIAM BLACKWELL "

- At a Court held for Fauquier County the 23d day of May 1768
Present JOHN BELL, ARMISTEAD CHURCHHILL
JAMES SCOTT, JUNR. & JAMES BELL Gent.

- WILLIAM GRANT, Gent., is appointed to take the List of Tithes this year in the same precinct this year where WILLIAM EUSTACE, Gent. took them last year
- ARMISTEAD CHURCHHILL, Gent. in the room of JEREMIAH DARNALL, Gent.
- JAMES SCOTT, Gent. in the room of WILLIAM EDMONDS, Gent.
- Ordered that the Court be adjourned till tomorrow morning ten of the Clock
" JOHN BELL "

- At a Court continued and held for Fauquier County the 24th day of May 1768
Present JOSEPH BLACKWELL ARMISTEAD CHURCHHILL
JEREMIAH DARNALL & JOSEPH HUDNALL Gent.

- Ordered that THOMAS HARRISON, Gent. pay the several County Creditors their respective money claims out of the money which is in his hands

- a Lease from THOMAS LORD FAIRFAX to RICHARD CRAWLEY was proved by the Oaths of JAMES SCOTT, HUMPHREY BROOKE and MARTIN PICKETT witnesses thereto & ordered to be recorded

p. Fauquier County Court 24th of May 1768

357 - A Lease from THOMAS LORD FAIRFAX to WILLIAM ORGAN was proved by the Oaths of JAMES SCOTT, HUMPHREY BROOKE and MARTIN PICKETT, witnesses thereto, and ordered to be recorded

- A Lease from THOMAS LORD FAIRFAX to HENRY JONES was proved by the Oaths of JAMES SCOTT, HUMPHREY BROOKE and MARTIN PICKETT, witnesses thereto, and ordered to be recorded

- A Lease from THOMAS LORD FAIRFAX to JOHN ALLIS was proved by the Oaths of JAMES SCOTT, HUMPHREY BROOKE and MARTIN PICKETT, witnesses thereto, and ordered to be recorded

- A Lease from THOMAS LORD FAIRFAX to GEORGE SETTLE was proved by the Oaths of JAMES SCOTT, HUMPHREY BROOKE and MARTIN PICKETT, witnesses thereto, and ordered to be recorded

- A Lease from THOMAS LORD FAIRFAX to WILLIAM FLETCHER was proved by the Oaths of JAMES SCOTT, HUMPHREY BROOKE and MARTIN PICKETT, witnesses thereto, and ordered to be recorded

- Articles of Agreement between JAMES SCOTT, Clerk, and JAMES SCOTT, JUNIOR were acknowledged by the parties and ordered to be recorded

- A Release from JAMES SCOTT, JUNIOR to JAMES SCOTT, Clerk, was acknowledged by the said JAMES SCOTT, JUNIOR and ordered to be recorded

- Indenture of Lease and Release between JOHN DUNCAN, JUNIOR and DINAH his Wife of the one part and THOMAS POPE of the other part and Receit thereon endorsed were proved by the Oaths of EDWARD NEWGATE, THOMAS BENNITT and JAMES ARNOLD, witnesses thereto, to be the act and deed of the said JOHN DUNCAN and the same were acknowledged by the said DINAH his Wife, (she being first privily examined as the Law directs) and ordered to be recorded

- A Deed from JAMES SCOTT, Clerk, and SARAH his Wife to JAMES SCOTT, JUNIOR was acknowledged by the said JAMES SCOTT, Clerk, and SARAH his Wife (she being first privily examined as the Law directs) and ordered to be recorded

p. Fauquier County Court 24th of May 1768

358 - Absent. JEREMIAH DARNALL)
- Present. JAMES SCOTT) Gent.

- On the motion of JOHN MORGAN, Licence is granted him to keep ORDINARY at his House in this County for one year, he haveing executed and acknowledged Bond as the Law directs

- GAVIN LAWSON, Plt. agt. BENJAMIN TURNER, Deft. In Debt

This day came as well the Plt. by his Attorney as the Deft. in his proper person and the said Deft. acknowledged the action of the Plt. against him. Therefore it is considered by the Court that the Plt. recover against the said Deft. seven pounds, four shillings, the Debt in the Declaration mentioned, and his costs by him in this behalf expended, and the said Deft. in mercy, &c., But this Judgment is to be discharged by the paiment of three pounds, twelve shillings with Interest thereon to be computed after the rate of five per centum per annum from the eighteenth day of August 1767 till paid and the costs. Execution to be stayed till the twenty fifth day of December next

- On the motion of THOMAS BOGGES, Licence is granted him to keep ORDINARY at his House in this County for one year, he haveing executed and acknowledged Bond as the Law directs

- ARCHIBALD RITCHIE, Plt. agt. JOHN CONNOR, Deft. In Debt

This day came the Plt. by his Attorney and came also JOHN SMITH and became Special Bail and Pledge for the Deft. in this suit, and the said Defendant prays Oyer of the Writing in the Declaration mentioned and to him it is granted, &c.

- A Lease from RICHARD HENRY LEE to MARTIN PICKETT was proved by the Oath of JAMES WINN, a witness thereto and ordered to be recorded

- The persons appointed to view the Road petitioned for by WILLIAM

p. <u>Fauquier County Court 24th of May 1768</u>

359 KIRK returned their Report in these words, "In Obedience to an Order of Court to us directed, we the subscribers being first sworn have viewed the alteration in the Road that leads by Mr. KIRKs and find it convenient to take out of the Old Road near SOUTH RUN and continue Mr. KIRKs Line to the said Road near JOSEPH BAYLEYs where we split some bushes and then continue the Old Road to the Courthouse. Given under our hands this twenty fourth day of May 1768." WHARTN. RANSDELL, WM: RANSDELL, CHAS: MOREHEAD. And it is ordered that the said Road be established according to the Report

- WILLIAM STAMPS is appointed Surveyor of the Road in the room of CHARLES MOREHEAD and it is ordered that he with the Tithes belonging to the said Road do clear and keep the same in repair according to Law

- JOHN SUDDOTH is appointed Surveyor of the Road in the room of BEN WOOD and it is ordered that he with the Tithes belonging to teh said Road do clear and keep the same in repair according to Law

- GARNER BURGES is appointed Surveyor of the Road in the room of BENJAMIN POPE and it is ordered that he with the Tithes belonging to the said Road do clear and keep ths ame in repair according to Law

- JOHN & WILLIAM KNOX, Plt. agt. JOHN CONNOR, Deft. In Debt

This day came the Plt. by his Attorney and came also THOMAS WATTS and became Special Bail and Pledge for the Deft. in this suit, and the said Deft. by GEORGE BRENT, his Attorney, prays Oyer of the Writing in the Declaration mentioend

- BUSHORD DOGGETT, Foreman, JOHN KAMPER, HENRY KAMPER, THOMAS AYRES JACOB KAMPER, HARMAN BUTTON, JAMES CROCKETT, CHARLES MARTIN, JOHN BAILY, FREDERICK BURDITT, NATHANIEL DODD, WILLIAM GIBSON, JOHN SINCLAIR, JOHN HOPPER and BENJAMIN BALL were sworn a Grand Jury of Inquest for the body of this County and haveing received their charge withdrew to consider of their Presentments and after some time returned into Court and presented the Surveyor of the Road from the top of the NAKED MOUNTAIN to the top of (   ) BRIDGE for not keeping the same in repair according to Law within six months last past;

The Surveyor of the Road from CORBINS OLD MILL to GREAT RUN for not keeping the same in repair according to Law within six months

p. <u>Fauquier County Court 24th of May 1768</u>

360 last past, and

THOMAS BENNITT for profane swearing at Hamilton Parish in this County within two months;

And haveing nothing further to present were discharged

- BEN WOOD is appointed Surveyor of the Road in the room of JOHN RENOLDS and it is ordered that he with the Tithes belonging to the said Road do clear and keep the same in repair according to Law

- Ordered that the several persons presented by the Grand Jury be summoned to appear at the next Court to answer the same respectively

- Present. WILLIAM EDMONDS, Gent.

- Messieurs BOGLEs and COMPANY, Plts. agt. GEORGE RANKINS Deft. In Debt

This day came the Plts. by their Attorney and the said Deft. altho solemnly called came not but made default, Therefore it is considered by the Court that the Order of the last Court against the said Deft. and THOMAS ALLAN, his Security,b e confirmed and that the Plt. recover against the said Deft. twenty six pounds, eighteen shillings and eleven pency current money, the Debt in the Declaration mentioned, and their costs by them in this behalf expended, And the said Deft. in mercy, &c. But this Judgment is to be discharged by the payment of thirteen pounds, nine shillings and five pence, half penny with Interest thereon to be computed after the rate of five per centum per annum from the ninth day of May 1767 till paid and the costs

- WODROW and COMPAY, Plts. agt. BEDE JOHNSON, Deft. In Debt

This suit abates, the Sherif haveing returned that the Deft. is no Inhabitants of this County

- ALEXANDER WODROW, Admor. &c. of NIMROD ASHBY, Plt. agt.
ANDREW DAVIS, Deft. In Debt

This day came the Plt. by his Attorney and the said Deft. altho solemnly called came not but made default. Therefore it is considered by the Court that the Order of the last Court against the said Deft. and ANDREW DAVIS, SENIOR, his Security, be confirmed and that the Plt. recover against the

p. Fauquier County Court 24th of May 1768

361 said Deft. and the said ANDREW DAVIS, ten pounds, eight shillings, the Debt in the Declaration mentioned, and his costs by him in this behalf expended, And the said Deft. in mercy, &c., But this Judgment is to be discharged by the paiment of five pounds, four shillings Virginia currency with Interest thereon to be computed after the rate of five per centum per annum from the fourteenth day of March 1765 till paid and the costs

- THOMAS JETT, Assignee of ANDREW MONROE, Plt. agt. MARY SMITH, Deft.
In Debt

This day came the Plt. by his Attorney and came also AUGUSTINE SMITH and became Special Bail and Pledge for the Deft. in this suit, and the said Deft. by CUTHBERT BULLITT, her Attorney, prays Oyer of the Writing in the Declaration mentioned and she hath it, &c.

- JOHN JOHNSON, Assignee of WILLIAM BLACKWELL, Gent., Late Sherif of Fauquier County, Plt. agt. WILLIAM WOOD, Deft. In Debt

This suit abates, the Sherif haveing returned that the Defendant is no Inhabitant of this County

- ROBERT BRENT, Plt. agt. COSSOM HORTON, Deft. In Debt

This day came the Plt. by his Attorney and the said Deft. although solemnly called came not but made default. Therefore it is considered by the Court that the Order of the last Court against the said Deft. and JOHN HARRILL, his Security, be confirmed and that the Plt. recover against the said Deft. and the said JOHN HARRILL, eleven pounds, fourteen shillings and four pence, the Debt in the Declaration mentioned and his costs by him in this behalf expended, And the said Deft. in mercy, &c., But this Judgment is to be discharged by the payment of five pounds, seventeen shillings and two pence with Interest thereon to be computed after the rate of five per centum per annum from the first day of October 1765 till paid and the costs

- THOMAS RENOE, Plt. agt. THOMAS GARNER, JUNR., Deft. In Case

This day came the parties by their Attorneys and came also JOHN OREAR and JOHN ALLAN and became Special Bail and Pledge for the Deft. in this suit and the said Deft.

p. Fauquier County Court 24th of May 1768

362 defends the force and injury when &c. and pleads non assumpsit and the Trial of the issue is refered till the next Court

- JOSEPH KING, Plt. agt. JOHN RENOLDS and BENJAMIN POPE, Defts. In Debt

This day came the Plt. by his Attorney and the said Deft., BENJAMIN POPE, altho solemnly called came not but made default. Therefore it is considered by the Court that the Order of the last Court against the said Deft. and WILLIAM FOOTE, his Security, be confirmed and that the Plt. recover against the said Deft., POPE, and the said WILLIAM FOOTE, six pounds current money of Virginia, the Debt in the Declaration mentioned, and his costs by him in this behalf expended, And the said Deft. in mercy, &c., And this suit abates against RENOLDS

- On the motion of ELIZABETH RENNOLDS, who made Oath and executed and acknowledged Bond as the Law directs, Certificate is granted her for obtaining Letters of Administration of the Estate of JOHN RENNOLDS, deced.

- Ordered that THOMAS MARSHALL, JOHN SMITH, WILLIAM MARSHALL and WILLIAM SEATON or any three of them being first sworn do appraise the Estate of JOHN RENOLDS, deced., and return the appraisment to the Court

- JOHN GRAY and COMPANY, Plts. agt. WILLIAM TRIPLETT, Deft. In Case

This dayc ame the Plts. by their Attorney and came also JOHN JETT and became Special Bail and Pledge for the Deft. in this suit, and the said Deft. acknowledged the Plts. action against him for five pounds, sixteen shillings and eight pence. Therefore it is considered by the Court that the Plts. recover against the said Deft. the said five pounds, sixteen shillings and eight pence and their costs by them in this behalf expended, and the said Deft. in mercy, &c. Execution stayed till December Court

- MARTIN PICKETT Plt. agt. GEORGE BOSWELL, Deft. In Debt

This day came as well the Plt. by his Attorney as the said Deft. in

p. Fauquier County Court 24th of May 1768

363 his proper person and the said Deft. acknowledged the Plts. action against him for one hundred pounds with Interest thereon to be computed after the rate of five per centum per annum from the first day of November1767 till paid. Therefore it is considered by the Court that the Plt. recover against the said Deft. the said one hundred pounds with Interest as aforesaid and his costs by him in this behalf expended, And the said Deft. in mercy, &c., Execution stayed til first of October next

- Absent. WILLIAM EDMONDS)
- Present. JOHN MOFFETT) Gent.

- A Deed and Receit from JACOB HAYES and KATEY his Wife to WILLIAM STAMPS and ABRAHAM DODSON were acknowledged by the said JACOB HAYES and KATEY his Wife, she being first privily examined as the Law directs, to be their act and deed and ordered to be recorded

- An Indenture between ELIJAH NASH of the one part and ROBERT SANDERS of the other part was acknowledged by the parties and ordered to be recorded

ANN CLAYTON, Admrx. of SAMUEL PANNILL, deced., Plt. agt. JOHN WHEATLEY, Deft. In Case

This day came the Plt. by her Attorney and came also JAMES WHEATLEY and became Special Bail and Pledge for the Deft. in this suit, and the said Deft. prays and has leave to imparl specially to the Plts. Declaration at the next Court and then to plead

- JOHN BALLENDINE, Plt. agt. CHARLES TRIPLETT, Deft. In Debt

This suit abates, the Sherif haveing returned that the Deft. is no Inhabitant of this County

- JOHN TAYLOR, Plt. agt. WILLIAM BALL, Deft., In Debt

This day camethe Plt. by his Attorney and came also THOMAS MARSHALL and became Special Bail and Pledge for the Deft. in this suit and the said Deft. by CUTHBERT BULLITT, his Attorney, prays Oyer of the Writing in the Declaration mentioned and to him it is granted &c.

p. Fauquier County Court 24th of May 1768

364 - JAMES INGO DOZER, Plt. agt. WILLIAM WOOD, Deft. In Debt

This suit abates, the Sherif haveing returned that the Deft. is no Inhabitant of this County

- Messieurs ANDREW COCKRANE, WILLIAM CUNNINGHAME, & COMPANY, Plts. agt. JOHN CONNOR, Deft. In Debt

This day came the Plts. by their Attorney and came also MINOR WINN and became Special Bail and Pledge for the Deft. in this suit, and the said Deft. prays Oyer of the Writing in the Declaration mentioned and to him it is granted

- HUGH RYLY, an Infant by JOHN RYLY his next Friend, Plt. agt. BENJAMIN DOGGETT, Deft. In Case

Agreed, the Deft. paying costs

- WILLIAM BOGLE and COLIN DUNLOP, Surviving Partners of PATRICK & WILLIAM BOGLEs and COLIN DUNLOP of Glasgow, Plts. agt. CHARLES MORGAN, Deft. In Debt

This day came the Plts. by their Attorney and came also JAMES ARNOLD and became Special Bail and Pledge for the Deft. in this suit and the said Deft. acknowledged the action of the Plts. against him. Therefore it is considered by the Court that the Plts. recover against the said Deft. forty three pounds, the Debt in the Declaration mentioned, and his costs by him in this behalf expended, and thes aid Deft. in mercy, &c., But this Judgment is to be discharged by the paiment of twenty one pounds, seventeen shillings and six pence with Interest thereon to be computed after the rate of five per centum per annum from the ninth day of December 1766 till paid and the costs. Executuion stayed till September Court

- CUTHBERT BULLITT, Plt. agt. THOMAS CHINN, RAWLEIGH CHINN, AGATHA CHINN, WILLIAM SCOTT and BENNITT PRICE, Defts. In Chancery

Discontinued for want of prosecution

p. Fauquier County Court 24th of May 1768

365 - Indentures of Lease and Release between GEORGE ROGERS and BETTY his Wife of the one part and WILLIAM FLOURENCE, JUNIOR of the other part and the Receit thereon endorsed were acknowledged by the said GEORGE ROGERS and BETTY his Wife, (she being first privily examined as the Law directs) to be their act and deed and ordered to be recorded

- Messieurs WM: BOGLE and COLIN DUNLOP, Surviving Partners of PATRICK & WILLIAM BOGLEs & COLIN DUNLOP of Glasgow, Merchts., Plts. agt. PETER MARTIN, Deft. In Case

This suit abates, the Sherif haveing returned that the Deft. is no Inhabitant of this County

- Indentures of Lease and Release between JAMES BALL & LETTICE his Wife of the one part and HENRY LEE of the other part and Receit thereon endorsed were proved by the Oaths of ANN BLACKWELL, JAMES BLACKWELL and WILLIAM BALL, witnesses thereto, and together with aCommission thereto annexed for taking the acknowledgment and privy examination of the said LETTICE, and a Certificate of the Execution thereof, ordered to be recorded

- A Bond from JAMES BALL to HENRY LEE was proved by the Oaths of ANN BLACKWELL, JAMES BLACKWELL and WILLIAM BALL, witnesses thereto, and ordered to be recorded

- JAMES WHEATLEY is appointed Surveyor of the Road in the room of WILLIAM SMITH, And it is ordered that he with the Tithes belonging to the said Road do clear and keep the same in repair according to Law

- JOHN OBANNON, Exor. &c. of BRYANT OBANNON, Plt. agt. MICAJAH POOLE & THOMAS DODSON, Defts. On an Attachment

This day came the Plt. by his Attorney and the Sherif haveing returned that he had attached some tobacco and the said Deft. failing to appear and replevy the same altho called, It is considered by the Court that the Plt. recover against the said Deft. seven pounds, twelve shillings and seven pence half

p. Fauquier County Court 24th of May 1768

366 penny and his costs by him in this behalf expended, and the said Deft. in mercy &c., And it is ordered that the Sherif sell the attached effects and return an Account of the Sales to the Court

- JOHN WADDLE, Plt. agt. THOMAS CHINN, Deft. On an Attachment

This day came the Plt. by his Attorney and the Sherif haveing returned tht he had attached some tobacco and the Deft. failing to appear and replevy the sme altho called, it is considered by the Court that the Plt. recover against the said Deft. three pounds, five shillings and for pence and his costs by him in this behalf expended, And the said Deft. in mercy, &c., And it is ordered that the Sherif sell the attached effects and return an Account of the Sales to the Court

- On the motion of JOHN WHEATLEY, a Dedimus is awarded him to take the Deposition of WILLIAM STURDY at the suit of PANNILLs Administratrix

- JAMES FOLEY, Plt. agt. ALEXANDER FARROW, Deft. On an Attachment

This day came the Plt. by his Attorney and DANIEL FLOWREE, a Garnishee, being sworn declared that he had no effects of the Defts. in his hands, and JAMES NELLSON, another Garnishee, being sworn declared that he owes the Deft. five pounds, eight shillings, and the said Deft. failing to appear tho called, it is considered by the Court that the Plt. recover against the said Deft. eight pounds and his costs by him in this behalf expended, And the said Deft. in mercy, &c., And it is ordered that the money in the said NELLSONs hands be condemned towards satisfying this Judgment

- ROBERT BRENT, Plt. agt. GEORGE KENNOR, Deft. On a Petition

Judgment is granted the Plt. against the said Deft. for three pounds, three shillings and seven pence three farthings and his costs by him in this behalf expended

- JOHN ARISS, Plt. agt. THOMAS ALLAN, Deft. On a Petition

Judgment is granted the Plt. against the said Deft. for two pounds, five shillings and his costs by him in this behalf expended

- PHILIP PRICE, Assignee of DANIEL MORGAN, Plt. agt. PETER GRANT, Deft. In Debt

This day came as well the Plt. by his Attorney as the said Deft. in his

p. Fauquier County Court 24th of May 1768
367 proper peson and the said Deft. acknowledged the Plts. action against him.

Therefore it is considered by the Court that the Plt. recover against the said Deft. one hundred and eight pounds, the Debt in the Declaration mentioned, and his costs by him in this behalf expended; And the said Deft. in mercy, &c., But this Judgment is to be discharged by the paiment of fifty four pounds with Interest thereon to be computed after the rate of five per centum per annum from the fifteenth day of June 1767 till paid and the costs. Execution stayed four years

- JOHN SMITH, Plt. agt. SAMUEL HADDOX, Deft. On a Petition

Judgment is granted the Plt. against the said Deft. for three pounds, ten shillings and his costs by him in this behalf expended

- ROBERT COLEMAN, Plt. agt. WILLIAM PINKARD, Deft. On a Petition

Judgment is granted the Plt. against the said Deft. for one pound, seven shillings and five pence half penny and sixty five pounds of tobacco and his costs by him in this behalf expended

- Messieurs WILLIAM BOGLE and COLLIN DUNLOP, Surviving Partners of PATRICK & WILLIAM BOGLEs and COLLIN DUNLOP, of Glasgow, Merchts., & Partners, Plts. agt. JAMES ARNOLD, Deft. On a Petition

Judgment is granted the Plts. against the said Deft. for one pound, fifteen shillings and six pence half penny and their costs by them in this behalf expended

- The Same, Plts. agt. JOHN HARMAN, Deft. On a Petition

Judgment is granted the Plts. against the said deft. for two pounds, eleven shillings and ninepence and their costs by them in this behalf expended

- The Same, Plts. agt. JOHN LUTTRILL, Deft. On a Petition

Judgment is granted the Plts. against the said Deft. for two pounds, nine shillings and four pence and their costs by them in this behalf expended

- JOHN ASHLEY, Plt. agt. JOHN JETT, Deft. On a Petition

Judgment is granted the Plt. against the said Deft. for two pounds, eleven shillings and his costs by him in this behalf expended

- CUTHBERT BULLITT, Plt. agt. JEMIMA SETTLE, Deft. On a Petition

Discontinued

p. Fauquier County Court 24th of May 1768
368 - RICHARD HENRY LEE, Plt. agt. GEORGE HEAD, Deft. On a Petition

Judgment is granted the Plt. against the said Deft. for two pounds, seventeen shillings and six pence and his costs by him in this behalf expended

- WILLIAM HARDING, Exor. of JOHN HARDING, Plt. against JOHN POPE, Deft. On a Petition

Judgment is granted the Plt. against the said Deft. for two pounds and his costs by him in this behalf expended

- JOHN COCKE, Plt. agt. JOHN HALL, Deft. On a Petition

Agreed

- Ordered that the Sherif pay DANIEL RECTOR one hundred and fifty pounds of tobacco for three young wolves heads out of the fraction in his hands

- SAMUEL PEPER is appointed Surveyor of the Road in the room of JOSEPH NEAVILL and ordered that he with the Tithes belonging to the said Road do clear and keep the same in repair according to Law

- Ordered that the Court be adjourned till the Court in Course

" ARMISTEAD CHURCHHILL "

- At a Court held for Fauquier County the 27th day of June 1768
Present THOMAS HARRISON ARMISTEAD CHURCHHILL
JEREMIAH DARNALL JOSEPH HUDNALL
& JOHN MOFFETT Gent.

- An Indenture of Bargain and Sale between THOMAS HARRISON of the one part and WILLIAM HARRISON of the other part and a Receit thereon endorsed were acknowledged by the said THOMAS HARRISON and ordered to be recorded

p. Fauquier County Court 27th of June 1768
369 - Ordered that the Church Wardens of Hamilton Parish bind BENJAMIN MAHORNEY to JOHN MARTIN who is to learn him the Trade of a House Carpenter

- WILLIAM TRIPLETT is appointed Surveyor of the Road in the room of WILLIAM HOGAIN and it is ordered that he with the Tithes belonging to the Road do clear and keep the same in repair according to Law

- On the motion of GEORGE BOSWELL, leave is granted him to build a Water Mill on TURKEY RUN, it appearing that he has Land on both sides of the said Run and that the Land of no other person will be affected thereby

- An Indenture of Feofment between JOHN HENRY and MARY his Wife of the one part and JOHN HENRY, JUNIOR of the other part and a Memorandum of Livery of Seisin and a Receit thereon endorsed were acknowledged by the said JOHN HENRY and MARY his Wife, (she being first privily examined as the Law directs) to be their act and deed, ordered to be recorded

- THOMAS PORTER exhibitted and made Oath to an Account against ANGUS CAMERON, a Runaway Servant of his, for forty shillings expended in apprehending the said Runaway, and fifteen days absence. Ordered that the said Servant serve hjs said Master four months for the same after his time by Indenture or otherwise be expired

- Present. WILLIAM BLACKWELL, Gent.

- The Last Will and Testament of PETER PEARCE, deced., was proved by the Oaths of JOSEPH MORGAN & ELIZABETH MORGAN, witnesses thereto & ordered to be recorded; And on the motion of LYDIA PEARCE and JOHN PEARCE who made Oath and executed and acknowledged Bond as the Law directs, Certificate is granted them for obtaining a Proabt thereof in due form

- Ordered that CHARLES MARTIN, JAMES DUFF, CHARLES MORGAN and ALEXANDER BRADFORD or any three of them being first sworn do appraise the Estate of PETER PEARCE, deced., and return the appraisment to the Court

- On the motion of ROBERT SLAUGHTER setting forth that he has Land on one side of RHAPPAHANNOCK RIVER and that

p. Fauquier County Court 27th of June 1768
370 he intends to build a Water Mill thereon and praying that an acre of land on the opposite side may be laid of for that use, it is ordered that the Sherif summon a Jury of twelve Freeholders of the Vicinage to meet upon the land montion'd for who being met and duly sworn before a Majistrate or the Sherif shall diligently view and examine the said Land and the Land adjacent thereto which may be effected or laid under water by building such Mill, together with the Timber and other conveniences thereon and report the same with the true value of such acre and of the damages to the party holding the same or to any other person or persons under their hands and seals to the Court

- JOHN VINEY, Plt. agt. JAMES WINN, Deft. In Debt
This suit is dismissed

- WILLIAM JEFFRIES, a Servant Boy belonging to JOHN LAWS is adjudged by the Court to thirteen years old

- HENRY MILTON, a Servant Boy belonging to JOHN LAWS, is adjudged by the Court to be thirteen years old

- Indentures of Lease and Release between JOHN BARKER & MARY his Wife of the one part and JAMES GRINSTEAD of the other part and a Receit thereon endorsed were proved by the Oath of BENJAMIN BRADFORD, a witness thereto, and ordered to be recorded

- The persons appointed to view the Road from NEALES SCHOOL HOUSE on his Lorships Road to the Upper Church return'd their report in these words; to wit;

"In Obedience to an Order of Fauquier Court to us directed to view a way from BENJAMIN NEALEs SCHOOL HOUSE on his Lorships Road to the Upper Church, we find that the said way may be opened going as followeth from the said SCHOOL HOUSE along the Ridge to BARBEYs Spring Branch, thence to THUM RUN where BARBEYs Path crosses then to the Old Path near HENRY ROGERS Corn Field, then along the Old Path to LITTLE THUM RUN, thence up the Run between JOHN MOREHEAD & CHARLES SMITH to the Old Path by JOHN JOHNSONs Qr., thence along the Old Path by Capt. DIXONs Quarter into the Main Road above the said

p. Fauquier County Court 27th of June 1768

371 Church, we find the said way is not prejucicial to no one. Given under our hands this 28 day of March 1768." And it is ordered that the Road be established according to the said Report

- JOHN HALEY is appointed Surveyor of the Road from NEALS SCHOOL HOUSE on his Lordships Road to the Upper Church; And it is ordered that he with the Tithes to be appointed by THOMAS MARSHALL, Gent., do clear and keep the same in repair according to Law

- Present. WILLIAM EDMONDS, WILLIAM GRANT)
& GILLSON FOOTE) Gent.

- RICHARD CHICHESTER, JOHN BLACKWELL, JONATHAN GIBSON, WILLIAM BALL, MARTIN PICKETT, HENRY PEYTON, WILLIAM HARRISON, GEORGE BOSWELL & JOHN CHILTON, Gent. are recommended to his Honour the President as proper persons to be added to the Commission of the Peace for this County

- JOHN JAMES, Plt. agt. THOMAS SKINKER, Deft. In Trespass
Agreed, the Deft. paying costs

- HENRY LEE, THOMAS LAWSON & JOHN LEE, Exors. &c. of ALLAN MACRAE, deced., Plts. agt. JOHN SYAS, Deft. In Case
Discontinued, being agreed by the parties

- Ordered that the Court be adjourn'd till tomorrow morning ten of the Clock
WILLIAM BLACKWELL

- At a Court continued and helf for Fauquier County the 28th day of June 1768
Present THOMAS HARRISON, WILLIAM BLACKWELL
WILLIAM EDMONDS & JOSEPH HUDNALL Gent.

- JOHN RECTOR, Plt. agt. BURGES SMITH, Deft. In Case
The Deft. produced his Majestys Writ of Certiorari commanding the

p. Fauquier County Court 28th of June 1768
372 Justices of this County or one of them to certify the Record and Proceedings in this Cause to the Justices of the General Court and they are certified accordingly

- JOHN BOLEY, Plt. agt. BURGES SMITH, Deft. In Case

The Deft. produced his Majestys Writ of Certiorari commanding the Justices of this County or one of them to certify the Record and Proceedings in this Cause to the Justices of the General Court and they are certified accordingly

- JAMES MURRY, Plt. agt. BURGES SMITH, Deft. In Case

The same Order

- DANIEL REDMAN, Plt. agt. BURGES SMITH, Deft. In Case

The same Order

- JOHN RALLS, Plt. agt. JAMES McDONALD, Deft. In Debt

This day came the Plt. by his Attorney and the Sherif haveing returned on the Attachment awarded against the said Defts. Estate that he had attached one Chaff Bed and one old blankett, and the said Deft. failing to appear and replevy the same, tho called, It is considered by the Court that the Plt. recover against the said Deft. six pounds, nine shillings and eight pence, the Debt in the Declaration mentioned, and his costs by him in this behalf expended; and the said Deft. in mercy, &c., But this Judgment is to be discharged by the payment of three pounds, four shillings & ten pence current money of Virginia with Interest thereon to be computed after the rate of ifve per centum per annum from the thirteenth day of November 1767 till paid and the costs; And it is ordered that the Sherif sell the attached effects and return an Account of the Sales to the Court

- WILLIAM BOGLE & COLLIN DUNLOP, Surviviong Partners of PATRICK & WILLIAM BOGLEs, & COLLIN DUNLOP, of Glasgow, Merchants, Plts. agt. WILLIAM ROUSAU, Deft. In Debt

p. Fauquier County Court 28th of June 1768
373 This day came the Plts. by their Attorney and came also HENRY MAUZY and became Special Bail and Pledge for the Deft. in this suit, and the said Deft. defends the force and injury when &c., and pleads payment and the Trial of the issue is refered untill the next Court

- The Same, Plts. agt. HENRY BOATMAN, Deft. In Debt

This day came the Plts. by their Attorney and came also JOHN BAILY and became Special Bail and Pledge for the Deft. in this suit, and the said Deft. prays Oyer of the Writing in the Declaration mentioned & he hath it &c.

- ANDREW COCKRANE, WILLIAM CUNNINGHAME & CO., Plts. agt. PATRICK BREWTON & WILLIAM FOOTE, Defts. In Debt

Discontinued, being agreed by the parties

- Messieurs WILLIAM BOGLE & COLLIN DUNLOP, Surviving Partners of PATRICK & WILLIAM BOGLEs & COLLIN DUNLOP, of Glasgow, Merchants, Plts. agt. EDWARD TURNER, Deft. In Debt

This suit abates, the Sherif haveing returned that the Deft. is no Inhabitant of this County

- JAMES BUCHANAN, Assignee of MARTIN PICKETT & CO., Plt. agt. ALEXANDER WOODSIDES, Deft. In Debt

This day came as well the Plt. by his Attorney as the Deft. in his proper person & the said Deft. acknowledged the action of the Plt. against him. Therefore it is considered by the Court that the Plt. recover against the said Deft. twenty seven pounds, eight shillings and six pence current money, the Debt in the Declaration mentioned, and his costs by him in this behalf expended and the said Deft. in mercy, &c., But this Judgment is to be discharged by the paiment of thirteen pounds, fourteen shillings and three pence with Interest thereon to be computed after the rate of five per centum per annum from the first day of April 1768 till paid and costs. Execution stayed nine months

p. Fauquier County Court 28th of June 1768
374 - JAMES BUCHANAN, Plt. against ALEXANDER WOODSIDES, Deft. In Debt
Judgment is granted the Plt. against the said Deft. for his costs by him in this behalf expended

- Messieurs WILLIAM BOGLEs & COLLIN DUNLOP, Surviving Partners of PATRICK & WILLIAM BOGLEs & COLLIN DUNLOP, of Glasgow, Merchants, Plts. agt. ALEXANDER WOODSIDES, Deft. In Debt

This day came as well the Plts. by their Attorney as the Deft. in his proper person and the said Deft. acknowledged the action of the Plts. against him. Therefore it is considered by the Court that the Plts. recover against the said Deft. fourteen pounds, seventeen shillings current money, the Debt in the Declaration mentioend, and their costs by them in this behalf expended; And the said Deft. in mercy &c., But this Judgment is to be discharged by the payment of four pounds, sixteen shillings & six pence with Interest thereon to be computed after the rate of five per centum per annum from the twenty seventh day of June 1768 till paid & the costs

- WILLIAM THORNTON, Plt. agt. AUGUSTINE SMITH & JOSEPH SMITH, Defts. In Debt

This day came the Plt. by his Attorney and came also WILLIAM McCLANAHAM and became Special Bail and Pledge for the Defts. in this suit, and the said Defts. by CUTHBERT BULLITT, their Attorney, prays Oyer of the Writing in the Declaration mentioned and to them it is granted &c.

- ORIGINAL YOUNG & JOHN BLACKWELL, Plts. agt. JAMES GARNER, Deft. In Debt

This day came the parties in their proper persons and the Deft. acknowledged the action of the Plts. against him. Therefore it is considered by the Court that the Plts. recover against the said Deft. twenty five pounds, fifteen shillings and eight pence, the Debt in the Declaration mentioned, and their costs by them in this behalf expended, And the said Deft. in mercy, &c., But this Judgment

p. Fauquier County Court 28th of June 1768
375 is to be discharged by the paiment of twelve pounds, seventeen shillings and ten pence current money with Interest thereon to be computed after the rate of five per centum per annum from the twenty first day of September 1767 till paid & the costs

- JOHN WILLIAMS is appointed Surveyor of the Road in the room of HENRY RECTOR and it is ordered that he with the Tithes belonging to the said Raod do clear and keep the same in repair according to Law

- Aminadab Seekright, Plt. agt. RICHARD COVINGTON, Deft. In Ejectment for one Messuage Tenement & one hundred acres of Land with the appurtenances in the Parish of Hamilton in the County of Fauquier of the demise of EDWARD BALL

Agreed, the Deft. paying costs

- Aminadab Seekright, Plt. agt. STEPHEN McCORMACK, Deft. In Ejectment for one Messuage Tenement & two hundred acres of Land with the appurtenances in the Parish of Hamilton in the County of Fauquier of the demise of EDWARD TURNER

Discontinued, being agreed

- ANTHONY THORNTON, Plt. agt. MILES MURPHEW, Deft. In Debt

This day came the parties by their Attorneys and thereupon came also a Jury, to wit, SAMUEL MOORE, JOHN KEITH, HENRY RECTOR, JAMES WITHERS, JUNIOR, HENRY BOATMAN, GEORGE WILLIAMS, BUSHROD DOGGETT, JOHN SINCLAIR, WILLIAM ROUSAU, JOHN NELLSON, ISAAC CUNDIFF & BENJAMIN SNELLING, who being elected tried and sworn the truth to speak upon the issue joined upon their Oaths do say that the said Deft. doth owe to the Plt. one thousand and sixty pounds of Transfer tobacco, the Debt in the Declaration mentioned, and they assess the Plts. damages by occasion of the Defts. detention of that debt to one penny besides his costs; Therefore it is considered by the Court that the Plt. recover against the said Deft. the said one thousand and sixty pounds of tobacco together with the damages aforesaid in form aforesaid assessed and his costs by him in this behalf expended, and the said Deft. in mercy, &c.

p. <u>Fauquier County Court 28th of June 1768</u>

376 - On the motion of JOHN CORBIN, it is ordered that ANTHONY THORNTON pay him three hundred and sixty five pounds of tobacco for five days attendance & four times comeing twenty miles and returning, as a witness for him against MILES MURPHEW

- RAWLEIGH CHINN, Plt. agt. JOHN CHAPMAN & JOHN KEEBLE, Defts. In Debt

This day came the parties by their Attorneys & thereupon came also a Jury, to wit, MAXIMILLIAN BERRYMAN, JAMES WITHERS, JOHN BARBEE, WILLIAM JENNINGS, JOHN DAVIS, BEN SETTLE, STEPHEN MORRIS, PARNACH GEORGE, HENRY MAUZY, WILLIAM MORGAN, JACOB ADAMS & SAMUEL THORNBERRY, who being elected tried and sworn the truth to speak upon the issue joined, upon their Oaths do say that the said Defts. do owe to the Plt. five poounds, ten shillings, the Debt in the Declaration mentioned, And they do assess the Plts. damages by occasion of the Defts. detention of that Debt to one penny besides his costs; Therefore it is considered by the Court that the Plt. recover against the said Deft. the said five pounds, ten shillings together with his damages aforesaid in form aforesaid assessed and his costs by him in this behalf expended, And the said Deft. in mercy, &c.

- A Lease between the Right Honourable THOMAS LORD FAIRFAX of the one part and JOHN CRIMM of the other part was proved by the Oaths of JAMES SCOTT, HUMPHREY BROOKE and MARTIN PICKETT, witnesses thereto, and ordered to be recorded

- A Lease between the Right Honourable THOMAS LORD FAIRFAX of the one part and JOHN CRIM, JUNIOR of the other part was proved by the Oaths of JAMES SCOTT, HUMPHREY BROOKE and MARTIN PICKETT,witnesses thereto, and ordered to be recorded

- A Lease between the Right Honourable THOMAS LORD FAIRFAX of the one part and JOHN CRIMM, JUNR. of the other part as proved by the Oaths of JAMES SCOTT, HUMPHREY BROOKE and MARTIN PICKETT, witnesses thereto, and ordered to be recorded

- On the motion of JOHN RECTOR, SENR., It is ordered that RAWLEIGH CHINN pay him two hundred & twenty five pounds of tobacco for nine days attendance as a witness for him against CHAPMAN and KEEBLE

p. <u>Fauquier County Court 28th of June 1768</u>

377 - On the motion of HENRY RECTOR, SENR., it is ordered that RAWLEIGH CHINN pay him three hundred pounds of tobacco for twelve days attendance as a witness for him against CHAPMAN & KEEBLE

- On the motion of ISAAC CUNDIFF, it is ordered that RAWLEIGH CHINN pay him three hundred pounds of tobacco for twelve days attendance as a witness for him against CHAPMAN & KEEBLE

- On the motion of JOHN RECTOR, JUNIOR, it is ordered that RAWLEIGH CHINN pay him one hundred and seventy five pounds of tobacco for seven days attendance as a witness for him against CHAPMAN and KEEBLE

- On the motion of JOHN RECTOR, JUNIOR, it is ordered that RAWLEIGH CHINN pay him two hundred pounds of tobacco for eight days attendance as a witness for him agaisnt CHAPMAN & KEEBLE

- On the motion of JACOB ADAMS, it is ordered that RAWLEIGH CHINN pay him three hundred and fifty pounds of tobacco for fourteen days attendance as a witness for him against CHAPMAN and KEEBLE

- Present JOS: BLACKWELL, Gent.

- STEPHEN McCORMACK, Plt. agt. JOHN KNOX, Exor. &c. of PETER HEDGEMAN, deced., Deft. In Case

This day came the parties by their Attornies and by their consent the Order of Reference in this Cause is discharged, and thereupon came a Jury, to wit, SAMUEL MOORE, JOHN KEITH, HENRY RECTOR, JAMES WITHERS, JUNR., HENRY BOATMAN, GEORGE WILLIAMS, BUSHROD DOGGETT, JOHN SINCLAIR, WILLIAM ROUSAU, JOHN NELLSON, ISAAC CUNDIFF & BENJAMIN SNELLING, who being elexted tried and sworn the truth to speak upon the issue joined, upon their Oaths do say that the said PETER HEDGEMAN, the Testator in his life time did assume upon himself in manner and form as the Plt. hath declared and they do assess the Plts. damages by means of the breach of that assumption to one hundred and sixty five pounds, seventeen shillings and four pence besides his costs; Therefore it is considered by the Court that the Plts. recover against the Deft.

p. Fauquier County Court 28th of June 1768

378 his damages aforesaid in form aforesaid assessed and his costs by him in this behalf expended, and the said Deft. in mercy, &c., to be levied of the goods & chattells of the said Testator in the hands of the said Deft. to be administered

- A Receit from THOMAS CHINN to THOMAS THORNTON was proved by the Oath of JOHN MATTHEWS, a witness thereto, & ordered to be recorded

- WILLIAM MOUNTJOY, Plt. agt. JOHN SINCLAIR, Deft. In Trespass

This day came the parties by their Attorneys and thereupon came also a Jury, to wit, MAXIMILLIAN BERRYMAN, JAMES WITHERS, JOHN BARBEE, WILLIAM JENNINGS, JOHN DAVIS, BENJAMIN SETTLE, STEPHEN MORRIS, PARNACH GEORGE, HENRY MAUZY, WILLIAM MORGAN, JACOB ADAMS & SAMUEL THORNBERRY, who being elected tried and sworn the truth to speak upon the issue joined, upon their Oaths do say that the Deft. is Not Guilty in manner and form as by pleading he hath alledged. Therefore it is considered by the Court that the Plt. take nothing by his Bill but for his false clamor be in mercy, &c., And that the said Deft. go thereof without day and recover against the said Plt. his costs by him in this behalf expended

- JAMES BUCHANAN, Plt. agt. DANIEL FLOWREE, Deft. On a Petition

Judgment is granted the Plt. against the said Deft. for five pounds and his costs by him in this behalf expended. Execution stayed till Christmas

- WILLIAM GRANT, Plt. agt. JOHN ASHBY, Deft. In Debt

This day came the parties by their Attorneys and thereupon came also a Jury, to wit, JAMES BAILY, JOHN DUNCAN, STEPHEN McCORMACK, JAMES GARNER, ALEXANDER MONROE, JOHN OBANNON, THOMAS OBANNON, LUKE HOLDER, JOSEPH LAVEL, JOHN BAILY, SANFORD CARROLL and JOHN JONES, whjo being elected tried and sworn the truth to speak upon the issue join'd, withdrew to consider of their Verdict

p. Fauquier County Court 28th of June 1768
379 - On the motion of ANN THRELKELD, it is ordered that STEPHEN McCORMACK pay her one hundred and twenty five pounds of tobacco for five days attendance as a witness for him against JOHN KNOX, Exor. &c. of PETER HEDGEMAN

- On the motion of JOHN WRIGHT, it is ordered that JOHN SINCLAIR pay him two hundred pounds of tobacco for eight days attendance as a witness for him at the suit of WILLIAM MOUNTJOY

- SARAH MAHORNEY, Plt. agt. BENJAMIN SNELLING, Deft. In Trespass, Assault and Battery

This day came the parties by their Attorneys and thereupon came also a Jury, to wit, JAMES WITHERS, JOHN BARBEE, WILLIAM JENNINGS, JOHN DAVIS, BENJAMIN SETTLE, STEPHEN MORRIS, HENRY MAUZEY, WILLIAM MORGAN, JACOB ADAMS, SAMUEL THORNBERRY, JOHN JAMES & TILLMAN WEAVER, who being elected tried and sworn the truth to speak, upon their Oaths do day that the said Deft. is Guilty in manner and form as the Plt. against him hath declared and they do assess the Plts. damages by occasion thereof to one penny. Therefore it is considered by the Court that the Plt. recover against the said Deft. her damages aforesaid in form aforesaid assessed and the said Deft. in mercy &c.

- On the motion of JAMES FRAZIER, it is ordered that JOHN SINCLAIR pay him two hundred and fifty pounds of tobacco for ten days attendance as a witness for him at the suit of WILLIAM MOUNTJOY

- On the motion of MAXIMILLIAN BERRYMAN, it is ordered that SARAH MAHORNEY pay him one hundred and fifty pounds of tobacco for six days attendance as a witness for her against BENJAMIN SNELLING

- On the motion of ELIZABETH MORGAN, it is ordered that SARAH MAHORNEY pay her fifty pounds of tobacco for two days attendance as a witness for her against BENJAMIN SNELLING

- GAVIN LAWSON, Assee. of CUTHBERT BULLITT, Plt. agt. JOHN CHAPMAN & ELIAS EDMONDS, Defts. In Debt

This day came the parties by their Attorneys and thereupon

p. Fauquier County Court 28th of June 1768
380 came also a Jury, to wit, SAMUEL MOORE, JOHN SMITH, BENJAMIN POPE, JOHN KEITH, BUSHROD DOGGETT, JAMES WITHERS, JUNR., JOHN HATHAWAY, JAMES HATHAWAY, RANDOLPH SPICER, WILLIAM JENNINGS, FRANCIS ATWELL & HENRY MAUZEY, who being elected tried and sworn the truth to speak upon the issue join'd upon their Oaths do say that the Deft. doth owe to the said Plt. three pounds, four shillings and six pence and seventy one pounds of tobacco with Interest thereupon to be computed after the rate of five per centum per annum from the twenty sixth day of August 1766 till paid; And they do assess the Plts. damages by occasion of the Defts. detention of that Debt to one penny, besides his costs. Therefore it is considered by the Court that the Plt. recover against the said Deft. his Debt and damages aforesaid in form aforesaid assessed and his costs by him in this behalf expended, and the said Deft. in mercy, &c.

- On the motion of WILLIAM COLLINS, it is ordered that STEPHEN McCORMACK pay him ninety seven pounds of tobacco for one days attendance, comeing twenty four miles & returning, as a witness for him against JOHN KNOX, Exor. &c. of PETER HEDGEMAN, deced., not to be taxed

- On the motion of JOHN DUNCAN, it is ordered that STEPHEN McCORMACK pay him one hundred & seventy five pounds of tobacco for seven days attendance as a witness for him against JOHN KNOX, Exor. &c. of PETER HEDGEMAN, deced.

- The same Order for LUKE HOLDER
- Ordered that the Court be adjourn'd till tomorrow ten of the Clock
" THOMAS HARRISON "

- At a Court continued and held for Fauquier County the 29th day of June 1768
Present JOSEPH BLACKWELL WILLIAM BLACKWELL
WILLIAM EDMONDS JEREMIAH DARNALL Gent.
& JOSEPH HUDNALL

p. Fauquier County Court 29th of June 1768
381 - EDWARD HOAR, Assee. of JOHN BARBEE, Plt. agt. GEORGE WILLIAMS, Deft. In Debt

This day came the parties by their Attorneys and thereupon came also a Jury, to wit, WILLIAM MORGAN, JAMES WITHERS, SENR., JAMES WITHERS, PHARNACH GEORGE, JAMES WITHERS, WILLIAM JENNINGS, HENRY MAUZEY, JOHN NELLSON, HENRY BOATMAN, WILLIAM ROUSAU, THOMAS CONWAY and PETER CORNWILL, who being elected tried and sworn the truth to speak upon the issue joined, upon their Oaths do say that the said Deft. hath paid the Debt in the Declaration mentioned as by pleading he hath alledged. Therefore it is considered by the Court that the Plt. take nothing by his Bill but for his false Clamor be in mercy, &c., And that the Deft. go thereof without day and recover against the said Plt. his costs by him in this behalf expended

- MARTIN PICKETT & COMPANY, Plts. agt. WILLIAM KITTSON & ALEXANDER JAMESON, Defts. In Debt

This day came the parties by their Attorneys and the said Defts. relinquishing their former plea acknowledged the action of the Plts. against them. Therefore it is considered by the Court that the Plts. recover against the said Defts. twenty four pounds current money, the Debt in the Declaration mentioned and their costs by them in this behalf expended; And the said Deft. in mercy, &c., But this Judgment is to be discharged by the payment of twelve pounds current money with Interest thereon to be computed after the rate of five per centum per annum from the fifteenth day of August 1764 till paid and the costs

- STEPHEN MORRIS, Plt. agt. THOMAS GARNER, JUNIOR, Deft. In Case

This day came the parties by their Attorneys and thereupon came also a Jury, to wit, WILLIAM MORGAN, JAMES WITHERS, SENR., JAMES WITHERS, PARNACH GEORGE, JAMES WITHERS,

p. Fauquier County Court 29th of June 1768
382 WILLIAM JENNINGS, HENRY MAUZEY, JOHN NELLSON, HENRY BOATMAN, WILLIAM ROUSAU, THOMAS CONWAY and PETER CORNWILL who being elected tried and sworn the truth to speak upon the issue joined, upon their Oaths do say that the Deft. did assume upon himself in manner and form as the Plt. against him hath declared and they do assess the Plts. damages by means of the Defts. breach of that assumption to nine pounds, three shillings and two pence besides his costs. Therefore it is considered by the Court that the Plt. recover against the said Deft. his damages aforesaid in form aforesaid assessed and his costs by him in this behalf expended; And the said Deft. in mercy, &c.

- JAMES PATON, Plt. agt. WILLIAM EMMONS, Exor. in his own wrong of DAVID EVANS, Defts. On a Petition

This Petition is dismist and it is ordered that the Plt. pay the Deft. his costs by him in this behalf expended

- On the motion of WILLIAM BLACKWELL, it is ordered that WILLIAM EMMONS pay him one hundred pounds of tobacco for four days attendance as a witness for him at the suit of JAMES PATON

- WILLIAM GRANT, Plt. agt. JOHN ASHBY, Deft. In Debt

The Jury sworn yesterday to try the issue in this Cause, returned into Court & upon their Oaths do say that the Arbitrators named in the Condition of the Writing Obligatory in the Declaration mentioned did make such an award between the Plt. and teh said Deft. within the time limitted in the said condition as by replying the Plt. hath alledged, and they find for the Plt. the sum of Five hundred pounds debt to be discharged by the payment of fifty pounds & also one penny damages. And the said Deft. prays that Judgment on the Verdict aforesaid may be arrested & stayed for the following reasons. First, that the award is not final & conclusive but manifestly uncertain, the Plt. yet being at liberty to prosecute his action of Trespass, Assault and Battery against the said Deft. Secondly, for that

p. 383 Fauquier County Court 29th of June 1768

no Breach is assigned by the said Plt. for which the Jury can assess damages against the Defendant; Thirdly, that the Verdict of the Jury aforesaid is imperfect and excessive and the Judgment cannot be ordered upon, Fourthly, that the fifty pounds found by the Jury for beach of the condition of the Cobnd ought to have been the damages, & the Cause is continued untill the next Court for the matters of Law arising thereupon to be argued

- Aminadab Seekright, Plt. agt. JOHN MAUZEY, Deft. In Ejectment for one Plantation & Messuage and three hundred acres of Land with the appurtenances situate lying and being in the Parish of Hamilton in the County of Fauquier of the demise of WILLIAM MOUNTJOY, Gent.

This day came the parties by their Attorneys, and thereupon came also a Jury, to wit, GEORGE BERRY, JOHN BARBEE, STEPHEN MORRIS, JOHN KEEBLE, BENJAMIN POPE, CHARLES SETTLE, BENJAMIN SETTLE, WILLIAM PINKARD, GEORGE HERRING, WILLIAM JENNINGS, JAMES WITHERS & JAMES WITHERS, who being elected tried and sworn the truth to speak upon the issue joined, brought in a Special Verdict in these words (to wit), We of the Jury find that MARY WAUGH, the Mother of the Plt. and Grand Mother of the Deft. was upon the 27th day of March Anno Domini one thousand seven hundred & forty nine seised of the premises in the Declaration mentioned in fee simple. We find that upon the same day she made her Last Will and Testament in Writing duly executed which said last Will is duly proved in the County Court of STAFFORD, We find that in and by the said Will, she devised the premises in the Declaration mentioned in manner following, Item. I give and bequeath to my Son, PETER MAUZEY three hundred acres of land upon ELK RUN in PRINCE WILLIAM County whereon FRANCIS WATTS now lives (being the premises in the said Declaration mentioned) and at his decease, then for the said Lands to be given to either of my said Sons Children as he shall think fit, as by the said Will may appear & to which we refer. We find that the said PETER MAUZEY afterwards upon the 12th day of February 1750/51 made his Last Will duly executed by which he devised the said premises in manner following; Item. I give to my loving Son, JOHN MAUZEY, all my Land on ELK RUN in PRINCE WILLIAM County and to his lawfull heirs for ever and in default of such to my

p. 384 Fauquier County Court 29th of June 1768

Son, PETER MAUZEY, and his lawfull heirs forever as by the said last Will may appear, to which we refer. We find that the Plt. is heir at Law to the said MARY

WAUGH. We find that the said PETER died in the life time of the said MARY WAUGH. We find that the said Deft. is the Son of PETER MAUZEY to whom he devised the said premises; We find that PETER MAUZEY after the said devise to him received the rents and profits of the said premises from FRANCIS WATTS, the Tenant, and that since his death the Deft. hath received the same. We find that the Testatrix, MARY WAUGH, expressed her approbation of PETER MAUZY's Will after his decease before one witness saying the land was given is as she intended it. We find that MARY WAUGH had jointly with the said PETER MAUZEY leased the said premises to the said FRANCIS WATTS which Lease we find and to which we refer. We find by the Testimony of one witness that she once made a Will and devised it to the Deft. but was advised to alter it and leave it in the Dower of his Father for that if he died it would go to his Eldest Brother (   ) would or not. We find that the Testatrix at the time of taking up the Land declared she intended it for her said Son, PETER MAUZEY. We find by the Testimony of one witness that after the death of PETER MAUZEY, a rent was offered to the Testatrix which she refused to receive saying the land was the Defts. and directed the Land to be paid to his Father in Law for the Defts. use upon the whole, if the Law is for the Plt. we find for him the premises in the Declaration mentioned and one penny damages, otherwise we find for the Deft. And the Cause is continued untill the next Court for the matters of law arising thereupon to be argued

- Indentures of Lease and Release between JEFFRY JOHNSON and RACHEL his Wife of the one part and PETER CORNWELL of the other part and a Receit thereon endorsed were acknowledged by the said JEFFRY JOHNSON to be his act and deed and together with the Commission for taking the acknowledgment and privy examination of the said RACHEL and a Certificate of the Execution thereof, ordered to be recorded

p. Fauquier County Court 29th of June 1768

385 - An Inventory and Appraisment of the Estate of JOHN LEE, deced., was returned and ordered to be recorded

- THOMASON ELLZEY, Plt. agt. BETTY MAUZEY, Executrix HENRY MAUZEY, & WM. ROUSAU, Exor. &s. of JOHN MAUZEY, deced., Defts. In Case

By consent of the parties, all matters in difference relative to this suit are refered to JOSEPH BLACKWELL & THOMAS MARSHALL, Gent., and their award or the award of such third person they shall chuse in case they disagree to be the Courts Judgment

- THOMAS OBANNON, Plt. agt. THOMAS GARNER, JUNR., Deft. In Debt

This day came the parties by their Attorneys and thereupon came also a Jury to wit, JOHN SMITH, JAMES BAILEY, JOHN DUNCAN, STEPHEN McCORMACK, ALEXANDER MONROE, JOSIAH HOLTZCLAW, LUKE HOLDER, JOSEPH LAVEL, JOHN BAILEY, JOHN JONES, GEORGE WILLIAMS & SANFORD CARREL, who being elected tried and sworn the truth to speak upon the issue joined upon their Oaths do say that the said Deft. is Guilty in manner and form as the Plt. against him hath declared and that the said Deft. doth owe to the Plt. seven pounds, and they do assess the Plts. damages by occasion of the Defts. detention of that Debt to one penny besides his costs, And the said Deft. by CUTHBERT BULLITT, his Attorney, prays that Judgment on the verdict aforesaid be arrested and stayed for the following reasons. First, that the Plt. hath in his Declaration declared in the Detinet only, whereas it ought to have been in the Debit & Detinet both; Secondly, that the Writ, Declaration & Verdict are insufficient and informal. And the suit is continued untill the next Court for the matters of Law ariseing thereupon to be argued

- MARY McNAMARA, Plt. agt. JAMES BAILEY, Deft. On a Petition

This Petition is dismist and it is ordered that the Plt. pay

p. Fauquier County Court 29th of June 1768
386 to the Deft. his costs by him in this behalf expended

- BENJAMIN ASHBY, Assee. of MORDICAI (? BATSON), Plt. agt.
THOMAS CONNOR, Deft. On a Petition

Judgment is granted the Plt. against the said Deft. for thirteen shillings and eight pence and his costs by him in this behalf expended

- On the motion of HENRY BOATMAN, it is ordered that THOMAS OBANNON pay him four hundred and forty five pounds of tobacco for seven days attendance and three times comeing sixty miles and returning as a witness for him against THOMAS GARNER, JUNIOR

- RICHARD BRYAN & JANE MAHORNEY being summoned & not appearing as witnesses for SAMUEL THORNBERRY against JOHN MORGAN, it is ordered that an Attachment issue against them returnable to the next Court

- WILLIAM HARDING, Exor. of GEORGE HARDING, deced., Plt. agt.
WILLIAM HAMMITT, Deft. On Petition

The Act of Limitation pleaded and dismist

- WILLIAM CARR LANE, Plt. agt. WILLIAM KENTON, Deft. On a Petition

Judgment is granted the Plt. against the said Deft. for two pounds, three shillings and his costs by him in this behalf expended

- BENJAMIN HAMRICK, Plt. agt. JAMES BASHAW, Deft. On a Petition

Judgment is granted the Plt. against the said Deft. for three pounds, ten shillings and his costs by him in this behalf expended

- ABSALOM CORNELIOUS, Plt. agt. JACOB HAYS, Deft. On a Petition

Discontinued, being agreed by the parties

p. Fauquier County Court 29th of June 1768
387 - JOHN RALLS, Plt. agt. DANIEL McCOY, Deft. On a Petition

Judgment is granted the Plt. against the said Deft. for one pound, eighteen shillings and ten pence and his costs by him in this behalf expended

- On the motion of DANIEL KINCHELOE, it is ordered that BENJAMIN HAMRICK pay him one hundred and fifty pounds of tobacco for three days attendance and once comeing twenty five miles & returning as a witness for him against JAMES BASHAW

- The same Order for JOHN BUCHANAN

- On the motion of JOHN BARBEE, it is ordered that EDWARD HOAR pay him one hundred and seventy two pounds of tobacco for four days attendance and twice comeing twelve miles and returning as a witness for him against GEORGE WILLIAMS

- On the motion of JOHN MAUZEY, it is ordered that JOHN MAUZEY pay him three hundred and forty pounds of tobacco for four days attendance and twice comeing forty miles and returning as a witness for him at the suit of WILLIAM MOUNTJOY

- On the motion of MARY DONIPHAN, it is ordered that JOHN MAUZEY, JUNIOR pay her five hundred and seventy five pounds of tobacco for five days attendance and three times travelling fifty miles & returning as a witness for him as the suit of WILLIAM MOUNTJOY

- On the motion of THOMAS CONWAY, it is ordered that JOHN MAUZEY, JUNIOR pay him two hundred pounds of tobacco for eight days attendance as a witness for him at the suit of WILLIAM MOUNTJOY

- JAMES WITHERS, JUNIOR, Plt. agt. LEWIS CONNOR, Deft. On an Attachment

This day came the Plt. by his Attorney and the Sherif haveing returned that he had attached one small white Mare and one

p. Fauquier County Court 29th of June 1768
388 Saddle and the said Deft. failing to appear and replevy the attached effects, altho solemnly called, it is considered by the Court that the Plt. recover against the said Deft. five pounds and his costs by him in this behalf expended, and the said Deft. in mercy, &c., And it is ordered that the Sherif sell the attached effects and return an Account of the Sales to the Court

- GEORGE STUBBLEFIELD, Plt. agt. PETER GRANT, Deft. In Debt

This day came the parties by their Attorneys and the said Deft. relinquishing his former plea acknowledged the action of the Plt. against him. Therefore it is considered by the Court that the Plt. recover against the said Deft. sixteen pounds current money, the Debt in the Declaration mentioned and his costs by him in this behalf expended, and the said Deft. in mercy, &c. But this Judgment is to be discharged by the paiment of eight pounds current money with Interest thereupon to be computed after the rate of five per centum per annum from the first day of October 1766 till paid and the costs

- NEIL McCOOL, Assignee of THOMAS WIATT, who was Assignee of BENJAMIN WINSLOW, Plt. agt. PETER GRANT, Deft. In Debt

This day came the parties by their Attornies and the said Deft. relinquishing his former plea acknowledged the action of the Plt. against him. Therefore it is considered by the Court that the Plt. recover against the said Deft. eighteen pounds, the Debt in the Declaration mentioned, and his costs by him in this behalf expended; And the said Deft. in mercy, &c., But this Judgment is to be discharged by the payment of nine pounds current money of Virginia with Interest thereon to be computed after the rate of five per centum per annum from the first day of November 1766 till paid and the costs

p. Fauquier County Court 29th of June 1768
389 - JAMES WINN, Plt. agt. PETER GRANT, Deft. In Debt

This day came the parties by their Attornies and the said Deft. relinquishing his former plea acknowledged the action of the Plt. against him. Therefore it is considered by the Court that the Plt. recover against the said Deft. eighty pounds, ten shillings, the Debt in the Declaration mentioned and his costs by him in this behalf expended, And the said Deft. in mercy, &c., But this Judgment is to be discharged by the payment of forty pounds, five shillings with Interest thereon to be computed after the rate of five per centum per annum from the twenty fifth day of March 1767 till paid and the costs

- WILLIAM BALL, Plt. agt. PETER GRANT, Deft. In Debt

This day came the parties by their Attorneys and the said Deft. relinquishing his former plea acknowledged the action of the Plt. against him. Therefore it is considered by the Court that the Plt. recover against the said Deft. thirty two pounds current money, the Debt in the Declaration mentioned, and his costs by him in this behalf expended, And the said Deft. in mercy, &c., But this Judgment is to be discharged by the paiment of sixteen pounds current money with Interest thereon to be computed after the rate of five per centum per annum from the twenty fifth day of Decemer 1766 till paid and the costs

- MARTIN HARDIN, Plt. agt. GEORGE TURBEFIELD KENNER, Deft. In Debt

This day camethe parties by their Attornies and the said Deft. relinquishing his former plea acknowledged the action of the Plt. against him. Therefore it is considered by the Court that the Plt. recover against the said Deft. eighteen pounds

p. Fauquier County Court 29th of June 1768
390 twelve shillings current money of Virginia, the Debt in the Declaration mentioned and his costs by him in this behalf expended, And the said Deft. in mercy

But this Judgment is to be discharged by the payment of nineteen shillings and eight pence with Interest thereon to be computed after the rate of five per centum per annum from the thirtieth day of June 1763 till paid & the costs

- On the motion of JAMES CAMPBELL, it is ordered that ANN CONNOR pay him seventy five pounds of tobacco for three days attendance as a witness for her at the suit of JAMES WITHERS

- BETTY MAUZEY, HENRY MAUZEY & WILLIAM ROUSAU, Exors. &c. of JOHN MAUZEY, deced., Plts. agt. JOHN KNOX, Exor. &c. of WILLIAM HEDGEMAN, deced., Deft. In Case

This came came the parties by their Attorneys and the said Deft. relinquishing his former plea acknowledged the Plts. action against him. Therefore it is considered by the Court that the Plt. recover against the said Deft. fourteen pounds & their costs by them in this behalf expended, to be levied of the goods and chattells which belonging to the said WILLIAM HEDGEMAN at the time of his death being in the hands of the said JOHN KNOX to b administered, together with their costs by them in this behalf expended and the said Deft. in mercy, &c.

- JOHN CORBIN, Plt. agt. DANIEL MORGAN, Deft. In Trespass, Assault & Battery

Agreed, the Deft. paying costs

- On the motion of WILLIAM MORGAN, it is ordered that BETTY MAUZEY, HENRY MAUZEY & WILLIAM ROUSAU, Exors. &c. of JOHN MAUZEY, deced., pay him two hundred and twenty five pounds of tobacco for nine days attendance as a witness for them against JOHN KNOX, Exor. &c. of WILLIAM HEDGEMAN, deced.

p. Fauquier County Court 29th of June 1768

391 - THOMAS FOLEY, Plt. agt. JOHN WINN, Deft. In Case

This day came the parties by their Attorneys and thereupon came also a Jury, to wit, GEORGE WILLIAMS, JAMES BAILEY, JOSEPH LAVEL, JOHN BAILEY, WILLIAM JENNINGS, JAMES WITHERS, JAMES WITHERS, GEORGE GRANT, PETER KAMPER and ALEXANDER MONROE (only ten named) who being elected tried and sworn the truth to speak upon the issue joined, upon their Oaths do say that the Deft. did assume upon himself in manner & form as the Plt. against him hath declared and they do assess the Plts. damages by means of the Defts. breach of that assumption to five pounds, eighteen shillings besides his costs; Therefore it is considered by the Court that the Plt. recover against the said Deft. his damages aforesaid in form aforesaid assessed and his costs by him in this behalf expended, and the said Deft. in mercy, &c.

- JAMES WITHERS, Plt. agt. JOSEPH HUDNALL, Deft. In Case

This day came the parties by their Attorneys and thereupon came also a Jury, to wit, GEORGE WILLIAMS, JAMES BAILEY, ALEXANDER MONROE, JOSEPH LAVEL, JOHN BAILEY, STEPHEN MORRIS, GEORGE GRANT, PETER KAMPER, BENJAMIN SETTLE, JACOB ADAMS WILLIAM HUTCHINSON and FRANCIS PAYNE who being elected tried and sworn the truth to speak upon the issue joined, withdrew to consider of their verdict

- Ordered that the Court be adjourned untill tomorrow morning Eight of the Clock JOSEPH BLACKWELL

- At a Court continued and held for Fauquier County the 30th day of June 1768

Present	JOSEPH BLACKWELL		WILLIAM BLACKWELL	
	WILLIAM EDMONDS		JEREMIAH DARNALL	
		&	JOSEPH HUDNALL	Gent.

- THOMAS GARNER, Plt. agt. DANIEL MORGAN, Deft. In Case
This suit is dismist and it is ordered that the Plt. pay to

p. Fauquier County Court 30th of June 1768
392 the Deft. his costs by him in this behalf expended

- THOMAS GARNER, who sues as well for the Parish of HAMPSHIRE as for himself, Plt. agt. JOHN HORD, Deft. In Debt
This suit is dismist and it is ordered that the Plt. pay to the Deft. the costs by him in this behalf expended

- MICHAEL MARR, Plt. agt. GEORGE SKINKER, Deft. In Case
Agreed, the deft. paying costs

- JOSHUA KING,Plt. agt. WILLIAM WAITE, Deft. In Debt
Discontinued

- The Attachment obtained by JOHN SYAS against the Estate of ANDREW LEACHMAN is dismis'd

- THOMAS GARNER, JUNIOR, Plt. agt. THOMAS GARNER, Deft. On an Attachment
Discontinued

- GUSTAVUS SCOTT,. Plt. agt. THOMAS CHINN, Deft. On an Attachment
Discontinued

- MOSES HAYS, Plt. agt. GEORGE BETHEL, Deft. On an Attachment
This day came the Plt. by his Attorney and the Sherif haveing returned that he had attached one bed, one linnen wheel, one iron pot, one shovel, one bason, six basketts and some Cotton, one paid and eleven spoons, some shoemakers tools, three bottles, seven hens, one crok & twenty two Chickens and geese & one bridle, twelve hogs

p. Fauquier County Court 30th of June 1768
393 marked with a Crop in the left and under keel in the right year and some trifles, and the Deft. failing to appear and replevy the attached effects, altho solemnly called, it is considered by the Court that the Plt. recover against the said Deft. two pounds, sixteen shillings and three pence and his costs in this behalf expended, and the said Deft. in mercy, &c., And it is ordered that the Sherif sell the attached effects and return an Account of the Sales to the Court

- WILLIAM CARR & THOMAS CHAPMAN, Plts. agt. THOMAS CHINN, Deft. On an Attachment
This day came the Plts. by their Attorney and the Sherif haveing return that he had attached some old Casks and the said Deft. failing to appear and replevy the attached effects although solemnly called, It is considered by the Court that the Plts. recover against the said Deft. fifty eight pounds and their costs by them in this behalf expended and the said Deft. in mercy, &c. But this Judgment is to be discharged by the paiment of twenty nine pounds with Interest thereon to be computed after the rate of five per centum per annum from the tenth day of April 1765 till paid and the costs. And it is ordered that the Sherif sell the attached effects and return an Account of the Sales to the Court

- JAMES WINN, Plt. agt. ISAAC ROBERTS, Deft. On an Attachment
This day came the Plt. by his Attorney and the Sherif haveing returned that he had attached one new markett Coat and the Deft. failing to appear and replevy the attached effects although solemnly called, It is considered by the Court that the Plt. recover against the said Deft. his costs by him in this behalf expended and the said Deft. in mercy &c.

- JAMES WINN, Plt. agt. THOMAS CHINN, Deft. On an Attachment

This day came the Plt. by his Attorney and the Sherif

p. Fauquier County Court 30th of June 1768

394 haveing returned that he had attached some tobacco and the said Deft. failing to appear and replevy the attached effects altho solemnly called, It is considered by the Court that the Plt. recover against the said Deft. three pounds, eighteen shillings and his costs by him in this behalf expended, and the said Deft. in mercy, &c. And it is ordered that the Sherif sell the attached effects and return an Account of the Sales to the Court

- SARAH DODSON, Plt. agt. GEORGE LINTON, Deft. On an Attachment

Discontinued

- ROBERT ASHBY, Plt. agt. JOHN STACY, Deft. On an Attachment

This day came the Plt. by his Attorney and SAMUEL MOORE, a Garnishee, being sworn declared he has one pound, thirteen shillings in his hands of the Defts. Estate, and this suit is continued untill the next Court

- BENJAMIN POPE, Plt. agt. FRANCIS MOORE, Deft. On an Attachment

This day came the Plt. by his Attorney and the Sherif haveing returned that he had attached a parcell of tobacco in the possession of SAMUEL MOORE, and the said Deft. failing to appear and replevy the attached effects altho solemnly called, It is considered by the Court that the Plt. recover against the said Deft. three shillings and ten pence half penny and his costs by him in this behalf expended; and the said Deft. in mercy, &c. And it is ordered that the Sherif sell the attached effects and return an Account of the Sale to the Court; And JAMES WINN, a Garnishee, being sworn, declared he ows the said Deft. seventeen shillings and one penny. And it is ordered that the money in the said WINNs hands be condemned towards satisfying this Judgment

- An Inventory & Sale of MARY LEE's Estate was returned and ordered to be recorded

p. Fauquier County Court 30th of June 1768

395 - GEORGE NEAVILL, JUNIOR, Plt. agt. WILLIAM OBANNION, Deft. On an Attachment

This day came the Plt. by his Attorney and MARTIN PICKETT, a Garnishee, being sworn declares that he ows the Deft. three pounds, sixteen shillings and eight pence and the Deft. failing to appear and replevy the same altho solemnly called, It is considered by the Court that the Plt. recover against the said Deft. five pounds and his costs by him in this behalf expended, and the said Deft. in mercy, &c. And it is ordered that the money in the hands of the said MARTIN PICKETT be condemned towards satisfying this Judgment

- GERARD BANKS, Plt. agt. THOMAS BRONAUGH, Deft. In Case

This day came the Plt. by his Attorney and thereupon came also a Jury, to wit, WILLIAM PICKETT, HANCOCK LEE, JOHN OBANNION, WILLIAM JENNINGS, BENJAMIN POPE, SAMUEL MOORE, JOSEPH SMITH, JOHN ALLAN, JAMES WINN, JAMES WITHERS, JAMES GARNER and FRANCIS ATWELL, who being sworn well and truly to enquire of damages in this suit, upon their Oaths do say that the said Plt. hath sustained damages by means of the Defts. breach of the promise and assumption in the Declaration mentioned to two pounds four shillings and one penny besides his costs; Therefore it is considered by the Court that the Plt. recover against the said Deft. his damages aforesaid in form aforesaid assessed and his costs by him in this behalf expended; And the said Deft. in mercy, &c,.

- JAMES WITHERS, Plt. agt. JOSEPH HUDNALL, Deft. In Case

The Jury sworn yesterday in this Cause returned into Court and upon their Oaths do say that the said Deft. is Not Guilty in manner and form as the said Deft. pleading hath alledged. Therefore it is considered by the Court tht the Plt. take nothing by his Bill but for his false clamor be in mercy, &c., And the Deft. go thereof without day and recover against the said Plt. his costs by him in this behalf expended

p. Fauquier County Court 30th of June 1768

396 - JOHN RALLS, Plt. agt. JOHN CROSBY, JUNIOR, Deft. In Case

This day came the Plt. by his Attorney and thereupon came also a Jury, to wit, WILLIAM PICKETT, HANCOCK LEE, JOHN OBANNION, WILLIAM JENNINGS, BENJAMIN POPE, SAMUEL MOORE, JOSEPH SMITH, JOHN ALLAN, JAMES WINN, JAMES WITHERS, JAMES GARNER & FRANCIS ATWELL, who being sworn well and truly to enquire of the damages in this suit, upon their Oaths do day that the Plt. hath sustained damages by means of the Deft. breach of promise and assumption in the Declaration mentioned to seven pounds, nineteen shillings and four pence, besides his costs. Therefore it is considered by the Court that the Plt. recover against the said Deft. his damages aforesaid in form aforesaid assessed and his costs by him in this behalf expended and the said Deft. in mercy, &c., And it is ordered that the Sherif sell the attached effects and return an Account of the Sales to the Court

- JOHN RALLS, Plt. agt. GEORGE CROSBY, Deft. In Case

This day came the Plt. by his Attorney and thereupon came a Jury, to witt, (the same Jury as RALLS against CATLETT) who being sworn well & truly to enquire of damages in this suit, upon their Oaths do say that the Plt. hath sustained damages by means of the Defts. breach of promise and assumption in the Declaration mentioned to six pounds, nineteen shillings and three pence farthing besides his costs. Therefore it is considered that the Plt. recover against the said Deft. his damages aforesaid in form aforesaid assessed and his costs by him in this behalf expended and the said Deft. in mercy, &c. And it is ordered that the Sherif sell the attached effects and return an Account of the Sales to the Court

- Ordered that the Court be adjourned till the Court in Course

JOS: BLACKWELL

p. - At a Court held for Fauquier County the 25th day of July 1768

397 Present THOMAS HARRISON WILLIAM GRANT
WILLIAM EDMONDS & JOSEPH HUDNALL Gent.

- Messieurs WILLIAM BOGLE & COLLIN DUNLOP, Surviving Partners of PATRICK, & WILLIAM BOGLEs & COLLIN DUNLOP, of Glasgow, Merchants, Plts. agt. WILLIAM ROUSAU, Deft. In Debt

This day came the parties by their Attornies and the said Deft. relinquishing his former plea acknowledged the action of the Plts. against him. Therefore it is considered by the Court that the Plts. recover against the said Deft. one hundred and sixty pounds current money, the Debt in the Declaration mentioned, and their costs by them in this behalf expended, and the said Deft. in mercy, &c. But this Judgment is to be discharged by the payment of seventy six pounds, ten shillings & ten pence with Interest thereon to be computed after the rate of five per centum per annum from the first day of July 1767 till paid and the costs

- ELY THOMPSON, Plt. agt. ANDREW HUME, Deft. In Case

Agreed, the Deft. paying costs

- A Lease between FRANCIS HACKLEY of the one part and JOSEPH ODOR of the other part was proved by the Oaths of JOHN MORGAN, THOMAS CONWAY & ALEXANDER WOODSIDES, witnesses thereto, and ordered to be recorded

- WILLIAM BALL, Plt. agt. PETER GRANT, Deft. In Case

This day came the parties by their Attornies and the said Deft.

p. Fauquier County Court 25th of July 1768

398 relinquishing his former plea acknowledged the action of the Plt. against him

Therefore it is considered by the Court that the Plt. recover against the said Deft. seven pounds and his costs by him in this behalf expended and the said Deft. in mercy, &c.,

- A Deed of Gift between GEORGE HOPPER of the one part and JOSEPH HOPPER and THOMAS HOPPER of the other part was proved by the Oaths of JOSEPH BLACKWELL, JOHN CHILTON & THOMAS MATTHEWS, witnesses thereto, ordered to be recorded

- An Indenture of Feofment between GEORGE HOPPER, JOSEPH HOPPER & THOMAS HOPPER of the one part and JOSEPH BLACKWELL of the other part and a Memorandum of Livery of Seisen & Receit thereon endorsed were proved by the Oaths of THOMAS SMITH, THOMAS MATTHEW & JOHN SMITH, witnesses thereto, ordered to be recorded

- ROBERT BOULT is appointed Surveyor of the Road from his Lordships New Road into the Main Road leading from GOOSE CREEK and it is ordered that he with the persons using the said Road do clear and keep the same in repair according to Law

- An Indenture of Bargain and Sale between JAMES SCOTT, JUNIOR of the one part and WILLIAM STAMPS of the other part and a Receit thereon endorsed were acknowledged by the said JAMES SCOTT to be his act and deed, ordered to be recorded

- A Bond from JAMES SCOTT, JUNIOR & WILLIAM ELLZEY to WILLIAM STAMPS was acknowledged by the said JAMES SCOTT & WILLIAM ELLZEY, ordered to be recorded

- Indentures of lease and Release between JOHN BALENDINE & MARY his Wife of the one part and JAMES SCOTT of the other part & Receit thereon endorsed were proved by the Oaths of JOHN CHILTON & WILLIAM HUNTON, witnesses thereto, ordered to be certified

- An Indenture of Feofment between JOHN BALENDINE & MARY his Wife of the one part and JAMES SCOTT of the other part and Receit thereon endorsed were proved by the Oaths of JOHN CHILTON & WILLIAM HUNTON, witnesses thereto, ordered to be certified

- AMBROSE KEMP, Plt. agt. WILLIAM PINKARD, Deft. In Case

This day came the Plt. by his attorney and came also (? ELLMORE GEORG)

p. Fauquier County Court 25th of July 1768

399 and became Special Bail & Pledge for the Deft. in this suit, and the said Deft. by

WILLIAM ELLZEY, his Attorney, prays & has leave to imparl specially to the Plts. Declaration untill the next Court and then to plead

- An Indenture of Feofment between JOHN BALLENDINE & MARY his Wife of the one part and JOHN CHILTON of the other part and a Receit thereon endorsed were proved by the Oaths of JAMES SCOTT and WILLIAM HUNTON, witnesses thereto. ordered to be certified

- An Indenture of Feofment between JOHN BALLENDINE and MARY his Wife of the one part and WILLIAM HUNTON of the other part and a Receit thereon endorsed were proved by the Oaths of JAMES SCOTT and JOHN CHILTON, witnesses thereto, ordered to be certified

- A Release from HECTOR ROSS to JAMES SCOTT, JOHN CHILTON & WILLIAM HUNTON was proved by the Oaths of WHARTON RANSDELL & WILLIAM RANSDELL, witnesses thereto, and ordered to be certified

- Indentures of Lease and Release between JOSEPH COMBS and ELIZABETH his Wife of the one part and ORIGINAL YOUNG of the other part & a Receit thereon endorsed were proved by the Oaths of JOHN LEE, JOSEPH BARBEE & SINNETT YOUNG, witnesses thereto & together with a Commission for takeing the acknowledgment and privy examination of the said ELIZABETH & a Certificate of Execution thereof, ordered to be recorded

- WILLIAM WAITE came into Court and exhibitted & proved an Account against the Estate of JOHN FELTON, deced., ordered to be certified

- On hearing the Petition of SAMUEL WALKER against CHARLES MORGAN and WILLIAM WOOD, the same is dismissed and it is ordered that the Plt. pay to the Defts. their costs by them in this behalf expended

- WILLIAM ELLZEY, Plt. agt. JEFFREY JOHNSON, JUNR., Deft. On a Petition
Judgment is granted the Plt. against the said Deft. for three pounds, one shilling and seven pence and his costs by him in this behalf expended

- SARAH LEE, an Infant by HANCOCK LEE her next Friend, Plt. agt.
GEORGE GRANT, Deft. On a Petition
Discontinued, being agreed by the parties

p. Fauquier County Court 25th of July 1768

400 - RICHARD BRYAN & JANE MAHORNEY being summoned as witnesses for SAMUEL THORNBERRY against JOHN MORGAN and not appearing, it is ordered that an Attachment issue against them returnable to the next Court

- ROBERT BOULT, Plt. agt. JOHN REED, Deft. On a Petition
Judgment is granted the Plt. against the said Deft. for three pounds, four shillings and his costs by him in this behalf expended

- Absent. WILLIAM EDMONDS & JOSEPH BLACKWELL)
- Present. JOSEPH BLACKWELL, ARMISTEAD CHURCHHILL, & JEREMIAH DARNALL) Gent.

- On the motion of ALEXANDER WOODSIDES, it is ordered that a Dedimus issue to take the Deposition of a certain witness who lives in the Province of PENSYLVANIA at the suit of JOHN SHUMATE, he giving the Plt. legal notice of the time & place of executing the same

- HANCOCK LEE, Assignee of MARTIN PICKETT & COMPANY, Plt.
agt. WILLIAM FELKINS, Deft. On a Petition
Judgment is granted the Plt. against the said Deft. for two pounds, seventeen shillings & six pence with Interest thereon to be computed after the rate of five per centum per annum from the first day of October 1767 till paid and his costs by him in this behalf expended

- The Same, Plt. agt. EDWARD ELLSMORE, Deft. On a Petition
Judgment is granted the Plt. against the said Deft. for three pounds and his costs by him in this behalf

p. Fauquier County Court 25th of July 1768

401 expended, But this Judgment is to be discharged by the paiment of one pound, ten shillings with Interest thereon to be computed after the rate of five per centum per annum from the eleventh day of May 1767 till paid & the costs

- The Same, Plt. agt. JOHN WILLOUGHBY, Deft. On a Petition
Judgment is granted the Plt. against the said Deft. for two pounds with Interest thereon to be computed after the rate of five per centum per annum from the fifteenth day of July 1767 till paid & his costs by him in this behalf expended

- Ordered that the Court be adjourned till tomorrow morning ten of the Clock
THOMAS HARRISON

- At a Court continued and held for Fauquier County the 26th day of July 1768
Present THOMAS HARRISON, JOSEPH BLACKWELL
WILLIAM EDMONDS & JEREMIAH DARNALL Gent.

- On the motion of EUPHIMA DAVIS, who made Oath & executed and acknowledged Bond as the Law directs, Certificate is granted her for obtaining Letters of Administration of the Estate of THOMAS DAVIS, deced.

- Ordered that JAMES FREEMAN, LUKE HOLDER, JOHN BELL & STEPHEN McCORMACK or any three of them being first sworn do appraise the Estate of THOMAS DAVIS, deced., and return the appraisment to the Court

- JOHN WIATT, Assee. of JOHN ARIS, Plt. agt. WILLIAM WAITE, Survivor of JOHN FELTON & WILLIAM WAITE, Deft. In Debt.
This day came the Plt. by his Attorney and the Sherif haveing

p. Fauquier County Court 26th of July 1768
402 returned on the Attachment awarded against the said Defts. Estate that he had attached one Chest of Drawers and the said Deft. not appearing to replevy the same altho solemnly called, It is considered by the Court that the Plt. recover against the said Deft. sixteen pounds current money, the Debt in the Declaration mentioned, and his costs by him in this behalf expended; and the said Deft. in mercy, &c., But this Judgment is to be discharged by the payment of eight pounds with Interest thereon to be computed after the rate of five per centum per annum from the seventeenth day of June 1767 till paid and the costs, And it is ordered that the Sherif sell the attached effects and return an Account of the Sales to the Court

- WILLIAM SETTLE, Assignee of AMY SETTLE, Plt. agt. JOHN JETT, Deft. In Debt
This day came the Plt. by his Attorney and the said Deft. altho solemnly called came not but made default. Therefore it is considered by the Court that the Order of the last Court against the said Deft. and WILLIAM TRIPLETT, his Security, be confirmed and that the Plt. recover against them forty eight pounds, four shillings & eight pence current money, the Debt in the Declaration mentioned, and his costs by him in this behalf expended, And the said Deft. in mercy &c., But this Judgment is to be discharged by the paiment of twenty four pounds, two shillings & four pence with Interest thereon to be computed after the rate of five per centum per annum from the seventh day of June 1766 till paid & the costs

- ARCHIBALD McCALL, Assignee of JOHN ARISS, Plt. agt. WILLIAM WAITE, Survivor of WILLIAM WAITE & JOHN FELTON, Deft., In Debt
This day came the Plt. by his Attorney and the Sherif haveing returned on the Attachment awarded against the said Defts. Estate

p. Fauquier County Court 26th of July 1768
403 that he had attached one Desk and the said Deft. failing to appear and replevy the same altho solemnly called, It is considered by the Court that the Plt. recover against the said Deft. fourteen pounds, six shillings, the Debt in the Declaration men-

tioned, and his costs by him in this behalf expended, and the said Deft. in mercy, &c., But this Judgment is to be discharged by the payment of seven pounds, three shillings with Interest thereon to be computed after the rate of five per centum per annum from the seventh day of December 1767 till paid and the costs; And it is ordered that the Sherif sell the attached effects and return an Account of the Sales to the Court

- Present. WILLIAM GRANT & JAMES SCOTT, Gent.

- JAMES NEAVILL, Plt. agt. ALEXANDER JEFFRIES, Deft. In Trespass, Assault & Battery

Discontinued being agreed by the parties

- BENJAMIN SETTLE, Plt. agt. JOSEPH SETTLE, Deft. In Chancery

Discontinued being agreed by the parties

- JAMES LANE, Plt. agt. MARY ISHAM KEITH, Deft. In Case

This day came the parties by their Attorneys and the said Deft. acknowledged the action of the Plt. against her for seven pounds, three shillings & nine pence. Therefore it is considered by the Court that the Plt. recover against the said Deft. the said seven pounds, three shillings & nine pence and his costs by him in this behalf expended and the said Deft. in mercy &c.

- An Indenture of Bargain and Sale between JOSEPH SETTLE and MARY his Wife of the one part and BENJAMIN SETTLE of the otehr part and Receit thereon endorsed were acknowledged by the said

p. Fauquier County Court 26th of July 1768

404 JOSEPH & MARY his Wife (she being first privily examined as the Law directs) to be their act and deed, ordered to be recorded

- CHARLES LYNCH, Plt. agt. SAMUEL BLACKWELL, Deft. In Case

This suit is dismist and it is ordered that the Plt. pay the Deft. his costs by him in this behalf expended

- An Indenture of Bargain and Sale between BENJAMIN SETTLE & CATHARINE his Wife of the one part and GEORGE SETTLE of the other part and a Receit thereon endorsed were acknowledged by the said BENJAMIN SETTLE & CATHARINE his Wife, (she being first privily examined as the Law directs) to be their act and deed, ordered to be recorded

- ANDREW KENNEDY & JOHN GLASSELL, Admors. of ROBERT BURGIS, deced., Plts. agt. SAMUEL EARLE, Deft. In Case

Continued untill the next Court and by the consent of the parties this suit is not to abate by the death of either party

- On the motion of BRYAN BRUIN, it is ordered that a Dedimus issue to take the Deposition of ALEXANDER WHITE, a witness for him against JOHN OBANNION & FRANCES his Wife

- JOHN CHURCHHILL, Plt. agt. JOHN ARIS, Deft. In Case

By consent of the parties, all matters in difference relation to this suit are refered to WHATON RANSDELL, WILLIAM GRANT & JOHN HATHAWAY, or any two of them & their award to be the Judgment of the Court

- On the motion of WILLIAM WITHERS, it is ordered that JOSEPH LAVEL pay him twenty five pounds of tobacco for one days attendance as a witness for THOMAS WITHERS against him, the suit being continued at his costs

p. Fauquier County Court 26th of July 1768

405 - On the motion of JAMES WITHERS, it is ordered that JOSEPH LAVEL pay him fifty pounds of tobacco for two days attendance as a witness for THOMAS WITHERS against him, the suit being continued at his costs

- ALEXANDER WODROW & JOHN NEILSON, Plts. agt. JOSEPH SETTLE, Deft.
On an Attachment
Discontinued

- Present. ARMISTEAD CHURCHHILL, Gent.

- JOHN BAILEY, Plt. agt. JAMES WINN, Deft. In Debt
This day came the parties by their Attorneys and thereupon came also a Jury, to wit, DAVID KALE, EPHRAIM HUBBARD, JAMES HATHAWAY, PHARNACH GEORGE, JAMES GARNER, GEORGE BERRY, HENRY MAUZEY, GEORGE BENNITT, BUSHROD DOGGETT, THOMAS HATHAWAY, PHILIP WATERFIELD & THOMAS WATTS who being elected tried & sowrn the truth to speak upon the issue joined, upon their Oaths do say that the Deft. is Guilty in manner and form as the Plt. against him hath declared and that the Deft. doth owe to the Plt. five pounds; and they do assess the Plts. damages by occasion of the detention of that debt to one penny besides his costs, and the said Deft. prays that Judgment on the Verdict aforesaid may be arrested & stayed for the following reasons; to wit, First, the Declaration lays the receiving the money after the gameing alledged; Secondly, that the Writ is irregular not mentioning any sum as to the Debt., And this suit is continued untill the next Court for the matters of Law arriseing thereupon to be argued

- ADAM HUNTER, Plt. agt. MINOR WINN & JAMES WINN, Defts. In Debt
Dismist being agreed by the parties

p. Fauquier County Court 26th of July 1768

406 - HENRY LEE, DANIEL PAYNE and JANE BAYLIS, Exors. &c. of JOHN BAYLIS, deced., Plts. agt. ALEXANDER PARKER, Deft. Upon a Writ of Scire Facias to revive a Judgment obtained by the said JOHN BAYLIS, deced., in his life time against the said Deft. for twenty seven pounds, twelve shillings & one penny damages and five hundred and thirty three pounds of nett tobacco and fifteen shillings or one hundred and fifty pounds of tobacco for costs;
It is considered by the Court that the Plts. may have their Execution against the said Deft. for his damages & costs aforesaid according to the force form & effect of the recovery aforesaid, And it is further considered by the Court that the Plts. recover against the said Deft. their costs by them in this behalf expended and the said Deft. in mercy, &c.

- JOHN BEVERLEY ROY, Assignee of GEORGE STUBBLEFIELD, Plt. against PETER GRANT, Deft. In Debt
This day came the parties by their Attorneys and the said Deft. relinquishing his former plea, acknowledged the action of the Plt. against him. Therefore it is considered by the Court that the Plt. recover against the said Deft. thirty six pounds current money, the Debt in the Declaration mentioned, and his costs by him in this behalf expended; and the said Deft. in mercy, &c., But this Judgment is to be discharged by the payment of eighteen pounds with Interest thereon to be computed after the rate of five per centum per annum from the first day of November 1766 till paid & the costs

- On the motion of JAMES BAILEY, it is ordered that JOHN BAILEY pay him fifty pounds of tobacco for two days attendance as a witness for him against JAMES WINN

p. Fauquier County Court 26th of July 1768

407 - On the motion of JOHN HALL, it is ordered that JOHN BAILEY pay him fifty pounds of tobacco for two days attendance as a witness for him against JAMES WINN.

- The same Order for BENNITT PRICE

- Messieurs WILLIAM BOGLE & COLLIN DUNLOP, Surviving Partners of PATRICK & WILLIAM BOGLEs & COLLIN DUNLOP of Glasgow, Merchants, Plts. against SAMUEL BLACKWELL, Deft. In Debt

This day came the parties by their Attorneys and the said Deft. relinquishing his former plea acknowledged the action of the Plts. against him, Therefore it is considered by the Court that the Plts. recover against the said Deft. thirty three pounds current money, the Debt in the Declaration mentioned and their costs by them in this behalf expended, and the said Deft. in mercy, &c., But this Judgment is to be discharged by the paiment of sixteen pounds, ten shillings & six pence half penny with Interest thereon to be computed after the rate of five per centum per annum from the eighth day of April 1766 till paid & the costs

- ANDREW COCKRANE, WILLIAM CUNNINGHAME & COMPANY, Plts. agt. JOHN DUNCAN, JUNR. (Son of JOHN), Deft. In Case

This day came the Plts. by their Attorney and thereupon a Jury to wit, DAVID KALE, THOMAS WITHERS, JAMES HATHAWAY, PHARNACH GEORGE, JAMES GARNER, GEORGE BERRY, HENRY MAUZEY, GEORGE BENNITT, BUSHROD DOGGETT, THOMAS HATHAWAY, PHILIP WATERFIELD & THOMAS WATTS, JUNR., who being sworn well & truly to Enquire of damages in this suit, upon their Oaths do say that the Plts. have sustained damages by means of the Defts. breach of the promise & assumption in the Declaration mentioned

p. Fauquier County Court 26th of July 1768

408 to forty two pounds, sixteen shillings & six pence besides their costs; Therefore it is considered by the Court that the Plts. recover against the said Deft. & CHARLES WRIGHT & WILLIAM KEIRNES, his Securitys, their damages aforesaid in form aforesaid assessed and their costs by them in this behalf expended, and the said Deft. in mercy, &c.

- HENRY ELLISON of Whitehaven, Plt. agt. THOMAS BRONAUGH, Deft. In Debt

This day came the parties by their Attorneys and the said Deft. relinquishing his former plea acknowledged the action of the Plt. against him. Therefore it is considered by the Court that the Plt. recover against the said Deft. eighty four pounds current money, the Debt in the Declaration mentioned, and his costs by him in this behalf expended, and the said Deft. in mercy, &c., But this Judgment is to be discharged by the payment of forty one pounds, eighteen shillings & eight pence with Interest thereon to be computed after the rate of five per centum per annum from the first day of August 1765 till paid & the costs

- Absent. ARMISTEAD CHURCHHILL, Gent.

- PHILIP WATERFIELD, Plt. agt. JOHN CHURCHHILL, Deft. In Case

Thsi day came the parties by their Attornies and thereupon came allso a Jury, to wit, DAVID KALE, JAMES GARNER, GEORGE BERRY, HENRY MAUZEY, GEORGE BENNITT, BUSHROD DOGGETT, THOMAS HATHAWAY, THOMAS WATTS, BEN SETTLE, GEORGE SETTLE, WILLIAM SMITH and EPHRAIM HUBBARD, who being elected tried & sworn the truth to speak upon the issue joined, upon their Oaths do say that the said Deft. is Guilty in manner and form as the Plt. against him hath declared and they do assess the Plts. damages by reason thereof to ten pounds besides his costs; Therefore it is considered by the Court that the Plt. recover against the said deft. his damages aforesaid in form aforesaid assessed and his costs by him in this behalf expended; And the said Deft. in mercy, &c.

p. Fauquier County Court 26th of July 1768

409 - THOMAS DOUGLAS & COMPANY of MONTROSE, Merchants, Plts. agt. JOHN BAYLIS, Deft. In Debt

This day came the parties by their Attorneys and the said Deft. relinquishing his former plea acknowledged the Plts. action against him. Therefore it is considered by the Court that the Plts. recover against the said Deft. six pounds, the Debt in the Declaration mentioned, and their costs by them in this behalf expended, and the said Deft. in mercy, &c., But this Judgment is to be discharged by the paiment of two pounds, ten shillings with Interest thereon to be computed after the rate of five per centum per annum from the first day of October 1765 till paid and the costs

- On the motion of JOHN BAYLIS, an Injunction is granted him to stay the Execution of a Judgment obtained by THOMAS DOUGLASS & COMPANY against him untill the matter thereof can be heard in Equity, his giving Bond and Security as the Law directs before next Court

- MARTIN HARDIN, Plt. agt. HUMPHREY BROOKE, Deft. In Debt

This day came as well the Plt. by his Attorney as the Deft. in his proper person and the said Deft. relinquishing his former plea and acknowledged the action of the Plt. against him. Therefore it is considered by the Court that the Plt. recover against the said Deft. seven pounds, the Debt in the Declaration mentioned, and his costs by him in this behalf expended, And the said Deft. in mercy, &c., But this Judgment is to be discharged by the paiment of two pounds, eighteen shillings & two pence current money with Interest thereon to be computed after the rate of five per centum per annum from the 17th day of June 1767 till paid & the costs

- Messieurs WILLIAM BOGLE & COLLIN DUNLOP, Surviving Partners of PATRICK & WILLIAM BOGLEs & COLLIN DUNLOP, of Glasgow, Merchants, Plts. agt. PETER GRANT, Deft. In Case

This day came the parties by their Attornies and the said Deft.

p. 410 Fauquier County Court 26th of July 1768

relinquishing his former plea acknowledged the action of the Plts. against him for thirty seven pounds, thirteen shillings & an half penny. Therefore it is considered by the Court that the Plt. recover against the said Deft. the thirty seven pounds, thirteen shillings & an half penny and their costs by them in this behalf expended, and the said Deft. in mercy, &c.

- The Same, Plts. agt. HANCOCK LEE, Deft. In Debt

This day came the parties by their Attornies and the said Deft. relinquishing his former plea acknowledged the action of the Plts. against him; Therefore it is considered by the Court that the Plts. recover against the said Deft. one hundred and eighteen pounds & four pence current money of Virginia, the Debt in the Declaration mentioned, and their costs by them in this behalf expended, and the said Deft. in mercy, &c., But this Judgment is to be discharged by the paiment of fifty four pounds, fourteen shillings & two pence with Interest thereon to be computed after the rate of five per centum per annum from the thirtieth day of September 1767 till paid & the costs

- The Same, Plts. agt. HANCOCK LEE, Admor. of MARY LEE, deced., Deft. In Case

This day came the parties by their Attornies and the said Deft. relinquishing his former plea acknowledged the Plts. action against him for six pounds, twelve shillings & eleven pence half penny. Therefore it is considered by the Court that the Plts. recover against the said Deft. the said six pounds, twelve shillings & eleven pence half penny to be levied of the goods & chattells of the said MARY LEE in the hands of the said HANCOCK LEE to be administered, and their costs by them in this behalf expended, And the said Deft. in mercy, &c.

- ANTHONY GARRETT is appointed Constable in this County in the

p. Fauquier County Court 26th of July 1768

411 room of WILLIAM ROBERTSON, and it is ordered that he take the Oaths prescribed by Law before a Justice of this County

- JOHN JETT is appointed Surveyor of the Road from CEDAR RUN to ELK RUN and it is ordered that he with the Tithes belonging to the said Road do clear and keep the same in repair according to Law

- On the motion of JOHN DUNCAN, JUNR., it is ordered that PHILIP WATERFIELD pay him fifty pounds of tobacco for two days attendance as a witness for him against JOHN CHURCHHILL

- On the motion of JAMES YOUNG, it is ordered that PHILIP WATERFIELD pay him fifty pounds of tobacco for two days attendance as a witness for him against JOHN CHURCHHILL.

- On the motion of JAMES HATHAWAY, it is ordered that JOHN CHURCHHILL pay him twenty five pounds of tobacco for one days attendance as a witness for him at the suit of PHILIP WATERFIELD

- Ordered that the Court be adjourned till the Court in Course

" JOSEPH BLACKWELL "

(Fauquier County Minute Book, 1764-1768, ends.).

FAUQUIER COUNTY, VIRGINIA
MINUTE BOOK
1768-1773

p. 1 At a Court held for Fauquier County the 22nd day of August 1768
Present THOMAS HARRISON, WILLIAM EDMONDS
JEREMIAH DARNALL & JOSEPH HUDNALL Gent.

- JOHN GRIGSBY, Plt. agt. GEORGE RANKINS, Deft. In Case
This day came the Plt. by his Attorney and thereupon came a Jury, to wit, WILLIAM SEATON, JOHN MAUZEY, JOHN KEITH, JOHN SINCLAIR, JUNR., JOSEPH LAVELL, WILLIAM ROUSAU, JOSEPH HUDNALL, JAMES WITHERS, CHARLES DUNCAN, EDWAD HAMPTON, JAMES DUNCAN & CHARLES GARNER, who being sworn well and truly to enquire of the damages in this suit, upon their Oaths do say that the Plt. hath sustained damages by means of the Defts. breach of promise and assumption in the Declaration mentioned to six pounds, nineteen shillings & four pence farthing besides his costs; Therefore it is considered by the Court that the Plt. recover against the said Defendant his damages aforesaid in form aforesaid assessed and his costs by him in this behalf expended, and the said Deft. in mercy, &c., And it is ordered that the Sherif sell the attached effects and return an account of the sales to the Court

- A Lease between the Right Honourable THOMAS LORD FAIRFAX of one part and DAVID DARNALL of the other part was proved by the Oaths of JAMES SCOTT, WILLIAM RANSDELL and JOHN MOFFETT, witnesses thereto, & ordered to be recorded

- A Lease between the Right Honourable THOMAS LORD FAIRFAX of one part and THOMAS HICKERSON of the other part was proved by the Oaths of JAMES SCOTT, WILLIAM RANSDELL

p. 2 Fauquier County Court 22nd of August 1768
and JOHN MOFFETT, witnesses thereto, & ordered to be recorded

- A Lease between the Right Honourable THOMAS LORD FAIRFAX of one part and WILLIAM GRIMSLEY of the other part was proved by the Oath sof JAMES SCOTT, WILLIAM RANSDELL and JOHN MOFFETT, witnesses thereto, and ordered to be recorded

- A Lease between the Right Honourable THOMAS LORD FAIRFAX of one part and DANIEL RECTOR of the other part was proved by the Oaths of JAMES SCOTT, WILLIAM RANSDELL and JOHN MOFFETT, witnesses thereto, and ordered to be recorded

- A Lease between the Right Honourable THOMAS LORD FAIRFAX of one part and JOHN MARSHALL of the other part was proved by the Oaths of JAMES SCOTT, WILLIAM RANSDELL and JOHN MOFFETT, witnesses thereto. and ordered to be recorded

- A Lease between the Right Honourable THOMAS LORD FAIRFAX of one part and WILLIAM DAY of the other part was proved by the Oaths of JAMES SCOTT, WILLIAM RANSDELL & JOHN MOFFETT, witnessess thereto and ordered to be recorded

- A Lease between the Right Honourable THOMAS LORD FAIRFAX of one part and WILLIAM FELKINS of the other part was proved by the Oaths of JAMES SCOTT, WILLIAM RANSDELL & JOHN MOFFETT, witnesses thereto, and ordered to be recorded

- A Lease between the Right Honourable THOMAS LORD FAIRFAX of one part and DAVID BARTON of the other part was proved by the Oaths of JAMES SCOTT, WILLIAM RANSDELL and JOHN MOFFETT, witnesses thereto, and ordered to be recorded

- A Lease between the Right Honourable THOMAS LORD FAIRFAX of one part and LEWIS WOODYARD of the other part was proved by the Oaths of JAMES SCOTT, WILLIAM RANSDELL & JOHN MOFFETT, witnesses thereto, and ordered to be recorded

p. Fauquier County Court 22nd of August 1768

3 - A Lease between the Right Honourable THOMAS LORD FAIRFAX of one part and BENJAMIN ROPER of the other part was proved by the Oaths of JAMES SCOTT, WILLIAM RANSDELL & JOHN MOFFETT, witnesses thereto, and ordered to be recorded

- A Lease between the Right Honourable THOMAS LORD FAIRFAX of one part and JACOB UTTERBACK of the other part was proved by the Oaths of JAMES SCOTT, WILLIAM RANSDELL & JOHN MOFFETT, witnesses thereto, and ordered to be recorded

- A Lease between the Right Honourable THOMAS LORD FAIRFAX of one part and WILLIAM DULING of the other part was proved by the Oaths of JAMES SCOTT, WILLIAM RANSDELL & JOHN MOFFETT, witnesses thereto, and ordered to be recorded

- JOHN RALLS, Assignee of WILLIAM SCOTT, Plt. agt. ROBERT CLEVELAND & EDWARD DICKENSON, Defts. In Debt

Discontinued being agreed by the parties

- JOHN RALLS, Plt. agt. BAILEY WOOD, Deft. On a Petition

Judgment is granted the Plt. against the said Deft. for his costs by him in this behalf expended

- PRESLY THORNTON & FRANCIS THORNTON, Exors. of FRANCIS THORNTON, deced., who was Assignee of ALSMEDON GESSITH, Plt. agt. ALLAN GUTTRIDGE, Def.t In Debt

Judgment is granted the Plts. against the said Deft. for their tobacco costs by them in this behalf expended

p. Fauquier County Court 22nd of August 1768

4 - CHARLES MORGAN, Plt. agt. SCARLETT MADDIN, Deft. In Case

This day came the parties by their Attornies and thereupon came also a Jury, to wit, JONAS WILLIAMS, JAMES WRIGHT, SAMUEL THORNBERRY, JAMES OLDHAM, RICHARD OLDHAM, THOMAS WATTS, THOMAS ELLIOTT, JAMES BASHAW, JOHN McCOR-MACK, FRANCIS McCORMACK, JOHN MOREHEAD and JOHN HUTCHINGS who being elected tried and sworn the truth to speak upon the issue joined, upon their Oaths do say that the Deft. did assume upon himself in manner and form as the Plt. against him hath declared and they do assess the Plts. damages by means of the Defts. breach of that assumption to one shilling besides his costs. Therefore it is considered by the Court that the Plt. recover against the said Deft. his damages aforesaid in form aforesaid assessed and his costs by him in this behalf expended, and the said Deft. in mercy, &c.

- BENJAMIN SNELLING, Plt. agt. JOHN BURK, Deft. In Trespass

This day came the parties by their Attorneys and teh said Deft. relinquishing his former plea acknowledged the Plts. action against him for ten shillings. Therefore it is considered by the Court that the Plt. recover against the said Deft. the said ten shillings and his costs by him in this behalf expended and the said Deft. in mercy. &c.

- On the Petition of CHARLES CHINN, leave is granted him to erect a Water Mill on CROMWELLS RUN, it appearing that he has Land on both sides the said Run and that the Land of no other person will be affected thereby

p. Fauquier County Court 22nd of August 1768

5 - HANNAH CORBIN, Plt. agt. JOHN ARISS, Deft. In Case

This suit is dismist and it is ordered that the Plt. pay to the Deft. his costs by him in this behalf expended

- CHARLES RECTOR, Plt. agt. ROBERT JARVIS, Deft. In Trespass, Assault & Battery Discontinued, being agreed by the parties

- Absent. JOSEPH HUDNALL)
- Present. JOHN MOFFETT,) Gentlemen

- THOMAS WITHERS, Plt. agt. JOSEPH LAVEL, Deft., In Case

This day came the parties by their Attorneys and thereupon came also a Jury, to wit, BAILEY WOOD, JAMES WRIGHT, SAMUEL THORNBERRY, JAMES OLDHAM, RICHARD OLDHAM, THOMAS WATTS, THOMAS ELLIOTT, JAMES BASHAW, JOHN McCORMACK, FRANCIS McCORMACK, JOHN MOREHEAD and JOHN HUTCHINGS, who being elected tried and sworn the truth to speak upon the issue joined, upon their Oaths do say that the said Deft. is Guilty in manner and form as the Plt. against him hath declared and they do assess the Plts. damages by occasion thereof to eight pounds besides his costs. Therefore it is considered by the Court that the Plt. recover against the said Deft. his damages aforesaid in form aforesaid assessed and his costs by him in this behalf expended; And the said Deft. in mercy, &c. And on the motion of the Deft.

p. Fauquier County Court 22nd of August 1768

6 and it apparing to the Court that the Jury found contrary to the Evidence, a new Trial is awarded him in this Cause, he paying the costs of this Tryal

- ARMISTEAD CHURCHHILL, Gent., returned his List of Tithes

- Absent. WILLIAM EDMONDS,)
- Present. JAMES SCOTT) Gentlemen

- Indentures of Lease and Release between JOSEPH THOMAS and KATEY his Wife of the one part and JOSEPH HOLTZCLAW of the other part were acknowledged by the said JOSEPH and KATEY (she being first privily examined as the Law directs) and with the Receit on the Release endorsed which was also acknowledged by the said JOSEPH, ordered to be recorded

- WILLIAM GRANT, Gent., returned his List of Tithes

- A Lease between the Right Honourable THOMAS LORD FAIRFAX of the one part and SIMON HEFLIN of the other part was proved by the Oaths of JAMES SCOTT, HUMPHREY BROOKE and MARTIN PICKETT, witnesses thereto, and ordered to be recorded

- Absent. THOMAS HARRISON,
- Present JOSEPH BLACKWELL & JOSEPH HUDNALL Gent.

- A Lease between the Right Honourable THOMAS LORD FAIRFAX of the one part and ELIZABETH MARSHALL of the other part was proved by the Oaths of JAMES SCOTT, HUMPHREY BROOKE and MARTIN PICKETT, witnesses thereto, and ordered to be recorded

- An Indenture of Feofment between GEORGE HENRY and LYDIA his Wife of the one part and RICHARD LEWIS of the other part was acknowledged by the said GEORGE & LYDIA (she being first privily examined as the Law directs) and together with a Memorandum of Livery of Seisen and Receit thereon endorsed, which were

p. Fauquier County Court 22nd of August 1768

7 also acknowledged by the said GEORGE and ordered to be recorded

- On the motion of THOMAS JAMES, a Licence is granted him for keeping ORDINARY at his House in this County for one year, he haveing executed and acknowledged Bond as the Law directs

- Present WILLIAM BLACKWELL, Gent.

- JOHN MARSHALL, Plt. agt. JOHN ARISS, Deft. In Case

This day came the parties by their Attornies (and by their consent the Order of Reference in this suit is discharged), And thereupon came also a Jury, to wit, WILLIAM

JENNINGS, THOMAS HATHAWAY, JAMES WITHERS, JAMES HATHAWAY, CHARLES WICKLIFF, WILLIAM PARKER, GEORGE SETTLE, WILLIAM SUTTON, JOHN COCKE, FRANCIS PAYNE, THOMAS WILLIAMS & JOHN KEITH, who being elected tried and sworn the truth to speak upon the issue joined, withdrew to consider of their Verdict

- JAMES SCOTT, Gent. returned his List of Tithes

- RICHARD LANGHAM HALL, Plt. against HUMPHREY BROOKE, Deft. In Case

This day came as well the Plt. by his Attorney as the Deft. in his proper person and the Deft. acknowledged the action of the Plt. against him for twenty pounds. Therefore it is considered that the Plt. recover against the said Deft. the said twenty pounds and his costs by him in this behalf expended, and the said Deft. in mercy, &c.

- On the motion of JAMES GARNER, it is ordered that JOSEPH LAVEL pay him one hundred pounds of tobacco for four days attendance as a witness for him at the suit of THOMAS WITHERS, the suit being continued at his cost

p. Fauquier County Court 22nd of August 1768

8 - On the motion of JAMES WITHERS, it is ordered that JOSEPH LAVEL pay him twenty five pounds of tobacco for one days attendance as a witness for THOMAS WITHERS against him, the suit being continued at his cost

- The same for WILLIAM WITHERS

- A Lease between the Right Honourable THOMAS LORD FAIRFAX of the one part and JOHN PAYNE of the other part was proved by the Oaths of JAMES SCOTT, HUMPHREY BROOKE and MARTIN PICKETT, witnesses thereto, and ordered to be recorded

- Ordered that two Tithes belonging to JOHN ROUT be added to the List of Tithes

- ANDREW DILLON, Plt. agt. JOHN TWENTYMAN, Deft. In Debt

By consent of the parties, all matters in dispute relating to this suit are refered to THOMAS SLAUGHTER, HENRY FIELD, JUNR. and BENJAMIN ROBERTS, Gent., and their award or the award of any two of them to be Judgment of the Court

- Ordered that JOHN HOPPER, DIXON BROWN, WILLIAM DAY and JOHN CRIMM or any three of them being first sworn do view the most convenient way from the Road cleared by the County of CULPEPER near WILLIAM DAYs into his Lordships road and return their Report to the Court

- DAVID PANNILL, Plt. agt. JAMES BROWN, Deft. In Debt

This day came the Plt. by his Attorney and came also JAMES BROWN and became Special Bail and Pledge for the Deft. in this suit, and the said Deft. prays and has leave to imparl specially to the Plts. Declaration untill the next Court and then to plead

p. Fauquier County Court 22nd of August 1768

9 - Ordered that three Tithes belonging to JOHN JOHNSON be added to the Lists of Tithes

- MARTIN PICKETT, Assignee of REUBIN BRAMLETT, Plt. agt. WILLIAM SMITH & WILLIAM BALL, Deft. On a Petition

This day came as well the Plt. by his Attorney as the Deft., BALL, in his proper person and the said Deft. ackdnowledged the action of the Plt. against him. Therefore it is considered by the Court that the Plt. recover against the said Deft. three pounds, fifteen shillings current money and his costs by him in this behalf expended. And teh said Deft. in mercy, &c. And the Petition abates against the Deft., SMITH, the Sherif haveing returned that he is no Inhabitant of this County

- On the motion of SARAH SHIP, it is ordered that ARMISTEAD CHURCHHILL pay her eighty five pounds of tobacco for one days attendance, and once comeing twenty mines and returning, as a witness for him at the suit of THOMAS WATTS, JUNR.

- An Indenture of Feofment between EDWARD BALL and ELIZABETH his Wife of the one part and RICHARD COVINGTON of the other part was acknowledged by the said EDWARD and ELIZABETH his Wife (she being first privily examined as the Law directs) and together with a Memorandum of LIvery of Seisen and Receit thereon endorsed were also acknowledged by the said EDWARD, ordered to be recorded

- Ordered that the Court be adjourned til tomorrow morning nine of the Clock

JOSEPH BLACKWELL

p. - At a Court continued and held for Fauquier County the 23d day of August 1768
10 Present JOSEPH BLACKWELL WILLIAM BLACKWELL
WILLIAM GRANT & JEREMIAH DARNALL Gent.

- HENRY BOATMAN, Plt. agt. WILLIAM SUTTON, Deft., On a Petition Judgment is granted the Plt. against the said Deft. for his costs by him in this behalf expended

- On hearing the Petition of THOMAS WATTS against ARMISTEAD CHURCHHILL, the same is dismist and it is ordered that the Plt. pay to the Deft. his costs by him in this behalf expended

- MARTIN PICKETT and COMPANY, Plts. agt. BENJAMIN SEBASTIN, Deft. In Debt This day came as well the Plts. by their Attorney as the Deft. in his proper person and the said Deft. acknowledged the Plts. action against him. Therefore it is considered by the Court that the Plts. recover against the said Deft. thirty pounds, eleven shillings and three pence current money, the Debt in the Declaration mentioned, and their costs by them in this behalf expended; And the said Deft. in mercy, &c., But this Judgment is to be discharged by the payment of three pounds, four shillings and six pence like money with Interest thereupon to be computed after the rate of five per centum per annum from the twenty fourth day of May 1763 till paid and the costs. Execution stayed till Christmas

- Present. JOSEPH HUDNALL & ARMISTEAD CHURCHHILL, Gent.

- BRYAN BRUIN, Plt. agt. JOHN OBANNION & FRANCES his Wife, Defts. In Case This day came the parties by the Attorneys and the said Defts. relinquishing their former plea acknowledged the Plts. action against them for seven pounds, five shillings & three pence

p. Fauquier County Court 23d of August 1768
11 Therefore it is considered by the Court that the Plt. recover against the said Defts. the said seven pounds, five shilings and three pence and his costs by him in this behalf expended, and the said Defts. in mercy, &c.

- THOMAS OBANNION, Plt. agt. THOMAS GARNER, Deft. In Debt This day came the parties by their Attornies and thereupon the matters of Law ariseing on the Errors in Arrest of Judgment filed in this Cause being argued and the Court here fully understood, it seems that the Law is with the Plt. Therefore it is considered by the Court that the Plt. recover against the said Deft. seven pounds, five shillings, the Debt., and one penny Damage, the Debt and Damages by the Jury in this Cause found and his costs by him in this behalf expended, and the said Deft. in mercy, &c.

- JOHN HORD, Plt. agt. THOMAS GARNER, JAMES ARNOLD and THOMAS POPE, Defts. In Debt This day came the parties by their Attornies and thereupon the matters of Law arriseing upon the Errors in Arrest of Judgment filed in this Cause being argued and by the Court fully understood, it seems that the Law is with the Plt. Therefore it is considered by the Court that the Plt. recover against the said Defts. one Watch of the value of eight pounds and a Gun of the value of one pound, ten shillings, the Debt in the Declaration mentioned, and one penny damage, the Debt and Damages by the Jury in this Cause found. And his costs by him in this behalf expended, and the said Defts. in mercy, &c.

p. Fauquier County Court 23d of August 1768
12 - JOHN TAYLOR, Plt. agt. WILLIAM BALL, Deft. In Debt

This day came the parties by their Attorneys and the said Deft. acknowledged the action of the Plt. against him. Therefore it is considered by the Court that the Plt. recover against the said Deft. sixteen pounds, eight shillings and ten pence current money, the Debt in the Declaration mentioned, and his costs by him in this behalf expended, and the said Deft. in mercy, &c., But this Judgment is to be discharged by the paiment of eight pounds, four shillings and five pence with Interest thereon to be computed after the rate of five per centum per annum from the first day of January 1768 till paid and the costs

- Ordered that JOSEPH BLACKWELL, GEORGE THRELKELD, THOMAS SMITH and RICHARD COVINGTON or any three of them, being first sworn, do view the most convenient way from RICHARD COVINGTONs into the AQUIA ROLLING ROAD & return their Report to the Court

- MARTIN PICKETT and COMPANY, Plts. agt. THOMAS GRUBS, Deft. In Debt

This day came as well the Plts. by their Attorney as the said Deft. in his proper person and the said Deft. acknowledged the Plts. action against him. Therefore it is considered by the Court that the Plts. recover against the said Deft. six pounds, eight shillings & four pence current money, the Debt in the Declaration mentioned, and their costs by them in this behalf expended, and teh said Deft. in mercy, &c., But this Judgment is to be discharged by the paiment of three pounds, seven shillings

p. Fauquier County Court 23d of August 1768
13 and four pence with Interest thereon to be computed after the rate of five per centum per annum from the twenty fourth day of May 1763 till paid and the costs

- WILLIAM CAGE, Plt. agt. ELY THOMPSON, Deft. In Case

This day came the parties by their Attorneys and thereupon came also a Jury, to wit, BENJAMIN POPE, THOMAS WATTS, STEPHEN MORRIS, CHARLES GARNER, FRANCIS McCORMACK, JOHN McCORMACK, EDWIN FIELDING, EDWARD HAMPTON, JEFFRY JOHNSON, JOHN MORGAN, SANFORD CARREL and SAMUEL PEPPER, who being elected tried and sworn the truth to speak upon the issue joined, brought in a Special Verdict in these words, (to wit);

"We the Jury find by the witnesses, EDWARD TURNER and JOSEPH GRIMSLY, that ELY THOMPSON did play at Cards with WILLIAM DAY and WILLIAM CAGE and lost in Notes of hand and a Horse to the amount of twenty or thirty pounds and to redeem the said Notes and Horse he gave an order on Mr. BENNITT PRICE for twelve pounds which was protested. Now if the Law is for the Plt., we find for him, if for the Deft., we find for him."

And this Cause is continued untill the next Court for the matters of Law arriseing thereupon to be argued

- HENRY NEAVILL haveing misbehaved himself in Prison as of the Court, it is ordered that he be committed untill he gives security for his good behaviour, himself in the sum of twenty pounds, and his Securities in the sum of ten pounds each

- A Deed of Partition between JOHN ADAMS of the one part and ZEPHANIAH TURNER of the other part was proved by the Oaths of ROBERT ASHBY, HEZEKIAH TURNER and JOHN ASHBY to be the act and deed of the said JOHN & ZEPHANIAH, ordered to be recorded

- An Indenture of Bargain and Sale between ZEPHANIAH

p. Fauquier County Court 23d of August 1768

14 TURNER of the one part and HEZEKIAH TURNER of the other part and Receit thereon endorsed were proved by the Oaths of ROBERT ASHBY, JOHN ADAMS and JOHN ASHBY witnesses thereto & ordered to be recorded

- The persons appointed to assign the Wife of PAUL WILLIAMS her Dower in the Land whereof JAMES FOX, deced., was seised, returned their Report to the Court which was ordered to be recorded

- Ordered that MATHEW ADAMS and JOHN GLASSCOCK be added to the List of Tithes

- JAMES BUCHANAN, Assignee of MARTIN PICKETT & COMPANY, Plt. agt. JAMES OLDHAM, Deft. In Debt

This day came as well the Plt. by his Attorney as the said Deft. in his proper person and the said Deft. acknowledged the action of the Plt. against him. Therefore it is consided by the Court that the Plt. recover against the said Deft. nineteen pounds, eight shillings, the Debt in the Declaration mentioned, and his costs by him in this behalf expended, And the said Deft. in mercy, &c. But this Judgment is to be discharged by the paiment of six pounds, sixteen shillings & eight pence with Interest thereon to be computed after the rate of five per centum per annum from the twenty fourth day of August 1768 till paid and the costs. Execution stayed till next April

- THOMAS MOFFETT, Plt. agt. FRANCIS MOORE, Deft. On a Petition

This Petition is dismist, and it is ordered that the Plt.

p. Fauquier County Court 23d of August 1768

15 pay the Deft. his costs by him in this behalf expended

- WILLIAM ELLZEY, Plt. agt. THOMAS WILLIAMS, Deft. On a Petition

Judgment is granted the Plt. against the said Deft. for five pounds, nine shillings and his costs by him in this behalf expended

- JANE MAHORNEY and RICHARD BRYAN being summoned as witnesses for SAMUEL THORNBERRY against JOHN MORGAN and failing to appear, tho called, it is ordered that they be fined according to Law unless they appear and shew cause to the contrary at the next Court

- WILLIAM PINKARD, Plt. agt. JOHN WHITESIDE, Deft. In Case

By consent of the parties all matters in difference relative to this suit are refered to JOHN BLACKWELL, WILLIAM BLACKWELL and JOHN WRIGHT, JUNR., or any two of them and their award to be the Judgment of the Court

- CHARLES DUNCAN, Plt. agt. WILLIAM SMITH, Deft. On a Petition

Agreed, the Deft. paying costs

- ELIZABETH STRIBLING, Admrx. to WILLIAM STRIBLING, deced., Plt. agt. EDWARD BURGES, Deft. On a Petition

This Petition abates, the Sherif haveing returned tht the Deft. is no Inhabitant of this County

p. Fauquier County Court 23d of August 1768

16 - On the motion of SAMUEL JOHNSON, it is ordered that SUSANNAH SMITH pay him fifty pounds of tobacco for two days attenance as a witness for DANIEL McCOY at the suit of the said SMITH, the suit being continued at her costs

- JOHN CHURCHHILL, Plt. agt. JOHN ARISS, Deft. In Case

The Jury sworn yesterday in this Cause returned into Court and upon they Oaths do say that the Deft. did assume upon himself in manner and form as the Plt. against him hath declared and they do assess the Plts. damages by means of the Defts. breach of the promise and assumption in the Declaration mentioned to two pounds, three shillings and four pences besides his costs. Therefore it is considered by the Court that the Plt. recover against the said Deft. his damages aforesaid in form aforesaid assessed and his costs by him in this behalf expended, and the said Deft. in mercy, &c.

- On the motion of AGATHA HOLDER, it is ordered that CHARLES DUNCAN pay her fifty pounds of tobacco for two days attendance as a witness for him against WILLIAM SMITH

- On the motion of ELIZABETH DUNCAN, it is ordered that CHARLES DUNCAN pay her eighty six pounds of tobacco for two days attenance, once comeing twelve miles and returning, as a witness for him against WILLIAM SMITH

- WILLIAM KITTSON, Plt. agt. FRANCIS JAMES, Deft. In Trespass, Assault & Battery

Thsi day came the parties by their Attornies and thereupon came also a Jury, to wit, JAMES WHEATLEY, JOHN SMITH, JOHN

p. Fauquier County Court 23d of August 1768

17 OLDHAM, WILLIAM PINKARD, JAMES FLETCHER, WILLIAM DAY, WILLIAM ROBERTSON, JOSEPH WILLIAMS, LUKE HOLDER, BENJAMIN BUTLER, ROBERT BOULT and ELY THOMPSON, who being elected tried and sworn the truth to speak upon the issue joined, upon their Oaths do say that the Deft. is Guilty in manner and form as the Plt. against him hath declared and they do assess the Plts. damages by occasion thereof to twelve pounds besides his costs. Therefore it is considered by the Court that the Plt. recover against the said Deft. his damages aforesaid in form aforesaid assessed and his costs by him in this behalf expended, But the Court being of opinnion that the Jury found contrary to Evidence in this Cause, a new Trial is awarded the Deft. at the next Court, he paying the costs occasioned thereby

- JAMES BUCHANAN, Assignee of MARTIN PICKETT & COMPANY, Plt. agt. MOSES JOHNSON, Deft. On a Petition

Discontinued, being agreed by the parties

- JOSEPH JONES, Esqr. Plt. agt. ABSALOM CORNELIOUS, Deft. On a Petition

Discontinued, being agreed by the parties

- On the motion of MINOR WINN, a Licence is granted him to keep an ORDINARY at his House in this County for one year, he haveing executed and acknowledged Bond as the Law directs

- CHARLES MORGAN, Plt. agt. JOHN MORGAN, Exor. &c. of CHARLES MORGAN, deced., Deft. In Case

This day came the parties by their Attornies and thereupon came also a Jury, to wit, JOHN WRIGHT, JOSEPH HUDNALL, JOSEPH HITT, BENJAMIN TURNER, PHILIP DAVIS, WILLIAM CAGE, EDWARD

p. Fauquier County Court 23d of August 1768

18 TURNER, RICHARD LUTTRILL, RHODAM TULLOS, JOHN SMITH, JOHN HEADLEY & FRANCIS JAMES, who being elected tried and sworn the truth to speak upon

the issue joined upon their Oaths do say that the said Testator in his life time did within five years next before the prosecution of the originall Writ assume upon himself in manner and form as the Plt. against him hath declared and they do assess the Plts. damages by means of the breach of that assumption to two shillings and seven pence half penny besides his costs. Therefore it is considered by the Court that the Plt. recover against the said Deft. his damages aforesaid in form aforesaid assessed to be levied of the goods and chattells of the said Testator in the hands of the said Deft. to be administered & together with his costs by him in this behalf expended, And the said Deft. in mercy, &c.

- On the motion of JOSEPH HUDNALL, it is ordered that FRANCIS JAMES pay him fifty pounds of tobacco for two days attendance as a witness for him at the suit of KITTSON, the suit being continued at his costs

- CUTHBERT BULLITT, Special Bail for ELY THOMPSON at the suit of WILLIAM CAGE, came into Court and surrendered up the said THOMPSON in discharge of his recognizance and THOMAS MARSHALL, Gent., came into Court and became Special Bail and Pledge for the Deft. in this suit

- On the motion of DANIEL MORGAN, it is ordered that FRANCIS JAMES pay him one hundred and seventy pounds of tobacco for two days attendance and once travelling forty miles and returning as a witness for WILLIAM KITTSON against the said JAMES, the Cause being continued at his costs

- On the motion of EDWARD TURNER, It is ordered that ELY THOMPSON pay him ninety five pounds of tobacco for two days attendance, once comeing fifteen miles and returning

p. Fauquier County Court 23d of August 1768
19 as a witness for him at the suit of WILLIAM CAGE

- The same Order for JOSEPH GRIMSLY

- On the motion of BENJAMIN POPE, it is ordered that FRANCIS JAMES pay him twenty five pounds of tobacco for one days attendance as a witness for him at the suit of THOMAS MOFFETT

- JEFFERY JOHNSON, Plt. agt. JOHN MOFFETT, Deft. In Detinue

This day came the parties by their Attornies and thereupon came also a Jury, to wit, WILLIAM JENNINGS, JAMES WITHERS, WILLIAM PICKETT, JOHN COCKE, JOHN HATHAWAY, JAMES HATHAWAY, THOMAS HATHAWAY, SAMUEL PORTER, WILLIAM PARKER, JAMES BASHAW, JOHN WRIGHT & JOHN KEITH, who being elected trtied and sworn the truth to speak upon the issue joined, and after evidence to them of and upon the premises given from the Bar of this Court to consult of their verdict upon the premises withdrew and after the said Jury had consulted among themselves and agreed to the Barr to give their Verdict in this behalf, returned, upon which the said JEFFREY JOHNSON being solemnly called doth not come nor further prosecute his Bill against the said JOHN MOFFETT. Therefore it is considered by the Court that the Deft. recover against the said Plt. the sum of five shillings and his costs by him in this behalf expended, and the said Plt. in mercy, &c.

- MARTIN PICKETT and COMPANY, Plts. agt. RHODAM TULLOS, Eft. In Debt

This day came as well the Plt. by his Attorney as the Deft. in his proper person and the said Deft. acknowledged the action of the Plts. against them. Therefore it is considered by the Court

p. Fauquier County Court 23d of August 1768
20 that the Plts. recover against the said Deft. seventeen pounds, eleven shillings current money, the Debt in the Declaration mentioned, and his costs by him in

this behalf expended, And the said Deft. in mercy, &c. But this Judgment is to be discharged by the paiment of nine pounds, eight shillings and eight pence with Interest thereon to be computed after the rate of five per centum per annum from the twenty fourth day of May 1768 till paid and the costs

- MARTIN PICKETT & COMPANY, Plts. agt. DAVID DERNALL, Deft. In Debt

This day came as well the Plts. by their Attorney as the Deft. in his proper person and the said Deft. acknowledged the Plts. action against him. Therefore it is considered by the Court that the Plt. recover against the said Deft. twenty four pounds, one shilling current money, the Debt in the Declaration mentioned, and their costs by them in this behalf expended, and the said Deft. in mercy, &c., But this Judgment is to be discharged by the payment of ten pounds, thirteen shillings and four pence with Interest thereon to be computed after the rate of five per centum per annum fromthe twenty fourth day of May 1768 till paid and the costs

- JAMES BUCHANAN, Assignee of MARTIN PICKETT & COMPANY, Plt. agt. ANN BROWN, Deft. On a Petition

Judgment is granted the Plt. against the said Deft. for one pound, sixteen shillings and nine pence with Interest thereon to be computed after the rate of five per centum per annum from the twenty four day of

p. Fauquier County Court 23d of August 1768

21 May 1768 till paid and the costs

- JAMES BUCHANAN, Assignee of MARTIN PICKETT & COMPANY, Plts. agt. JAMES GODDARD, Deft. On a Petition

Judgment is granted the Plts. against the said Deft. for two pounds, thirteen shillings and a penny half penny with Interest thereon from the twenty fourth day of May 1768 till paid and the costs

- The Same, Plts. agt. EDWARD FIELDING, Deft. On a Petition

Judgment is granted the Plt. against the said Deft. for two pounds, two shillings & six pence with Interest thereon to be computed after the rate of five per centum per annum from the first day of May 1768 till paid and the costs

- JAMES BUCHANAN, Plt. agt. JOHN BRAGG, Deft. On a Petition

Judgment is granted the Plt. against the said Deft. for four pounds, eighteen shillings and his costs by him in this behalf expended

- A Deed of Mortgage between PETER GRANT of one part and THOMAS MARSHALL and JAMES SCOTT of the other part was proved by the Oaths of WILLIAM PICKETT, THOMAS SMITH & MARTIN PICKETT, witnesses thereto, and ordered to be recorded

- On the motion of SAMUEL PEPPER, it is ordered that JOHN MOFFETT pay him fifty pounds of tobacco for two days attendance as a witness for him at the suit of JEFFERY JOHNSON

- The same Order for HENRY MOFFETT

- The same Order for HANNAH MOFFETT

- The same Order of JEFFERY JOHNSON

- On the motion of ANDERSON MOFFETT, it is ordered that

p. Fauquier County Court 23d of August 1768

22 JOHN MOFFETT pay him two hundred and ninety pounds of tobacco for two days attendance and once comeing eighty miles and returning as a witness for him at the suit of JEFFERY JOHNSON

- On the motion of THOMAS MARSHALL, it is ordered that JEFFERY JOHNSON pay him fifty pounds of tobacco for two days attendance as a witness for him against JOHN MOFFETT

- JOHN RALLS, Assignee of WILLIAM SCOTT, Plt. agt. JOHN COCKE and JOSEPH TAYLOR, Defts. In Debt

This day came as well the Plt. by his Attorney at the Defts. in their proper person and the said Defts. acknowledged the action of the Plt. against them. Therefore it is considered that the Plt. recover against the said Defts. fourteen pounds, fifteen shillings current money, the Debt in the Declaration mention, and his costs by him in this behalf expended, And the said Deft. in mercy &c., But this Judgment is to be discharged by the paiment of four pounds, fifteen shillings and three pence with Interest thereon to be computed after the rate of five per centum per annum from the twenty third day of August 1768 till paid and the costs

- WILLIAM EDMONDS and JOHN BLACKWELL took the susual Oaths to his Majesties person and Government and subscribed the Test

- ALEXANDER KEITH having first taken the usual Oaths to his Majesties person and Government and subscribed the Test, had the Oath of a SHERIF administered to him

- On the motion of ORIGINAL YOUNG, it is ordered that JOHN MOFFETT pay him fifty pounds of tobacco for two days attendance as a witness for him at the suit of JEFFREY JOHNSON

p. Fauquier County Court 23d. of August 1768

23 - On the motion of CHARLES WRIGHT, it is ordered that JAMES ADKINS pay him fifty pounds of tobacco for two days attendance as a witness for him at the suit of the said ADKINS, this suit being continued at his costs

- The same Order for FRANCIS PAYNE

- JOHN RALLS, Assignee of WILLIAM SCOTT, Plt. agt. JAMES BASHAW & PETER BASHAW, Defts. In Debt

This day came the Plt. by his Attorney and came also JOHN COOKE and became Special Bail and Pledge for the Defts. in this suit, and the said Defts. altho solemnly called did not come nor say any thing in bar or preclusion of the action aforesaid of the said Plt. but hath made default, whereby the said Plt. remains against the said Defts. therein undefended. Therefore it is considered by the Court that the Plt. recover against the said Defts. seven pounds, thirteen shillings and eight pence current money, the Debt in the Declaration mentioned, and his costs by him in this behalf expended, and the said Deft. in mercy &c., But this Judgment is to be discharged by the payment of three pounds, sixteen shillings and eight pence with Interest thereon to be computed after the rate of five per centum per annum from the twelfth day of July 1768 till paid and the costs

- On the motion of JOHN CHURCHHILL, it is ordered that a Dedimus issue to take the Deposition of JOHN BELL, an infirm witness for him at the suit of ELIZABETH KEIRNS, he giveing the Plt. legal notice of the time and place of executing the same

p. Fauquier County Court 23d of August 1768

24 - JOHN JOHNSON, Plt. agt. JAMES BROWN, Deft. On a Petition

Judgment is granted the Plt. against the said Deft. for five pounds, eighteen shillings and his costs by him in this behalf expended

- On the motion of MARY SETTLE, who made Oath and executed and acknowledged Bond as the Law directs, Certificate is granted her for obtaining Letters of Administration of the Estate of MARTIN SETTLE, deced.

- Ordered that WILLIAM WITHERS, VINCENT GARNER, WILLIAM SMITH and THOMAS WITHERS or any three of them being first sworn do appraise the Estate of MARTIN SETTLE, deced., and return the Appraisment to the Court

- Ordered that the Court be adjourned till tomorrow morning ten of the Clock
WILLIAM BLACKWELL

- At a Court continued and held for Fauquier County the 24th day of August 1768
Present JOSEPH BLACKWELL WILLIAM BLACKWELL
WILLIAM GRANT & WILLIAM EDMONDS Gent.

- HENRY LEE, DANIEL PAYNE and JANE BAYLIS, Exors. &c. of JOHN BAYLIS, deced., Plts. agt. GEORGE COULSON, Deft. Upon a Writ of Scire Facias to revive a Judgment obtained by the said JOHN BAYLIS in his life time against the said Deft. for nine pounds, fifteen shillings and a penny with Interest thereon to be computed after the rate of five per centum per annum from the first day of March 1763 for Debt,

p. Fauquier County Court 24th of August 1768
23 and one hundred and thirty eight pounds of tobacco and fifteen shillings or one hundred and fifty pounds of tobacco for Costs;

It is considered by the Court that the Plts. may have their Execution according to the force form and effect of the recovery aforesaid, And it is further considered by the Court that the Plts. recover against the said Deft. their costs by them in this behalf expended

- JAMES BUCHANAN, Plt. agt. TARPLY BRAGG, Deft. In Case
This suit abates, the Sherif haveing returned that the Deft. is no Inhabitant of this County

- JOHN RALLS, Assignee of WILLIAM SCOTT, Plt. agt. BENJAMIN TAYLOR and GEORGE LYNTON, Defts. In Debt
This suit abates, the Sherif haveing returned that the Defts. are no Inhabitants of this County

- JOHN TOMLIN, Plt. agt. LEROY GEORGE HULIT, Deft. In Trespass
This suit is agreed and it is ordered that the Deft. pay the Plt. his costs by him in this behalf expended

- JOHN SHUMATE, Plt. agt. GAVIN LAWSON, Deft. In Case
This day came the parties by their Attorneys and the said Deft. to the Plt. here in Court doth tender six pounds, ten shillings and three pence which by the said Plt. accepted and the said Deft. pleads non assumpsit as to the redidue and the Tryal of the issue is refered untill the next Court

p. Fauquier County Court 24th of August 1768
26 - HONOR WILLIAMS, Plt. agt. THOMAS WITHERS, Deft. In Case
By consent of the parties all matters in difference relative to this suit are refered to JOHN DUNCAN and PAUL WILLIAMS and their award to be the Judgment of this Court

- MARTIN PICKETT & COMPANY, Plts. agt. JAMES STROTHER, Deft. On a Petition
Judgment is gratned the Plts. against the said Deft. for two pounds, eighteen shillings and six pence with Interest thereon to be computed after the rate of five per centum per annum from the twenty fourth day of May 1768 till paid and the costs

- MARTIN PICKETT & COMPANY, Plts. agt. THOMAS GRUBBS, Deft. On a Petition
Judgment is granted the Plts. against the said Deft. for two pounds, seven shillings and nine pence with Interest thereon to be computed after the rate of five per centum per annum from the twenty fourth day of May 1768 till paid and the costs

- RICHARD SPURR, Exor. &c. of JAMES SPUR, deced., Plt. agt.
WILLIAM ROBERTS, Deft. On a Petition

Discontinued

- AMUS DAVIS, Plt. agt. BENJAMIN POPE, Deft. On a Petition

Judgment is granted the Plt. against the said Deft. for two pounds and his costs by him in this behalf expended

- THOMAS WHITE, Plt. agt. SAMUEL GRIGSBY, Deft. On a Petition

p. Fauquier County Court 24th of August 1768

27 Judgment is granted the Plt. against the said Deft. for four pounds, seven shillings and his costs by him in this behalf expended

- JOHN MORGAN, Plt. agt. SWANSON BROWN, Deft. On a Petition

Judgment is granted the Plt. against the said Deft. for four hundred and fourty five pounds of tobacco and one shilling and nine pence and his costs by him in this behalf expended

- Indentures of Lease and Release between HENRY PEYTON of the one part and CUTHBERT BULLITT of the other part and a Receit on the Release endorsed were proved by the Oaths of WILLIAM ELLZEY and GEORGE BRENT, witnesses thereto, and ordered to be certified

- On the motion of WILLIAM ASBURY, it is ordered that THOMAS WHITE pay him seventy five pounds of tobacco for three days attendance as a witness for him against SAMUEL GRIGSBY

- WILLIAM TURNER, Plt. agt. ANN FINNIE and JOHN JAMES, Exors. &c. of JOHN FINNIE, deced., Defts. In Chancery

This suit abates by teh death of the Complainant

- ELIZABETH ETHERINGTON, Plt. agt. JOHN ETHERINGTON, Deft. In Chancery

This suit abates by the death of the Deft.

- Present. JOSEPH HUDNALL, Gentleman

- GEORGE BERRY, Plt. agt. HENRY LEE, THOMAS LAWSON & JOHN LEE, Exors. &c. of ALLAN MACRAE, deced., Defts. In Chancery

p. Fauquier County Court 24th of August 1768

28 This suit is agreed and it is ordered that the Defts. pay to the Plt. his costs by him in this behalf expended

- THOMAS KEITH, Plt. agt. ALEXANDER KEITH and ISHAM KEITH, Devisees of JAMES KEITH, Clerk, deced., Defts. In Chancery

By consent of the parteis, it is ordered that HENRY PEYTON, JOHN KEITH and JAMES FOLEY in Company with the Surveyor do divide the Land in the Bill mentioned according to the Will of the said JAMES KEITH, Clerk, deced.

- Ordered that the Court be adjourned till the Court in Course

JOSEPH BLACKWELL

- At a Court held for Fauquier County the 26th day of September 1768

Present THOMAS HARRISON WILLIAM GRANT
GILSON FOOTE JOSEPH HUDNALL Gent.

- On the Petition of CHARLES CHINN and others, it is ordered that HENRY PEYTON, JAMES FOLEY, JOHN SIAS, JOHN RECTOR and JACOB RECTOR or any three of them being first sworn do view the most convenient way from the County Line following COMBS's MILL ROAD to CRUMMILLS RUN and from thence to the Upper Church and return their report to the Court

- LOTT HACKLEY is appointed Surveyor of the Road from FIELDS FORD into the Main Road and it is ordered that he with the Tithes that shall be appointed by

p. Fauquier County Court 26th of September 1768
29 WILLIAM GRANT, Gent., do clear and keep the same in repair according to Law

- Ordered that the Church Wardens of Hamilton Parish bind DUDLY MATTHIS to GEORGE BROWN, who is to learn him the Trade of a Carpenter and House Joiner

- Present. JEREMIAH DERNAL, Gent.

- An Indenture of Bargain and Sale between JAMES EWELL and CHARLOTTE his Wife and JESSE EWELL and MARY his Wife of the one part and ROBERT SCOTT of the other part and Receit thereon endorsed were proved by the Oaths of THOMAS CHAPMAN and WILLIAM ELLZEY, witnesses thereto, and together with a Commission thereto annexed for takeing the acknowledgement and privy examination of the said CHARLOTTE and MARY and a Certificate of the Execution thereof, ordered to be recorded

- WILLIAM PINKARD, Plt. agt. JOHN WHITESIDES, Deft. In Case

The persons appointed to settle all matters in dispute between the parties relateing to this suit returned their report in these words, (to wit);

"Fauquier County 26th September 1768. Pursuant to the within Order, we the Subscribers on hearing the witnesses relative to suit depending between the parties within named doth hereby award that the within named JOHN WHITESIDES, JUNR. do pay unto the within named WILLIAM PINKARD the sum of five pounds, five shillings current money and costs. Witness our hands the day and year above written."

" JOHN BLACKWELL "
" JOHN WRIGHT "

p. Fauquier County Court 26th of September 1768
30 Therefore it is considered by the Court that the Plt. recover against the said Deft. the said five pounds, five shillings and his costs by him in this behalf expended, And the said Deft. in mercy, &c.

- HONOR WILLIAMS, Plt. agt. THOMAS WITHERS, Deft. In Case

The persons appointed to settle all matters in dispute between the parties relateing to this Cause returned their report in these words, (to wit);

"In Obedience to the within Order, we the Subscribers have met the third day of September 1768 and find for HONOUR WILLIAMS fourteen pounds, eight shillings current money. PAUL WILLIAMS, JOHN DUNCAN."

Therefore it is considered by the Court that the Plt. recover against the said Deft. the said fourteen pounds, eight shillings and her costs by her in this behalf expended, and the said Deft. in mercy, &c.

- Ordered that THOMAS HARRISON, Gent., pay JOHN BLACKWELL and ORIGINAL YOUNG, late Sherifs of this County, four thousand nine hundred and eighty three pounds of tobacco at twelve shillings and six pence percentum (out of the Publick money which is in his hands) for Publick Levies which proved insolvent

- The persons appointed to view a Way from the Road cleared by the County of CULPEPER near WILLIAM DAYs into his Lordships Road returned their report in these words, (to wit);

Pursuant to the within Order, we the Subscribers being first sworn have viewed the Way within mentioend for a Road and do report that a Road from the CULPEPER ROAD near WILLIAM DAYs through

p. Fauquier County Court 26th of September 1768
31 his Lordships Manour with CRIMS ROLLING ROAD to the Manour Road by SIMON HEFLINs may be made. Given under our hands this 26th September 1768.
And the Road is established according to the above report

- WILLIAM DAY is appointed Surveyor of the Road from the Road cleared by the County of CULPEPER into his Lordships Road and it is ordered taht he with the Tithes that shall be appointed by JOSEPH HUDNAL, Gent., do clear and keep the same in repair according to Law

- DEKAR THOMPSON & COMPANY, Plts. agt. GEORGE SKINKER, Deft. In Case
Discontinued

- On the motion of GEORGE NEAVIL, it is ordered that PHILIP WATERFIELD pay him one hundred pounds of tobacco for four days attendance as a witness for him against JOHN CHURCHHILL

- JOHN RALLS, Plt. agt. RICHARD LEE, Deft. In Case
This day came the parties by their Attornies and the said Deft. acknowledged the action of the Plt. against him for six pounds, five shillings. Therefore it is considered by the Court that the Plt. recover against the said Deft. the said six pounds, five shillings and his costs by him in this behalf expended; And the said Deft. in mercy, &c.

p. Fauquier County Court 26th of September 1768
32 - THOMAS WITHERS, Plt. agt. JOSEPH LAVEL, Deft. In Case
This day came the parties by their Attorneys and thereupon came also a Jury, to wit, BUSHROD DOGGETT, JOSEPH SMITH, JOSEPH BRAGG, BENJAMIN PEPER, GEORGE BROWN, STEPHEN McCORMACK, JOHN DUNCAN, FRANCIS BRONAUGH, WILLIAM POPE PARNACH GEORGE, JOHN MORGAN and DANIEL SHUMATE, who being elected tried and sworn the truth to speak upon the issue joined; upon their Oaths do say that the Deft. is Not Guilty in manner and form as the Plt. against him hath declared by pleading the said Deft. hath alledged. Therefore it is considered by the Court that the Plt. take nothing by his Bill but for his false clamor be in mercy, &c. and that the Deft. go thereof without day and recover against the said Plt. his costs by him in this behalf expended

- ALEXANDER WODROW & JOHN NEILSON, Plts. agt. JACOB ADAMS, Deft. In Debt
This day cam ethe parties by their Attorneys and teh said Deft. relinquishing his former plea acknowledged the Plts. action against him. Therefore it is considered by the Court that the Plt. recover against the said Deft. thirteen pounds, ten shillings and eleven pence half penny current money, the Debt in the Declaration mentioned, and their costs by them in this behalf expended; And the said Deft. in mercy, &c., But this Judgment is to be discharged by the paiment of three pounds, three shillings and eleven pence with Interest thereon to be computed after the rate of five percentum per annum from the first day of Aprill 1765 till paid and the costs

p. Fauquier County Court 26th of September 1768
33 - ALEXANDER WODROW & JOHN NEILSON, Plts. agt. JACOB ADAMS, Deft. In Debt
This day came the parties by their Attornies and the said Deft. relinquishing his former plea acknowledged the Plts. action against him. Therefore it is considered by the Court that the Plts. recover against the said Deft. six pounds, sixteen shillings and nine pence current money, the Debt in the Declaration mentioned, and their costs by them in this behalf expended; And the said Deft. in mercy, &c. But this Judgment is to be discharged by the paiment of three pounds, eight shillings and four pence half penny with Interest thereon to be computed after the rate of five percentum per annum from the seventeenth day of August 1764 till paid and the costs

Memorandum; That the Plts. in the above suits acknowledge satisfaction for six pounds five shillings

- Ordered that twelve Tithes belonging to HENRY FITZHUGH be added to the List of Tithables

- Ordered that six Tithes belonging to FRANCIS WHITING be added to the List of Tithables

- An Account of Administration of the Estate of GEORGE FOOTE, deced.,was returned by GILSON FOOTE, Executor, who made Oath thereto & ordered to be recorded

- Ordered that twelve Tithes belonging to GEORGE SKINKER be added to the List of Tithables

- Indentures of Lease and Release between ROBERT SCOTT of the one part and JOHN KNOX of the other part and a Receit on the Release endorsed were acknowledged by the said ROBERT SCOTT & ordered to be recorded

- An Indenture of Release between JOHN KNOX of the one part and ROBERT SCOTT of the other part was acknowledged by the said JOHN KNOX and ordered to be recorded

p. Fauquier County Court 26th of September 1768

34 - A Deed of Assignment and Surrender between ROBERT SCOTT of one part and JESSE EWELL of the other part was acknowledged by the said ROBERT SCOTT & ordered to be recorded

- Ordered that two Tithes belonging to JOSEPH TAYLOR be added to the List of Tithables

- Indentures of Lease and Release between JOHN BELL and FRANKEY his Wife of the one part and WILLIAM BALL of the other part and a Receit on the Release endorsed were proved by the Oaths of FRANCIS ATWELL, RANDOLPH SPISER and JOHN WRIGHT, witnesses thereto and with the Commission for takeing the acknowledgement and privy examination of the said FRANKEY and the Certificate of the Execution thereof, ordered to be recorded

- A Bond from JOHN BELL to WILLIAM BALL was proved by the Oaths of FRANCIS ATWELL, RANDOLPH SPISER and JOHN WRIGHT, witnesses thereto, and ordered to be recorded

- JAMES BUCHANAN, Assignee of MARTIN PICKETT & COMPANY, Plt. agt.
PHILIP McNAMARR, Deft. In Debt

This day came the Plt. by his Attorney and came also EPHRAIM HUBBARD, THOMAS CONNOR and JOSEPH McNAMARR and became Special Bail and Pledge for the Deft. in this suit, and the said Deft. prays and has leave to imparl specially to the Plts. Declaration untill the next Court and then to plead

- JOSEPH LAVEL is appointed Surveyor of the Road in the room of BENJAMIN SETTLE, and it is ordered that he with the Tithes belonging to the said Road do clear and keep the same in repair according to Law

- HECTOR ROSS, Plt. agt. WILLIAM REDDING, Deft. On a Petition

p. Fauquier County Court 26th of September 1768

35 Judgment is granted the Plt. against the said Deft. for four hundred pounds of tobacco and his costs by him in this behalf expended

- On the motion of CHARLES GARNER, it is ordered that JOSEPH LAVEL pay him twenty five pounds of tobacco for one days attendance as a witness for him at the suit of THOMAS WITHERS

- On the motion of JAMES GARNER, it is ordered that JOSEPH LAVEL pay him twenty five pounds of tobacco for one days attendance as a witness for him at the suit of THOMAS WITHERS

- On the motion of WILLIAM WITHERS, it is ordered that THOMAS WITHERS pay him twenty five pounds of tobacco for one days attendance as a witness for him agaisnt JOSEPH LAVEL

= The same Order for JAMES WITHERS

- Ordered that three Tithables belonging to WILLIAM ROACH be added to the List of Tithables

- Ordered that the Court be adjourned till the Court in Course

" WILLIAM BLACKWELL "

- At a Court held for Fauquier County the 24th day of October 1768

Present	THOMAS HARRISON		ARMISTEAD CHURCHHILL	
	WILLIAM EDMONDS		JEREMIAH DERNALL	
		&	JOSEPH HUDNALL	Gentlemen

- An Indenture of Bargain and Sale between MORRIS HANSBOROUGH and JANE his Wife of the one part and JOHN INNAS of the other part and Receit thereon endorsed were

p. Fauquier County Court 24th of October 1768

36 acknowledged by the said MORRIS HANSBOROUGH and JANE his Wife (she being first privily examined as the Law directs) to be their act and deed and ordered to be recorded

- An Indenture of Bargain and Sale between CHARLES WALLER of the one part and CUTHBERT BULLITT of the other part and Receit thereon endorsed were acknowledged by the said CHARLES WALLER to be his act and deed and ordered to be recorded

- A Deed of Trust between CHARLES WALLER of the one part and JESSE NORMAN of the other part (for the use of ESTHER WALLER, Wife of the said CHARLES WALLER) and Receit thereon endorsed were acknowledged by the said CHARLES WALLER and ordered to be recorded

- Indentures of Lease and Release between WILLIAM KINCHELOE and MOLLY his Wife of the one part and JOHN KINCHELOE of the other part and a Receit on the Release endorsed were acknowledged by the said WILLIAM KINCHELOE and MOLLY his Wife (she being first privily examined as the Law directs) and ordered to be recorded

- Indentures of Lease and Release between JOHN MERCER and ANN his Wife of the one part and CARR BAILEY of the other part and a Receit on the Release endorsed were proved by the Oaths of JOHN BAILEY, JAMES BAILEY and JACOB MINTER, witnesses thereto, and with the Commission thereto annexed for takeing the acknowledgement and privy examination of the said ANN and a Certificate of the Execution thereof, ordered to be recorded

- The Last Will and Testament of JOHN MOREHEAD was proved by the Oaths of JOHN JETT and WILLIAM PRIMM, witnesses thereto, and ordered to be recorded, and on the motion of CHARLES ALEXANDER and WILLIAM MOREHEAD, Executors therein named, who made Oath

p. Fauquier County Court 24th of October 1768

37 and executed and acknowledged Bond as the Law directs, Certificate is granted them for obtaining a Probat thereof in due form

- Ordered that EDWARD HUMSTON, NICHOLAS GEORGE, JOHN JAMES and JOHN ASHBY or any three of them being first sworn do appraise the Estate of JOHN MOREHEAD deced., and return the appraisment to the Court

- An Indenture of Bargain and Sale between JOHN LEE of the one part and RICHARD HENRY LEE of the other part and a Receit thereon endorsed were proved by the Oaths of WILLIAM BLACKWELL, WILLIAM BLACKWELL, JUNR. and HANCOCK LEE, witnesses thereto, and ordered to be recorded

- A Bill of Sale between JOHN JETT of the one part and JOHN MOREHEAD of the other part was acknowledged by the said JOHN JETT and ordered to be recorded

And an Assignment of the same from the said JOHN MOREHEAD to SAMUEL MOREHEAD was proved by the Oaths of WILLIAM PRIM and JOHN JETT, witnesses thereto and ordered to be recorded

- An Indenture of Bargain and Sale between JOHN RECTOR of the one part and JOSEPH ROBINSON of the other part was acknowledged by the said JOHN RECTOR and ordered to be recorded

- An Indenture of Bargain and Sale between GEORGE SETTLE and MARY his Wife and THOMAS SETTLE, his Son, of the one part and THOMAS POPE of the other part was proved by the Oaths of JAMES SCOTT, CUTHBERT McMILLIAN and CUTHBERT HARRISON witnesses thereto, and ordered to be recorded

- A Certificate from the Right Honourable THOMAS LORD FAIRFAX to THOMAS POPE was proved by the Oath of JAMES SCOTT, a witness thereto, and ordered to be recorded

- Present. JOHN MOFFETT & WILLIAM BLACKWELL, Gentlemen

p. Fauquier County Court 24th of October 1768

38 - JOHN KNOX, Plt. agt. PETER DANIEL, Deft. In Case

This day came the parties by their Attorneys and thereupon came also a Jury, to wit, CUTHBERT HARRISON, THOMAS BRONAUGH, JOHN KEITH, JAMES BLACKWELL, CHARLES CHILTON, THOMAS HELMS, WILLIAM SETTLE, WILLIAM MOREHEAD, JAMES FOLEY, SAMUEL GRIGSBY, JOHN OBANNION & JOSEPH LAVEL, who being elected tried and sworn the truth to speak upon the issue joined,, withdrew to consider of their Verdict

- An Indenture of Feofment between WILLIAM COURTNEY of the one part and RICHARD LEWIS of the other part and a Memorandum of Livery of Seisen and Receit thereon endorsed were acknowledged by the said WILLIAM COURTNEY and ordered to be recorded

- Indentures of Lease and Release between WILLIAM PEARL and MARTHA his Wife of the one part and JOHN FRENCH of the other part and a Receit on the Release endorsed were acknowledged by the said WILLIAM PEARLE and MARTHA his Wife, (she being first privily examined as the Law directs) and ordered to be recorded

- An Agreement between JOSEPH HOPPER of the one part and THOMAS HOPPER of the other part was proved by the Oath of JOSEPH BLACKWELL and THOMAS MATTHEWS, witnesses theretto, and ordered to be recorded

- JOHN MOREHEAD, Plt. agt. THOMAS WATTS, Deft. In Case

By consent of the parties, all matters in difference relative to this suit are refered to THOMAS MARSHALL and JOHN MOFFETT and their award to be the Courts Judgment

- Ordered that the Court be adjourned till tomorrow morning ten of the Clock

THOMAS HARRISON

p. - At a Court continued and held for Fauquier County the 25th day of October 1768

39 Present THOMAS HARRISON ARMISTEAD CHURCHHILL
JEREMIAH DARNALL JOSEPH HUDNALL
and JOHN MOFFETT, Gent.

- The Last Will and Testament of ABRAHAM DODSON, deced., was proved by the Oaths of ABSALOM CORNELIOUS and JOHN BENNITT, witnesses thereto, and ordered to be recorded; And on the motion of BARBARY DODSON and JACOB HOLTZCLAW, Executors therein named, who made Oath and executed and acknowledged Bond as the Law directs, Certificate is granted them for obtaining a Probat thereof in due form

- Ordered that WILLIAM HUNTON, OBED CORNWELL, JACOB HAYS and JAMES BALLANGER or any three of them being first sworn do appraise the Estate of ABRAHAM DODSON, deced., and return the appraisment to the Court

- Present. WILLIAM BLACKWELL, Gent.

- An Indenture of Bargain and Sale between WILLIAM STAMPS and ANN his Wife of the one part and JAMES SCOTT of the other part and Receit thereon endorsed were acknowledged by the said WILLIAM STAMPS and ANN his Wife (she being first privily examined as the Law directs) and ordered to be recorded

- A Lease between JAMES SCOTT, JUNIOR, of the one part and WILLIAM STAMPS of the other part was acknowledged by the said JAMES SCOTT and ordered to be recorded

- A Bond from ELIZABETH ETHERINGTON to JOHN ETHERINGTON was acknowledged by the said ELIZABETH and ordered to be recorded

- A Bond from JOHN ETHERINGTON to ELIZABETH ETHERINGTON was acknowledged by the said JOHN and ordered to be recorded

p. <u>Fauquier County Court 25th of October 1768</u>

40 - On the motion of THOMAS WATTS, it is ordered that a Dedimus issue to take the Deposition of JOHN WATTS, a witnesses for him at the suit of PRESSLY THORNTON & FRANCIS THORNTON, Executors of FRANCIS THORNTON, deced.

- Ordered that the Church Wardens of Hamilton Parish bind SALLY TENNELL to RHODAM TULLOS according to Law

- Ordered that JOHN TOMLIN, GEORGE ROGERS and JAMES BAILEY divide the Estate of ROBERT MATTHIS, deced., among his Children according to his Last Will and Testament

- Ordered that THOMAS HARRISON pay JOHN HEADLY one pound, fourteen shillings current money out of the Publick Money that is in his hands

- JOSEPH & WILLIAM DELANIES, Plts. agt. JOHN SMITH, Deft. In Case

By consent of the parties, all matters in dispute relateing to this Cause are refered to JOSEPH BLACKWELL, THOMAS SLAUGHTER and JAMES SCOTT, Gent., or any two of them, and their Award to be the Judgment of the Court

- JOSEPH and WILLIAM DELANIES Plts. agt. ANDREW BARBEE, Deft. In Case

By consent of the parties, all matters in dispute relateing to this Cause are refered to JOSEPH BLACKWELL, THOMAS SLAUGHTER and JAMES SCOTT, Gent., and their Award to be the Judgment of the Court

- On the motion of GEORGE THRELKELD, it is ordered that JOSEPH and WILLIAM DELANIES pay him seventy five pounds of tobacco for three days attendance as a witness for them against JOHN SMITH

- On the motion of GEORGE RANKINS, it is ordered that JOSEPH and WILLIAM DELANIES pay him fifty pounds

p. <u>Fauquier County Court 25th of October 1768</u>

41 of tobacco for two days attendance as a witness for them against JOHN SMITH

- On the motion of WILLIAM BLACKWELL, it is ordered that JOSEPH and WILLIAM DELANIES pay him onE hundred and twenty five pounds of tobacco for five days attendance as a witness for them against JOHN SMITH

- On the motion of HENRY FIELDS, it is ordered that ANDREW BAXTER pay him two hundred and nineteen pounds of tobacco for three days attendance, twice comeing twenty four miles and returning, as a witness for him against JOSEPH and WILLIAM DELANIES

- An Account of Administration of the Estate of JAMES MORGAN, deced, was returned by HENRY MAUZEY, who made Oath thereto and ordered to be recorded

- On the motion of ALEXANDER HAMETT, it is ordered that JOSEPH and WILLIAM DELANIES pay him three hundred and ninety five pounds of tobacco for five days attenance, and three times comeing thirty miles and returning, as a witness for them against JOHN SMITH

- JOHN KNOX, Plt. agt. PETER DANIEL, Deft. In Case

The Jury sworn yesterday to try the issue in this Cause, returned into Court and upon their Oaths do say that the said Deft. maliciously and unjustly to vex, injure and oppress him the said Plt. did under colour and pretence of the said JOHN MERCERs Complaint without any just or reasonable cause, bind him, the said Plt. over to an Examineing Court upon suspicion of Felony as by replying the Plt. hath alledged, and they do assess the Plts. damages by occasion thereof to seventy five punds besides his costs. And the said Deft. prays that Judgment on the Verdict aforesaid

p. <u>Fauquier County Court 25th of October 1768</u>

42 may be arrested and stayed for the following reasons; to wit, First, for that the Declaration aforesaid and the matters therein contined are altogether insufficient in Law to maintain the said action; Second, for that the action aforesaid ought to have been brought in the County in which the fact is supposed to be committed, to wit, in STAFFORD, and not in this County; Third, for that it was snot proved that notice had been given to the said Deft. that the Plt. intended to bring the said action against him or was it insisted on at the Triall, Fourth, because the damages given by the Jury as excessive; Fifth, because the Jury after they were impannelled and sworn and heard some witnesses and sealed a privy verdict and the Jury haveing adjourned till next day, the Jury seperated and next day being called and appearing at the Barr heard further evdence and withdrew and returned a verdict for the Plt., Sixth for that the Jury eat and drunk after the riseing of the Court and before the ( ) of it next day at their own expence before they returned their verdict; Wherefore &c.

And the Cause is continued untill the next Court for the matters of Law ariseing thereupon to be argued

- JOHN KNOX, who sues as well for our Sovereign Lord the King for the use of the County of STAFFORD as for himself, Plt. agt. PETER DANIEL, Deft. In Debt

This day came the parties by their Attorneys and thereupon came also a Jury, to wit, BENJAMIN SNELLING, WILLIAM SUTTON, JAMES WRIGHT, WILLIAM STAMPS, JAMES WINN, JOHN McCORMACK, FRANCIS McCORMACK, JOHN OREAR, FRANCIS JAMES, BUSHROD DOGGETT, WILLIAM MORGAN and SINNETT YOUNG, who being elected tried and sworn the truth to speak upon the issue joined, upon their Oaths do say that the said Deft.

p. <u>Fauquier County Court 25th of October 1768</u>

43 is Not Guilty as by pleading he hath alledged. Therefore it is considered by the Court that the Plt. take nothing by his Bill but for his false Clamor be in mercy, &c., And that the Deft. go thereof without day and recover against the Plt. his costs by him in this behalf expended

- On the motion of PETER HANSBOROUGH, it is ordered that JOHN KNOX pay him five hundred and fifty pounds of tobacco for four days attendance, three times comeingfty miles and returning, as a witness for him against PETER DANIEL

- On the motion of JOSEPH PORTER, it is ordered that JOHN KNOX pay him three hundred and fifteen pounds of tobacco for three days attendance, comeing forty miles and returning, as a witness for him against PETER DANIEL

- The same Order for JOHN BROWN

- The same Order for CHARLES PORTER

- On the motion of JACOB ALLANTHARP, it is ordered that JOHN KNOX pay him five hundred and sixty eight pounds of tobacco for four days attendance, comeing fifty two miles & returning, as a witness for him against PETER DANIEL

- On the motion of JOHN ENGLISH, it is ordered that JOHN KNOX pay him five hundred and fifty pounds of tobacco for four days attendance and three times comeing fifty miles and returning, as a witness for him against PETER DANIEL

- On the motion of BRYAN CHADWELL, it is ordered that JOHN KNOX pay him three hundred and forty five pounds of tobacco for three days attendance and twice travelling forty five miles and returning as a witness for him against PETER DANIEL

- On the motion of WILLIAM MOUNTJOY, it is ordered that JOHN KNOX pay him five hundred and five pounds of tobacco for four days attendance and three times travelling forty five miles and returning as a witness for him against PETER DANIEL

- The same order of WILLIAM MOUNTJOY, JUNIOR

p. <u>Fauquier County Court 25th of October 1768</u>

44 - On the motion of CLEMENT BROOKE, it is ordered that JOHN KNOX pay him three hundred and forty five pounds of tobacco for three days attendance and twice comeing forty five miles and returning as a witness for him against PETER DANIEL (not to be taxed).

- On the motion of JOHN NELLSON, it is ordered that JOSEPH LAVEL pay him one hundred pounds of tobacco for four days attendance as a witness for him at the suit of THOMAS WITHERS (not to be taxed)

- On the motion of CHARLES MARTIN, it is rodered that JOHN KNOX pay him one hundred pounds of tobacco for four days attendance as a witness for him against PETER DANIEL, (not to be taxed)

- Ordered that twelve Tithes belonging to CHARLES and WILLIAM CHILTONs be added to the List of Tithables

- On the motion of SAMUEL SELDIN, it is ordered that PETER DANIEL pay him three hundred and forty five pounds of tobacco for three days attendance and twice comeing forty five miles and returning as a witness for him at the suit of JOHN KNOX

- Ordered that the Court be adjourned till the Court in Course

" THOMAS HARRISON "

(The remainder of this page is blank.)

p. <u>At a Court held for Fauquier County the third day of November 1768 for laying</u>

45 <u>the County Levy</u>

Present JOSEPH BLACKWELL WILLIAM BLACKWELL
ARMISTEAD CHURCHHILL WILLIAM EDMONDS
& JOSEPH HUDNALL, Gent.

- The County is made DR.		pounds of tobo.
To Mr. Secretlary Nelson		360
To HUMPHREY BROOKE, Clerk, his Salary		1248
To do. for copying the List of Tithes		400
To THOMAS MARSHALL, Sherif, his annual Salary		1248
To CUTHBERT BULLITT, Deputy Attorney		2000
To HUMPHREY BROOKE, Clerk, for attending a called Court on GEORGE LINTON		160
To the Sherif for summoning and attending a called Court on GEORGE LINTON		160
To WILLIAM BLACKWELL, late Sherif, his Account		3336
To JOHN HEADLY by Account	5/	
To WILLIAM BLACKWELL & THOMAS KEITH by Account	6/10	
To MINOR WINN, Assignee of JOSEPH WILLIAMS for Guarding GEORGE LINTON		175
To do. Assignee of WINFIELD ROBINSON, ELISHA ROBINSON THOMAS HATHAWAY & SANFORD CARROL for Guarding GEORGE LINTON		725
To WILLIAM JONES by Account		800
To JOHN KIRK, Constable, for viewing tobacco fields		652
To MINOR WINN by Account		1820
To JAMES STROTHER for one County Levy overpaid last year		6
To GEORGE SETTLE for one County Levy overpaid in 1766		8
To ALEXANDER MONROE for one do.		9
To 6 per cent for collecting		798
		14104
To Fraction in the Sherifs hands		1001
		15105
CR.		
By Last Years Fraction		369
By 2456 Tithes at 6 lbs. tobo. per poll		14736
		15105

p. Fauquier County Court 3rd of November 1768

46 The Levy of this County being six pounds of tobacco per poll, it is ordered that THOMAS MARSHALL collect the same of each person chargeable with the paiment thereof and pay the same to the several County Creditors, he haveing executed Bond for that purpose

signed by WILLIAM BLACKWELL

- At a Court held for Fauquier County the 28th day of November 1768
Present WILLIAM GRANT ARMISTEAD CHURCHHILL
WILLIAM EDMONDS JEREMIAH DERNALL
& JOSEPH HUDNALL Gent.

- MINOR WINN, Plt. agt. JAMES TAYLER, Deft. In Case
This suit is agreed and it is ordered that the Deft. pay to the Plt. his costs by him in this behalf expended

- A Commission for takeing the acknowledgement and privy examination of ANNE, the Wife of GEORGE DOBSON, upon certain Indentures of Lease and Release to

ROBERT SANDERS and a Certificate of the Execution thereof was returned and ordered to be recorded

- An Inventory and Appraisment of the Estate of THOMAS DAVIS, deced, was returned and ordered to be recorded

- An Inventory and Appraisment of the Estate of THOMAS MOREHEAD, deced., was returned and ordered to be rcorded

- Ordered that WILLIAM EUSTACE, JOHN NELLSON, TILLMAN WEAVER and JOSEPH MARTIN or any three of them do divide the Estate of JOHN MOREHEAD according to his Last Will

- ARMISTEAD CHURCHHILL is appointed Surveyor of the Road in the room of ZACHARIAH LEWIS and it is ordered that he with the Tithes belonging to the said Road do clear and keep the same in repair according to Law

p. Fauquier County Court 28th of November 1768

47 - THOMAS PORTER is appointed Surveyor of the Road from SAMUEL PORTER's to ARMISTEAD CHURCHHILL's Gate and it is ordered that he with the Tithes that shall be appointed by ARMISTEAD CHURCHHILL and JEREMIAH DERNALL, Gent., do clear and keep the same in repair according to Law

- JOHN MARTIN is appointed Surveyor of the Road from ARMISTEAD CHURCHHILL's Gate to LICKING RUN and it is ordered that he with the Tithes that shall be appointed by ARMISTEAD CHURCHHILL do clear and keep the same in repair according to Law

- CHARLES BURRUS is appointed Surveyor of the Road from LICKING RUN to the Forks of the Road in the room of ARMISTEAD CHURCHHILL and it is ordered that he with the Tithes that shall be appointed by ARMISTEAD CHURCHHILL and JEREMIAH DERNAL, Gent., do clear and keep the same in repair according to Law

- The persons appointed to view the Way petitioned for by CHARLES CHINN returned their Report in these words, to wit,

"In Obedience to an Order of Court to us directed, we the Subscribers being first sworn have viewed the Way from the County Line to Upper Church and find it more convenient beginning at the County Line and going between CHARLES CHINNs and JOHN FRENCHes, thence a straight course the lower side of JOHN SQUIERS, then a straight course the upper side of JOHN KINCHELOEs, and then by ISAAC CUNDIFFs and by JACOB RECTORs and the upper side of JOHN RHUST, and then by WILLIAM HUTCHINGSONs and the upper side of JAMES TAYLERs, from thence a straight course to the Church. Given under our hands this 24th day of October 1768; JOHN RECTOR, JACOB RECTOR, JOHN SIERS."

And it is ordered that the Road be established according to the said Report and the said CHARLES CHINN has liberty to clear the same

- The persons appointed to view the most convenient Way from COVINGTONs into AQUIA ROLLING ROAD returned their Report in these words, to wit,

" According to Order, we have viewed the Road from Mr. COVINGTONs to the place appointed

p. Fauquier County Court 28th of November 1768

48 and we find it to be as well where it is except turned between Mr. COVINGTONs and Mr. TULLOSes & a few small amendments besides. Test. GEO: THRELKELD, RICHARD COVINGTON, THOMAS SMITH,"

And the Road is established according to the said Report

- THOMAS CONWAY is appointed Surveyor of the Road from RICHARD COVINGTONs to AQUIA ROLLING ROAD and it is ordered that he with the Tithes that shall be appointed by WILLIAM GRANT, Gent., do clear and keep the same in repair according to Law

- On the motion of WILLIAM CARR, Judgment is granted him against ALEXANDER FARROW and LUKE COLLINS, his Security, for sixty five pounds, thirteen shillings and ten pence current money, it being the amount of a Replevy Bond taken by BENJAMIN KEYHANDALL, late Sherif of HAMPSHIRE by virtue of a Tirifacias to him directed and his costs by him in this behalf expended, and the said ALEXANDER FARROW and LUKE COLLINS, his Security, in mercy &c., But this Judgment is to be discharged by the paiment of twenty nine pounds, ten shillings and eleven pence and one hundred and eighty pounds of tobacco and fifteen shillings (and also one pound, seven shillings, the Sherifs fee on the aforesaid Execution) with Interest thereon to be computed after the rate of five percentum per annum from the eighteenth day of May 1768 till paid and the costs; it appearing that they had legal noice of this motion.

- A Lease between JAMES SCOTT of the one part and WILLIAM STAMPS of the other part was acknowledged by the said JAMES SCOTT and ordered to be recorded

- A Lease between RICHARD HENRY LEE of the one part and RANDOLPH SPISER of the other part was proved by the

p. Fauquier County Court 28th of November 1768

49 Oaths of JOHN HATHAWAY, MARTIN PICKETT and JAMES WINN, witnesses thereto, and ordered to be recorded

- On the motion of ANDREW COCKRANE, ALLAN DREGHORN and COMPANY, Judgment is granted them against JOSEPH ODOR and WILLIAM GRANT, his Security, for twenty eight pounds and two pence current money, (it being the amount of a Replevy Bond taken by the Sheriff of this County by virtue of a Tirifacias against the Estate of the said JOSEPH ODOR to him directed), and their costs by them in this behalf expended and the said JOSEPH ODOR and WILLIAM GRANT, his Security, in mercy, &c., But this Judgment is to be discharged by the paiment of fourteen pounds and one penny with Interest thereon to be computed after the rate of five percentum per annum from the twenty sixth day of May 1765 till paid and two hundred pounds of tobacco and fifteen shillings and the costs; it appearing that they had legal notice of this motion

- ZACHARIAS LEWIS, Plt. agt. CHARLES HOGAIN, Deft. On an Attachment

This day came the Plt. by his Attorney and the Sherif haveing returned that he had attached a parcell of Corn, one 'Chest, a parcel of tobacco, two potts, two pot reacks, one loom, two tables, four piggans, one can, four chairs, one pair pothooks, one pail, nine lasts, two pair woolen cards, four trays, one baskett, three pair pothooks, one plain, one pair hames, four basketts, twelve goards, three bottles, one shovel, a parcell of Walnut plank, a parcell of Flax, some fother, one sifter, two matts, one pair nippers, one Flax break and one butter pott, and the said Deft. failing to appear and replevy the attached effects, tho

p. Fauquier County Court 28th of November 1768

50 solemnly called, it is considered by the Court that the Plt. recover against the said Deft. five hundred pounds of tobacco and his costs by him in this behalf expended, and the said Deft. in mercy, &c., And it is ordered that the Sherif sell the attached effects and return and account of the sales to the Court

- JOHN WRIGHT, Foreman, JOHN DUNCAN, JOSEPH JEFFERIES, JOSIAH HOLTZCLAW, MAXIMILLIAN BERRYMAN, JOHN BAILEY, HENRY JONES, JAMES SUDDOTH,

THOMAS PORTER, JAMES STUART, SIMON MORGAN, JAMES BAILEY, EDMOND BASEY, CARR BAILEY, JOSEPH HITT and PHARNACH GEORGE were sworn a Grand Jury of Inquest for the body of this County and haveing received their charge withdrew to consider of their Presentments, and after some time returned into Court and brought in their Presentsment as followeth, to wit.,

"Fauquier, to wit, November 28th 1768. We the Jurors of our Lord the King for the County aforesaid do upon Oath present JAMES TAYLER of Hamilton Parish for being Drunk at the Parish aforesaid and profain swearing within two months last past by the knowledge of two of us;

"We present MARY TRIPLETT, the Wife of WILLIAM TRIPLETT, for retailing Liquors without a License at the Parish of Hamilton within six months last past by the knowledge of two of us;

"We present JOHN NELLSON for profane swearing at the Parish aforesaid within two months last past by the knowledge of two of us;

"We present HUMPHREY ARNOLD for turning out seconds of tobacco contrary to Act of Assembly at the Parish aforesaid within six months last past by the knowledge of two of us;

"We also present the same person, HUMPHREY ARNOLD, for being Drunk at the Parish aforesaid within two months last past by the knowledge of two of us;"

And it is ordered that the several persons presented be summoned to appear at the next Court to answer

p. <u>Fauquier County Court 28th of November 1768</u>

51 the same respectively

- RICHARD LEE haveing been in Prison upwards of twenty days at the suit of MITCHEL and CRUTCHER by virtue of a Warrant under the hand and seal of JOHN MOFFETT, Gent., was brought into Court and took the Oaths presented by Law and delivered a schedule of his Estate and made Oath thereto and it is ordered that he be discharged from his Imprisonment according to an Act of Assembly in that case made and provided

- Ordered that the Court be adjourned till the Court in Course

" WILLIAM GRANT "

- At a Court held for Fauquier County the 27th day of March 1769

Present	THOMAS HARRISON		WILLIAM GRANT	
	WILLIAM EDMONDS	&	JAMES SCOTT	Gent.

- Ordered that the Sherif summon a competent number of Freeholders qualified according to Law to be impannell'd and sworn a Grand Jury of Inquest for the body of this County in May next

- ALEXANDER WODROW & JOHN NEILSON, Plts. agt. EDWARD WILBURNE, Deft. In Chancery

The Deft. in his proper person agrees that he and his heirs and all persons claiming by from or under him may be forever foreclosed of all his & their Right, Title and Equity of Redemption of the mortgaged Land and premises in the Bill mentioned unless he pay the Plts. the sum of seventy five pounds with lawfull Interest thereon from December last

p. <u>Fauquier County Court 27th of March 1769</u>

52 - The Rates of Liquors continued as the last except the difference in Rum, to wit, West India Rum at ten shillings per gallon, Continent Rum at seven shil-

lings & six pence per gallon and Cyder at one shillings and eight pence per gallon

- Ordered that the Church Wardens of Hamilton Parish bind ANN BARR to THOMAS JAMES according to Law

- For certain reasons to the Court appearing, WILLIAM DUNCAN, Son of JOHN DUNCAN, JUNR., is discharged from paying County Levies dureing the Courts pleasure

- An Indenture of Bargain and Sale between JAMES ALLAN and JAMES HUNTER of the one part and GEORGE YATES and WILLIAM ROGERS of the other part and a Receit thereon endorsed were proved by the Oath of ANDREW BUCHANAN, a witness thereto, and ordered to be certified

- Ordered that BRERETON JONES, JOHN NELLSON, Black Smith, DANIEL HARRILL and SIMON CUMMINS or any three of them being first sworn do view the most convenient way from ELK RUN CHURCH to the Line of STAFFORD County and report the conveniences and inconveniences thereof to the Court

- An Inventory and Appraisment of the Estate of JOHN RENNOLDS, deced., was returned and ordered to be recorded

- Messieurs DAVID DALYELL, GEORGE OSWALD and COMPANY, Plts. agt.
EDWARD WILLBURNE, Deft. On an Attachment

This day came the Plts. by their Attorney and the Sherif haveing returned that he had attached one feather bed, one rug, one sheet & one womans saddle, which said attached effects by the Plts. consent are discharged and the said Deft., in his proper person acknowledged the Plts. action against him for fifteen pounds, ten shillings and one penny half penny. Therefore it is considered by the Court that the Plts. recover against the said Deft. the said fifteen pounds, ten shillings and one penny half penny and their costs by them in this behalf expended, and the said Deft. in mercy, &c.

- On the motion of MINOR WINN, Judgment is granted him against JOHN JETT, Security for JOHN CATLETT, JUNIOR, for five pounds,

p. Fauquier County Court 27th of March 1769
53 nine shillings and three pence and eight hundred and eighty and eight pounds of tobacco. the amount of a Replevy Bond executed by JOHN CATLETT, JUNIOR and the said JETT, his Security, and his costs by him in this behalf expended, and the said JOHN JETT in mercy, &c., But this Judgment is to be discharged by the paiment of two pounds, fourteen shillings and seven pence half penny and four hundred and forty four pounds of tobacco with Interest thereon to be computed after the rate of five percentum per annum from the twenty seventh day of September 1768 till paid and the costs; it appearing that the said JETT had legal notice of this motion

- WILLIAM GRANT is appointed Guardian to RICHARD FOOTE and WILLIAM FOOTE Orphans of GEORGE FOOTE, deced. he haveing executed and acknowledged Bond as the Law directs

- THOMAS HARRISON, JONATHAN GIBSON and HOWISON KENNER, Gent., are apponted to divide the Estate of JOHN MAUZEY, deced., among the several Devisees according to his Last Will and Testment

- JOHN PETERS, Plt. agt. THOMAS BRIDEWELL, Deft. On an Attachment

This day came the Plt. by his Attorney and the Sherif haveing returned that he had attached one Sow & one Mug and the Deft. failing to appear and replevy the attached effects, altho solemnly called, it is considered by the Court that the Plt. recover against the said deft. six hundred and ninety five pounds of tobacco and twelve shillings and six pence and his costs by him in this behalf expended, and the said Deft. in mercy, &c., And it is ordered that the Sherif sell the attached effects and return an account of the sales to the Court

- Ordered that the Court be adjourned till tomorrow morning ten of the Clock
THOMAS HARRISON

p. 54 - At a Court continued and held for Fauquier County the 28th day of March 1769
Present JOSEPH BLACKWELL WILLIAM GRANT
WILLIAM EDMONDS & JOSEPH HUDNALL Gent.

- JAMES BUCHANAN, Assignee of MARTIN PICKETT and COMPANY, Plt. agt. HENRY JONES, Deft. In Debt

This day came the Plt. by his Attorney and the Sherif haveing returned on the Attachment awarded against the said Defts. Estate that he had attached one Knife and the said Deft. failing to appear and replevy the same, altho solemnly called, it is considered by the Court that the Plt. recover against the said Deft. eleven pounds, thirteen shillings current money, the Debt in the Declaration mentioned, and his costs by him in this behalf expended, and the said Deft. in mercy, &c., But this Judgment is to be discharged by the paiment of three poudns, three shillings with Interest thereon to be computed after the rate of five percentum per annum from the twenty fourth day of June 1768 till paid and the costs; And it is ordered that the Sherif sell the attached effects and return an account of the sales to the Court

- JOHN RALLS, Plt. agt. JOHN EDGE, Deft. Upon a Writ of Scire Facias to revive a Judgment obtained by the Plt. against the said Deft. for six pounds for his damages which he sustained by means of the breach of a certain assumption by the said EDGE to him made and also one hundred and forty six pounds of nett tobacco and fifteen shillings or one hudnred and fifty pounds of tobacco for his costs

It is considered by the Court that the Plt. may have his

p. 55 Fauquier County Court 28th of March 1769

Execution against the said Deft. for his damages and costs aforesaid according to the force form and effect of the recovery aforesaid, And it is further considered by the Court that the Plt. recover against the said Deft. his costs by him in this behalf expended, and the said Deft. in mercy &c.

- HANCOCK LEE and COMPANY, Plts. agt. JOHN HEADLEY, Deft. In Case

This day came the Plts. by their Attorney and came also JAMES BAILY and became Special Bail and Pledge for the Deft. in this suit and the said Deft. prays and has leave to imparl specially to the Plts. Declaration untill the next Court and then to plead

- WILLIAM BOGLE and COLLIN DUNLOP, Surviving Partners of PATRICK & WILLIAM BOGLEs & COLLIN DUNLOP of Glasgow, Merchants, Plts. agt. JAMES FLETCHER, Deft. In Debt

Discontinued

- On the motion of GEORGE NEAVEILL, it is ordered that ELIZABETH KEIRNS pay him one hundred pounds of tobacco for four days attendance as a witness for him against JOHN CHURCHHILL

- On the motion of GEORGE NEAVILL, Licence is granted him to keep ORDINARY at his House in this County for one year and from thence till the next Court held for this County, he haveing executed and acknowledged Bond as the Law directs

- MARTIN PICKETT and COMPANY, Plts. agt. ELIZABETH RENNOLDS, Admrx. of JOHN RENNOLDS, deced., Deft. In Debt

Discontinued being agreed by the parties

- THOMAS HOGAIN & ROBERT FOSTER, Exors. of THOMAS LEACHMAN, deced., Plts. agt. RICHARD HALEY & JOHN SHURLY, Defts. In Debt

This suit abates, the Sherif haveing returned that the Defts. are no Inhabitants of this County

p. Fauquier County Court 28th of March 1769
56 - Present JEREMIAH DARNALL, Gent.

- JOHN MOREHEAD, Plt. agt. GAVIN LAWSON, Deft. In Case

Discontinued being agreed by the parties

- WILLIAM GAULD, Plt. agt. SAMUEL EARLE, Deft. In Trespass, Assault & Battery

This suit is dismist, the Plt. not appearing to prosecute the same

- JOSEPH MINOR, Plt. agt. PETER GRANT, Deft. In Debt

This day came the Plt. by his Attorney and came also WILLIAM GRANT and became Special Bail and Pledge for the Deft. in this suit, and the said Deft., altho solemnly called, doth not come nor say anything in bar or preclusion of the Plts. action against him but made default, whereby the said Plt. remains against the said Deft. therein undefended; Therefore it is considered by the Court that the Plt. recover against the said Deft. seven pounds current money, the Debt in the Declaration mentioned, and his costs by him in this behalf expended; And the said Deft. in mercy, &c.

- HANCOCK LEE, Assignee of MARTIN PICKETT & COMPANY, Plt. agt. VALENTINE FLYNN, Deft. In Debt

This day came the Plt. by his Attorney and came also THOMAS KEITH and became Special Bail and Pledge for the Deft. in this suit, and the said Deft., altho solemnly called, doth not come nor say anything in bar or preclusion of the Plts. action against him but hath made default, whereby the Plt. remains against the said Deft. therein undefended; Therefore it is considered by the Court that the Plt. recover against the said Deft. six pounds, four shillings and two pence current money, the Debt in the Declaration mentioned, and his costs by him in this behalf expended, and the said Deft., in mercy &c., But this Judg-

p. Fauquier County Court 28th of March 1769
57 ment is to be discharged by the paiment of three poudns, six shillings and eight pence with Interest thereon to be computed after the rate of five percentum per annum from the twenty fourth day of May 1768 till paid and the costs

- JOHN & WILLIAM KNOX, Plts. agt. WILLIAM WAITE and THOMAS HARRISON, Gent., Defts. In Debt

Judgment is granted the Plts. against the said Defts. for their costs by them in this behalf expended and the said Defts. in mercy, &c.

- GEORGE WILLSON, Assignee of CHARLES LYNCH, Plt. agt. SAMUEL BLACKWELL & MARTIN PICKETT, Defts. In Debt

This day came the Plt. by his Attorney and came also WILLIAM BLACKWELL and became Special Bail and Pledge for the Defts. in this suit, and the said Defts. acknowledge the Plts. action against them. Therefore it is considered by the Court that the Plt. recover against the said Defts. forty three pounds, ten shillings, the Debt in the Declaration mentioned, and his costs by him in this behalf expended, and the said Defts. in mercy, &c., But this Judgment is to be discharged by the paiment of fourteen pounds, eight shillings and seven pence with Interest thereon to be computed after the rate of five per centum per annum from December 1764 till paid and the costs. Execution stayed eleven months

- JAMES BUCHANAN, Plt. agt. PETER NEWPORT, Deft. In Debt

This day came the Plt. by his Attorney and came also JOSEPH HUDNALL and BUSHROD DOGGETT and became Special Bail and Pledge for the Deft. in this suit, and the said Deft. prays Oyer of the Writing Obligatory and he hath it, &c.

- ANDREW BUCHANAN, Assee. fo PICKETT & COMPANY, Plt. agt. WILLIAM PARKER, Deft. In Debt

This suit is agreed, and it is ordered that the Plt. pay to the Deft. his costs by him in this behalf expended

p. Fauquier County Court 28th of March 1769

58 - WILLIAM ALLASON, Plt. agt. THOMAS GRUBS, Deft. In Debt

This day came the Plt. by his Attorney and came allso MARTIN PICKETT and became Special Bail and Pledge for the Deft. in this suit, and the said Deft. prays Oyer of the Writing Obligatory & he hath it, &c.

- Present. JOHN MOFFETT, Gent.

- JOHN MOREHEAD, Plt. agt. THOMAS WATTS, Deft. In Case

The persons appointed to settle all matters in dispute relateing to this Cause returned their Report in these words., to wit,

"In Obedience to an Order of the Worshipfull Court of Fauquier dated October Court 1768, we have met according thereto in order to arbitrate and determine a certain matter of Scandal therein mentioend now depending and undetermined in the said Court between JOHN MOREHEAD, Plt. and THOMAS WATTS, Deft., And after haveing maturely considered the evidence introduced by the parties aforesaid, we find the Scandalous words on which the said suit was brought to have been spoken through excess of Liquor by the said Deft. to the prejudice of the character of the said Plt., and we also find the same to be groundless and without foundation. We therefore do award to the said Plt. all his costs lawfull expended in the prosecution of the said suit and no more (as the said Plt. has declared to us that he desires no damages against the said Deft. neither will he receive any if awarded, otherwise than his costs aforesaid. Given under our hands and seals this 23d day of December 1768.

THOMAS MARSHALL
JNO: MOFFETT"

- JOHN LEE, Plt. agt. THOMAS WATTS, Deft. In Case

This suit abates by the Defts. death

p. Fauquier County Court 28th of March 1769

59 - On the motion of BAILY JOHNSON, it is ordered that JOHN MOREHEAD pay him fifty pounds of tobacco for two days attendance as a witness for him against THOMAS WATTS

- A Bond between WILLIAM WHEATLY of the one part and JOHN WHEATLY of the other part was acknowledged by the said WILLIAM to be his act and deed, ordered to be recorded

- Ordered that an Attachment issue against RICHARD BRYAN and JANE MAHORNEY for a Contempt in not appearing as witnesses for SAMUEL THORNBERRY against JOHN MORGAN

- SUSANNAH SMITH, Plt. agt. DANIEL McCOY, Deft. On Petition

This suit is dismist and it is ordered that the Plt. apy to the Deft. his costs by him in this behalf expended

- JOHN RALLS, Plt. agt. SINNETT YOUNG, Deft. On a Petition

This suit is dismist and it is ordered that the Plt. pay to the Deft. his costs by him in this behalf expended

- On the motion of SAMUEL JOHNSON, it is ordered that DANIEL McCOY pay him one hundred and twenty five pounds of tobacco for five days attendance as a witness for him at the suit of SMITH

- SAMUEL EARLE, Plt. agt. MARK CANTON, Deft. On a Petition
Judgment is granted the Plt. against the said Deft. for one pound, fourteen shillins and six pence and fifty two pounds of tobacco and his costs by him in this behalf expended

- AUGUSTINE JENNINGS, Plt. agt. JONAS WILLIAMS, Deft. On a Petition
Judgment is granted the Plt. against the said Deft. for two pounds, fourteen shillings & ten pence and his costs by him in this behalf expended

p. Fauquier County Court 28th of March 1769
60 - NATHANIEL DODD, Plt. agt. JONAS WILLIAMS, Deft. On a Petition
Judgment is granted the Plt. against the said Deft. for two pounds, five shillings & four pence and his costs by him in this behalf expended

- EDWARD GODFREY, Plt. agt. CHARLES CASSON, Deft. On a Petition
Judgment is granted the Plt. against the said Deft. for four pounds, ten shillings and his costs by him in this behalf expended

- EDWARD BUSH, Plt. agt. EPHRAIM HUBBARD, Deft. On a Petition
Judgment is granted the Plt. against the said Deft. for two pounds, thirteen shillings and his costs by him in this behalf expended

- NATHANIEL STEPHENSON, Plt. agt. PETER GRANT, Deft. On a Petition
Judgment is granted the Plt. against the said Deft. for three pounds, seventeen shillings and his costs by him in this behalf expended

- A Bond from THOMAS MARSHALL & THOMAS KEITH to our Sovereign Lord the King was acknowledged by the said THOMAS MARSHALL and THOMAS KEITH and ordered to be recorded

- On the motion of CALVERT McDANIEL, it is ordered that SINNETT YOUNG pay him one hundred and fifty pounds of tobacco for six days attendance as a witness for him at the suit of JOHN RALLS

- SAMUEL (? P___) Plt. agt. TARPLY BRAGG, Deft. On a Petition
This Petition abates, the Sherif haveing returned that the Deft. is no Inhabitant of this County

p. Fauquier County Court 28th of March 1769
61 - On the motion of JOHN NELSON, it is ordered that WILLIAM HENDERSON pay him fifty pounds of tobacco for two days attendance as a witness for him at the suit of DARNALL

- The same Order of JOHN JOHNSON

- The same Order of WALLER JOHNSON

- On the motion of JAMES WILLIAMS, it is ordered that JOHN SHUMATE pay him one hundred and thirty nine pounds of tobacco for one days attendance and once comeing thirty eight miles and returning as a witness for him against ALEXANDER WOODSIDES

- JOSEPH HUDNALL, SENR., JOHN HUDNALL, JOSEPH HUDNALL, JUNR., WILLIAM HUDNALL, JAMES HUDNALL & Others, Plts. agt. JOHN WITHERS & THOMAS WITHERS, Admors. &c. of ELIZABETH WITHERS, deced., JAMES WITHERS and WILLIAM WITHERS, Defts. In Chancery
The Plts. Attorney moved that the Court would appoint a Guardian to prosecute this suit on behalf of JAMES HUDNALL, HENRY FIELDS, JUNR., NANCY MAUZEY, HENRY

MAUZEY, JUNR., PETER MAUZEY, WILLIAM MAUZEY, PRISCILLA MAUZEY, GEORGE MAUZEY, HESTER MAUZEY, JOHN WITHERS, JAMES WITHERS & WILLIAM WITHERS who are Infants, which the Court refused to do as no Guardian is mentioned in the Subpeana

- On the motion of RICHARD COVINGTON, Licence is granted him to keep ORDINARY at his House in this County, he haveing executed and acknowledged Bond as the Law directs

- RICHARD HOUGHLAND, Plt. agt. DAVID BARTON, Deft. On a Petition

Judgment is gratned the Plt. against the said Deft. for four pounds, six shillings and two pence half penny and his costs by him in this behalf expended

- SAMUEL DUNCAN, Plt. agt. EDWARD NEWGENT, Deft. On Petition

Judgment is granted the Plt. against the said Deft. for four pounds, nine shillings and his costs by him in this behalf expended

p. Fauquier County Court 28th of March 1769

62 - THOMAS HOGAIN & ROBERT FOSTER, Executors of THOMAS LEACHMAN, deced., Plts. agt. RICHARD HAILY & JOHN SHURLY, Defts On a Petition

This Petition abates, the Sherif haveing returned that the Defts. are not Inhabitants of this County

- GEORGE MYERS, Plt. agt. JOHN GREEN, Deft. On a Petition

Judgment is granted the Plt. against the said Deft. for two pounds, ten shillings and his costs by him in this behalf expended

- MICHAEL MARR, Plt. agt. THOMAS SKINKER, Deft. On a Petition

Judgment is granted the Plt. against the said Deft. for four pounds, nineteen shillings and four pence half penny and his costs by him in this behalf expended

- JOSEPH JEFFRIES, Plt. agt. EPHRAIM HUBBARD, Deft. On a Petition

Judgment is granted the Plt. against the said Deft. for two pounds, ten shillings and his costs by him in this behalf expended

- JOHN SHERMANS, Plt. agt. THOMAS STONE, Deft. On a Petition

Judgment is granted the Plt. against the said Deft. for his costs by him in this behalf expended

- Present. ARMISTEAD CHURCHHILL, Gent.

- ANDREW BUCHANAN, Assignee of PICKETT & CO., Plt. agt. WILLIAM DULING, SENR., Deft. On a Petition

Agreed

p. Fauquier County Court 28th of March 1769

63 - ANDREW BUCHANAN, Assee. of MARTIN PICKETT & COMPANY, Plt. agt. JOHN STONE, Deft. On a Petition

Judgment is granted the Plt. against the said Deft. for seven shillings and his costs by him in this behalf expended

- ANDREW BUCHANAN, Assee. of MARTIN PICKETT & COMPANY, Plt. agt. WILLIAM SUTTON, Deft. On Petition

Judgment is granted the Plt. against the said Deft. for three pounds, seventeen shillings with Interest thereon to be computed after the rate of five percentum per annum from the twenty fourth day of May 1768 till paid and the costs

- RHODAM TULLOS, Plt. agt. JOHN KNOX, Deft. On a Petition

This Petition abates by the Plts. death

- RICHARD GRAHAM, Plt. agt. BENJAMIN HAMRICK, Deft. On a Petition

Judgment is granted the Plt. against the said Deft. for four pounds, six shillings & six pence and fifty two pounds of tobacco and his costs by him in this behalf expended

- ABSALOM CORNELIOUS, Plt. agt. SIMON BOLEY, Deft. On a Petition
This Petition is dismist, the Plt. not appearing to prosecute the same
- MORRIS MORGAN, Plt. agt. DAVID BARTON, Deft. On a Petition
Judgment is granted the Plt. against the said Deft. for four pounds, six shillings and three pence and his costs by him in this behalf expended
- On the motion of BENJAMIN WHITE, it is ordered that JOHN MOREHEAD pay him fifty pounds of tobacco for two days attendance as a witness for him against THOMAS WATTS

p. Fauquier County Court 28th of March 1769

64 - On the motion of WILLIAM WHEATLY, it is ordered that JOHN MOREHEAD pay him twenty five pounds of tobacco for one days attendance as a witness for him against THOMAS WATTS
- HANCOCK LEE, Assee. of PICKETT & COMPANY, Plt. agt. ARTHUR HARRIS, Deft. On a Petition
This suit abates by return
- JAMES BUCHANAN, Assee. of PICKETT & COMPANY, Plt. agt. JOHN DAVIS, Deft. In Debt
This day came the Plt. by his Attorney and the Sherif haveing returned on the Attachment awarded against the said Defts. Estate that he had attached one Bridle Bitt and the Deft. failing to appear to replevy the same, altho solemnly called, It is considered by the Court that the Plt. recover against the said Deft. five pounds, eight shillings current money, the Debt in the Declaration mentioned, and his costs by him in this behalf expended; And the said Deft. in mercy, &c., But this Judgment is to be discharged by the paiment of two pounds, seventeen shillings and four pence with Interest thereon to be computed after the rate of five percentum per annum from the twenty fourth day of May 1768 till paid and the costs; And it is ordered that the Sherif sell the attached effect and return an account of the sales to the Court
- Ordered that the Court be adjourned till the Court in Course

ARMISTEAD CHURCHHILL

p. - At a Court held at Fauquier Courthouse the 24th day of April 1769 for Proof
65 of Publick Claims

Present WILLIAM EUSTACE, WILLIAM GRANT
ARMISTEAD CHURCHHILL JEREMIAH DARNALL
& JOSEPH HUDNALL Gent.

- Pursuant to the Act of Assembly, the Act concerning Claims was read
- A Claim of THOMAS CONWAY, JUNR. for takeing up a runaway slave therein mentioned was proved according to Law & ordered to be certified to the General Assembly
- A Claim of WILLIAM ASBURYs for takeing up a runaway slave therein mentioned, was proved according to Law and ordered to be certified to the General Assembly
- A Claim of JOHN ASHBYs for takeing up a runaway slave therein mentioned was proved according to Law and ordered to be certified to the General Assembly
- A Claim of THOMAS EMBRYs for takeing up a runaway slave therein mentioned was proved according to Law & ordered to be certified to the General Assembly
- A Claim of JOHN KIRK, JUNR., for takeing up a runaway slave therein mentioned was proved according to Law & ordered to be certified to the General Assembly

" WILLIAM BLACKWELL "

p. 66 - At a Court held for Fauquier County the 24th day of April 1769

Present WILLIAM EUSTACE, WILLIAM GRANT
ARMISTEAD CHURCHHILL JEREMIAH DARNALL
& JOSEPH HUDNALL Gent.

- Indentures of Lease & Release between ROBERT ELLISTON & ELLINOR his Wife of the one part and RICHARD LEWIS of the other part and a Receit on the Release endorsed were proved by the Oaths of THOMAS JAMES, JOSEPH WILLIAMS & JACOB ELLISTON, witness thereto, to be the act and deed of the said ROBERT & ELINOR his Wife, ordered to be recorded

- An Indenture of Feofment between THOMAS EAVES of the one part & ALEXANDER WOODSIDES of the other part and a Memorandum of Livery of Seisen & a Receit thereon endorsed were acknowledged by the said THOMAS & ordered to be recorded

- An Indenture of Feofment between THOMAS HOPPER and ANN HOPPER of the one part and JOSEPH BLACKWELL of the other part and a Memorandum of Livery of Seisen & a Receit thereon endorsed, were proved by the Oaths of WILLIAM BLACKWELL, THOMAS MATTHEWS & ELIZABETH MATTHEWS, witnesses thereto, ordered to be recorded

- On the motion of HANNAH FOOTE, who made Oath & executed & acknowledged Bond as the Law directs, Certificate is granted her for obtaining Letters of Administration of the Estate of GILLSON FOOTE, Gent., deceased

- Ordered that WILLIAM FOOTE, WILLIAM ALEXANDER, LINUM HELMS & RICHARD FOOTE or any three of them being first sworn do appraise the Estate of GILSON FOOTE, Gent., deceased, and return the appraisment to the Court

- For certain reasons to the Court appearing, JOSEPH WILLIAMS (DEEP RUN) is discharged from paying County Levies

- The persons appointed to divide the Estate of JOHN MAUZEY, deced., returned their Report which is ordered to be recorded

p. 67 Fauquier County Court 24th of April 1769

- WILLIAM BILLBOE, Assignee of ISRAEL MORRIS, Plt. agt.
THOMAS MIDDLETON, Deft., In Debt

This day came the Plt. by his Attorney and came also JOHN YOUNG and became Special Bail and Pledge for the Deft. in this suit and the said Deft. prays Oyer of the Writing Obligatory and to him it is granted, &c.

- PRESLY MOREHEAD, Orphan of JOHN MOREHEAD, deced., made choice of MARY MOREHEAD for his Guardian, who executed & acknowledged Bond as the Law directs

- On the motion of THOMAS MIDDLETON, it is ordered that a Dedimus issue to take the Deposition of JOHN BOTTS, an infirm witnesses for him at the suit of WILLIAM BILBOE

- On the motion of ELIZABETH CUMMINS, who made Oath & executed & acknowledged Bond as the Law directs, Certificate is granted her for obtaining Letters of Administration on the Estate of MALACHI CUMMINS, deced.

- Ordered that THOMAS BARTLETT, PHILIP FISHBACK, WILLIAM KINCHELOE & JOHN FISHBACK or any three of them being first sworn do appraise the Estate of MALACHI CUMMINS, deced., and return the appraisment to the Court

- An Indenture of Bargain & Sale between JAMES ALLAN & THOMAS SKINKER, Gent., Surviving Executors of the Last Will & Testament of JOHN ALLAN, deced., of the one part & GEORGE YATES & WILLIAM ROGERS, Executors of the Last Will and Testament of WILLIAM CONYERS, deced, of the other part, and a Receit thereon endorsed were proved by the Oaths of WILLIAM NEWTON & JAMES ROBISON, witnesses thereto and ordered to be rcorded

- JACOB ELLISTON made Oath to a Book of Accounts kept by him for CUTHBERT HARRISON, which is ordered to be recorded

p. Fauquier County Court 24th of April 1769
68 - An Indenture of Bargain & Sale between JOSEPH COMBS & ELIZABETH his Wife of the one part and CATHARINE STARK & JEREMIAH STARK of the other part and a Receit thereon endorsed were proved by the Oaths of CUTHBERT BULLITT, CUTHBERT HARRISON & THOMAS CHAPMAN, witnesses thereto, and with Commission thereto annexed for takeing the acknowledgement and privy examination of the said ELIZABETH & a Certificate of the Execution thereof, ordered to be recorded

- JOSEPH COMBS, Plt. agt. JOHN POPE, Deft. On an Attachment
This day came the Plt. by his Attorney and the Sherif haveing returned that he had attached one Horse Shoe and a parcell of tobacco, and the Deft. not appearing to replevy the said attached effects, altho solemnly called, it is considered by the Court that the Plt. recover against the said Deft. for one thousand and sixty pounds of Transfer tobacco and his costs by him in this behalf expended, and the said Deft. in mercy, &c. And it is ordered that the Sherif sell the attached effects & return an account of the sales to the Court

- Present. WILLIAM BLACKWELL, Gent.

- An Inventory & Appraisment of the Estate of PETER PEARCE, deced., was returned & ordered to be recorded

- JOHN BALLARD, Plt. agt. JOSEPH BLACKWELL & RICHARD LEWIS, Defts.
In Debt
This day came the parties by their Attorneys and thereupon came also a Jury, to wit, JAMES HATHAWAY, BENJAMIN NEALE, EPHRAIM HUBBARD, JOHN SMITH, WILLIAM DERNALL, WILLIAM WALKER, STEPHEN MORRIS, WILLIAM

p. Fauquier County Court 24th of April 1769
69 PARKER, AUGUSTINE JENNINGS, JOHN McCORMACK, SAMUEL RUST and BUSHROD DOGGETT, who being elected tried & sworn the truth to speak upon the issue joined, upon their Oaths do say that the Defts. have not paid to the said Plt. the said sum in the Declaration mentioned according to the form & effect of the said award, and in discharge of the said Obligation according to the condition of the same as by replying the Plt. hath alledged, and they find for the Plt. one hundred pounds current money, the Debt in the Declaration mentioned and they do assess the Plts. damages by means of the detention of that debt to two pounds, eighteen shillings & six pence. Therefore it is considered by the Court that the Plt. recover against the said Deft. his damages aforesaid in form aforesaid assessed and his costs by him in this behalf expended. And on the motion of the Defts., a new Trial is awarded them in this Cause they paying the cost of this Tiral, the Court being of opinion that the Jury found contrary to evidence

- A Bill of Sale from EPHRAIM HUBBARD to ANDREW COCKRANE & COMPANY was acknowledged by the said EPHRAIM to be his act and deed and ordered to be recorded

- An Indenture of Feofment between THOMAS MATTHEWS & ELIZABETH his Wife of the one part & JAMES ROBISON of the other part & Memorandum of Livery of Seisen & a Receit thereon endorsed were acknowledged by the said THOMAS & ELIZABETH (she being first privily examined as the Law directs) to be their act and deed and ordered to be recorded

- JOHN WOODSIDE, JUNR. is appointed Surveyor of the Road in the room of DANIEL BRADFORD and it is ordered that he with the Tithes belonging to the said Road do clear & keep the same in repair according to Law.

- THOMAS JACKMAN is appointed Surveyor of the Road in the room of THOMAS JAMES and it is ordered that he with the Tithes belonging thereto do clear and keep the same in repair according to Law

p. Fauquier County Court 24th of April 1769

70 - On the motion of WILLIAM NEWTON, it is ordered that JOHN BALL pay him three hundred & thirty three pounds of tobacco for three days attendance, twice comeing forty three miles & returning, as a witness for him against JOSEPH BLACKWELL & RICHARD LEWIS

- An Inventory and Appraisment of the Estate of MARTIN SETTLE, deced., was returned & ordered to be recorded

- Ordered that the Sherif pay JOHN COMBS three hundred & fifty pounds of tobacco out of the Fraction which is in his hands

- Ordered that the Court be adjourned till tomorrow morning ten of the Clock

" WILLIAM BLACKWELL "

- At a Court continued and held for Fauquier County the 25th day of April 1769

Present WILLIAM BLACKWELL WILLIAM EUSTACE
WILLIAM EDMONDS & JOSEPH HUDNALL Gent.

- RICHARD COTTA, who was committed to the Goal of this County on suspicion of his being a runaway was brought into Court and the Court being of opinion that he is not a runaway, It is ordered that he be discharged from his Imprisonment

- Present. JAMES SCOTT & WILLIAM GRANT, Gent.

- MARTIN PICKETT & COMPANY, Plts. agt. JAMES SYAS, Deft. In Debt

This day came the Plts. by their Attorney and the said Deft. altho solemnly called came not but made default. Therefore it is considered by the Court

p. Fauquier County Court 25th of April 1769

71 that the Order of the last Court against the said Deft. and GEORGE COULSON, his Security, be confirmed and that the Plts. recover against the said Deft. and his said Security the sum of twenty one pounds, four shillings & two pence current money, the Debt in the Declaration mentioned, and their costs by them in this behalf expended, and the said Deft. in mercy, &c., But this Judgment is to be discharged by the paiment of eleven pounds, five shillings & three pence with Interest thereon to be computed after the rate of five per centum per annum from the 24th day of May 1768 till paid and the costs

- MARTIN PICKETT & COMPANY, Plts. agt. JOSHUA TULLOS & RHODAM TULLOS, Defts. In Debt

This day came as well the Plts by their Attorney as the Deft., RHODAM, in his proper person & the said Deft., RHODAM, acknowledged the Plts. action against him. Therefore it is considered by the Court that the Plts. recover against the said Deft. twelve pounds, ten shillings current money, the Debt in the Declaration mentioned, with Interest thereon after the rate of five per centum per annum from the tenth day of March 1768 till paid & the costs by them in this behalf expended and the said Deft. in mercy, &c., And this suit is discontinued aginst the Deft., JOSHUA

- HANCOCK LEE, Assignee of MARTIN PICKETT & COMPANY, Plt. agt. JOHN McNEIL, Deft. In Debt

This day came the Plt. by his Attorney and the Sherif haveing returned on the Attachment awarded against the said Defts. Estate that he had attached one Ax, and the

Deft. failing to appear & replevy the attached effects, tho called, It is considered by the Court that the Plt. recover against the said Deft. sixteen pounds, nine shillings current money, the Debt in the Declaration

p. Fauquier County Court 25th of April 1769
72 mentioned & his costs by him in this behalf expended, and the said Deft. in mercy, &c., But this Judgment is to be discharged by the payment of seven pounds, seven shillings and eight pence with Interest thereon to be computed after the rate of five per centum per annum from the twenty fourth day of May 1768 till paid & the costs; And it is ordered that the Sherif sell the attached effects & return an account of the sales to the Court

- JOHN WRIGHT & ARMISTEAD CHURCHHILL, Church Wardens of Hamilton Parish, who sue for the use of the said Parish, Plts. agt. MARY SCOGGAN, Deft. In Debt

This day came the Plts. by their Attorney and the said Deft. altho solemnly called came not but made default. Therefore it is considered by the Court that the Order of the last Court against the said Deft. and WILLIAM SCOGGAN, her Security, be confirmed and that the Plts. recover against the said Deft. and her Security four hundred pounds of tobacco & cask or fifty shillings current money, the Debt in the Declaration mentioned (for the use of the said Parish) & their costs by them in this behalf expended & the said Deft. in mercy, &c.

- JOHN WRIGHT & ARMISTEAD CHURCHHILL, Church Wardens of Hamilton Parish, who sue for the use of the said Parish, Plts. agt. ELIZABETH FRYAR, Deft. In Debt

This day came the Plts. by their Attorney & the said Deft., altho solemnly called, came not but made default. Therefore it is considered by the

p. Fauquier County Court 25th of April 1769
73 Court that the Order of the last Court against the said Deft. & SAMUEL CONYERS, her Security, be confirmed and the Plts. recover against the said Deft. and her Security five hundred pounds of tobacco & cask or fifty shillings current money, the Debt in the Declaration mentioned (for the use of the said Parish) and their costs by them in this behalf expended, And the said Deft. in mercy, &c.

- MARY DONIPHAN & WILLIAM BRONAUGH, Executors &c. of ALEXANDER DONIPHAN, deced., Plts. agt. MOSES FLETCHER, Deft. Upon a Writ of Scire Facias to recover a Judgment obtained by the said ALEXANDER DONIPHAN in his life time against the said MOSES FLETCHER for five hundred & thirty pounds of tobacco with Interest thereon to be computed after the rate of five per centum per annum from the tenth day of October 1763 till paid for Debt, and one hundred & ten pounds of nett tobacco and fifteen shillings or one hundred & fifty pounds of tobacco for his costs by him in that behalf expended, and also eighty pounds of nett tobacco & fifteen shillings or one hundred and fifty pounds of tobacco which to him in our said Court were adjudged for his costs by him expended in executing our Writ of Scirefacias against the said MOSES

It is considered by the Court that the Plts. may have their Execution against the said Deft. for the Debt & Costs aforesaid according to the force form and effect of the recovery aforesaid, And it is further considered

p. Fauquier County Court 25th of April 1769
74 that the Plts. recover against the said Deft. their costs by them in this behalf expended, & the said Deft. in mercy, &c.

- JOHN RYLY, Plt. agt. JOSEPH BRAGG, JOSEPH BLACKWELL and RICHARD HENRY LEE, Defts. In Chancery

Continued for the Plt. to file his Bill of Complaint against the Defts. BRAGG & BLACKWEEL, and abates as to the Deft., LEE, for the Sherif haveing returned that the Deft., LEE, is no Inhabitant of this County

- JONATHAN (? POOE), Plt. agt. BENJAMIN DOUGLAS, Deft. In Case

This suit is agreed and it is ordered that the Deft. pay to the Plt. his costs by him in this behalf expended

- Absent. WILLIAM BLACKWELL, Gent.

- WILLIAM BLACKWELL, who sues as well for the use of the COLLEGE of WILLIAM & MARY as for himself, Plt. agt. PATRICK CARY, Deft., On Petition

This day came the parties by their Attornies and on hearing, it is considered by the Court that the Plt. recover against the said Deft, five pounds, one moiety thereof to the use of the COLLEGE of WILLIAM & MARY, and the other moiety for his own proper use & his costs by him in this behalf expended, and the said Deft. in mercy, &c.

Memorandum; the Plts. Attorney moved that this Petition should be called out of Course to which the Defts. Attorney objected, alledgeing that WILLIAM ELLZEY, an Attorney, who was employed by the Deft.

p. Fauquier County Court 25th of April 1769
75 was sick, but his objection was over ruled and the Petition ordered to be paid as ANDREW BUCHANAN, another of the Defts. Attorneys, was present. Then the Defts. Attorney objected to the regularity of the Petition as no time or place of selling, exposeing to sale & bartering the goods mentioned in the Petition, and that the Petition ought to have been brought in the name of the King for the use of the COLLEGE of WILLIAM & MARY, & the Prosecutor, which objection was also over ruled. On the Trial of the Petition, the Plt. gave in evidence by the Oath of JOSEPH WILLIAMS that on the twenty fifth day of August 1768, the Deft. did sell certain articles to the Plt. in this County in a room which the Deft. had at his first comeing rented of MINOR WINN several times for a week at the price of ten shillings & that he had sold goods at several other places

- Present. WILLIAM BLACKWELL & ARMISTEAD CHURCHHILL, Gent.

- JOHN WADDELL, Plt. agt. HENRY TAYLER, Deft. In Debt

This day came the Plt. by his Attorney and the said Deft., altho solemnly called, came not but made default. Therefore it is considered by the Court that the Order of the last Court against the said Deft. and BENJAMIN BALLARD, his Security, be confirmed and that the Plt. recover against the said Deft. and his said Security, twenty nine pounds current money, the Debt in the Declartion mentioned and his costs by him in this behalf expended, and the said Deft. in mercy &c., But this Judgment is to be discharged by the payment of fourteen pounds, ten shillings with Interest thereon to be computed after the rate of five per centum per annum from the first day of July 1763 till paid & the costs

p. Fauquier County Court 25th of April 1769
76 - EDWARD BUSH, Plt. agt. JOSHUA LAMPTON, Deft. On a Writ of Scirefacias to revive a Judgment obtained by the Plt. against the said Deft. for eighteen pounds, nine shillings with Interest thereon to be computed after the rate

of five per centum per annum from the first day of November 1764, and one hundred & fifty pounds of tobacco as well for Debt as for his costs by him in that behalf expended

It is considered by the Court that the Plt. may have his Execution against the said Deft. for the Debt and Costs aforesaid according to the force form and effect of the recovery aforesaid, And it is further considered that the Plt. recover against the said Deft. his costs by him in this behalf expended, and the said Deft. in mercy, &c.

- JAMES GWATKINS, a Surviving Executor of EDWARD GWATKINS, deced., Plt. agt. WILLIAM DOUGLASS & SARAH his Wife, Defts. On a Writ of Scirefacias to revive a Judgment obtained by the said EDWARD GWATKINS in his life time against the said Defts. for seven pounds, ten shilings & six pence, current money with Interest thereon to be computed after the rate of five per centum per annum from the sixth day of October 1764 for Debt, & one hundred and twenty five pounds of nett tobacco and fifteen shillings or one hundred & fifty pounds of tobacco for Costs

It is considered by the Court that the Plt. may have his Execution against

p. Fauquier County Court 25th of April 1769

77 ths said Deft. for the Debt and Costs aforesaid according to the force form & effect of the recovery aforesaid, And it is further considered that the Plt. recover against the said Deft. his costs by him in their behalf expended, And the said Deft. in mercy, &c.

- LETTICE THORNTON, Plt. agt. BENJAMIN BALLARD, Deft. In Trespass

This suit abates, the Sherif haveing returned that the Deft. is no Inhabitant of this County

- HANCOCK LEE, Assignee of MARTIN PICKETT & COMPANY, Plt. agt. JOHN NASH, Deft. In Debt

This suit abates, the Sherif haveing returned that the Deft. is no Inhabitant of this County

- ANDREW BUCHANAN, Assignee of MARTIN PICKET & COMPANY, Plt. agt. THOMAS HICKERSON, Deft. In Debt

This day came the Plt. by his Attorney and came also MARTIN PICKETT & became Special Bail & Pledge for the Deft. in this suit, and the said Deft., altho solemnly called, doth not come nor say any thing in bar or preclusion of the Plts. action against him, but hath made default whereby the Plt. remains against the said Deft. therein undefended. Therefore it is considered by the Court that the Plt. recover against the said Deft. fourteen pounds, sixteen shillings & eight pence and his costs by him in this behalf expended, and the said Deft. in mercy, &c., But this Judgment is to be discharged by the paiment of two pounds, eight shillings & two pence with Interest thereon to be computed after the rate of five per centum per annum from the twenty fourth day of May 1768 till paid & the costs

p. Fauquier County Court 25th of April 1769

78 - ANDREW BUCHANAN, Assignee of MARTIN PICKETT & COMPANY, Plt. agt. JOHN BODEN, Deft. In Debt

This day came the Plt. by his Attorney and the Sherif haveing returned on the Attachment awarded against the said Defts. Estate that he had attached one Hoe, and the said Deft. not appearing to replevy the same, tho called, It is considered by the Court that the Plt. recover against the said Deft. eleven pounds, three shillings & three pence current money, the Debt in the Declaration mentioned, and his costs by him in this behalf expended, And the said Deft. in mercy, &c. And it is ordered that the Sherif sell the attached effects and return an account of the sales to the Court

RICHARD GRAHAM, Plt. agt. RICHARD CUNDIFF, Deft. Upon a Writ of Scire Facias to revive a Judgment obtained by the Plt. against the said Deft. for four pounds, fifteen shillings and a half penny for Debt. and fifty two pounds of nett tobacco for Costs

It is considered by the Court that the Plt. may have his Execution against the said Deft. for the Debt and Costs aforesaid according to the force form and effect of the recovery aforesaid, And it is further considered that the Plt. recover against the said Deft. his costs by him in this behalf expended and the said Deft. in mercy, &c.

- RICHARD GRAHAM, Plt. agt. ALEXANDER HOLTON, Deft. Upon a Writ of Scire Facias to revive a Judgment obtained by the Plt. against the said Deft. for two pounds, nineteen shillings & seven pence, and five hundred

p. Fauquier County Court 25th of April 1769

79 & twelve pounds of tobacco for damages and one hundred and seventy pounds of nett tobacco and fifteen shillings or one hundred & fifty punds of tobacco for costs.

It is considered by the Court that the Plt. may have his Execution against the said Deft. for his Damages & Costs aforesaid according to the force form & effect of the recovery aforesaid, And it is further considered lthat the Plt. recover against the said Deft. his costs by him in this behalf expended; And the said Deft. in mercy, &c.

- ANDREW THOMPSON & COMPANY, Plts. agt. JOHN JETT SENIOR, Deft. In Debt

This day came the Plts. by their Attorney and the said Deft., altho solemnly called, came not but hath made default. Therefore it is considered by the Court that the Order of the last Court against the said Deft. and BENJAMIN DOUGLASS, his Security, be confirmed and that the Plts. recover against the said Deft. and his Security one hundred and nineteen pounds, twelve shillings and three pence current money, the Debt in the Declaration mentioned and their costs by them in this behalf expended, And the said Deft. in mercy, &c., But this Judgment is to be discharged by the paiment of fifty nine pounds, sixteen shillings and one penny half penny with Interest thereon to be computed after the rate of five per centum per annum from the first day of April 1767 till paid & the costs

- Messieurs ANDREW THOMPSON & COMPANY, Plts. agt. WILLIAM FINCH, Deft. In Debt

This suit abates, the Sherif haveing returned that the Deft. is no Inhabitant of this County

- GEORGE BOSWELL, Plt. agt. THOMAS BIRD, Deft. In Case

By consent of the parties all matters in difference relative to

p. Fauquier County Court 25th of April 1769

80 this suit are refered to JERMIAH DERNALL, JOHN WRIGHT, JUNR. & ZACHARIAH LEWIS and their Award to be the Courts Judgment

- JOSEPH MINTER, JUNR., Plt. agt. GEORGE GRUBS, Deft. In Case

Discontinued, being agreed by the parties

- SUSANNAH HOUCHMAN, Executrix &c. of HENRY HOUCHMAN, Exr. of HENRY HOUCHMAN, deced., Plt. agt. SAMUEL BLACKWELL, Deft. In Case

This day came the Plts. by their Attorney and came also WILLIAM BLACKWELL and became Special Bail & Pledge for the Deft. in this suit, and the said Deft., by his Attorney prays & has leave to imparl specially to the Plts. Declaration untill the next Court & then to plead

- Present. JOSEPH BLACKWELL, Gent.

- JAMES FOLEY, Assignee of THOMAS MARSHALL,, Gent., Sherif, Plt. agt. ALEXANDER FARROW, JOHN ASHBY & SAMUEL PORTER, Defts. In Debt
This suit is agreed, And it is ordered that the Defts. pay to the Plt. his costs by him in this behalf expended

- On the motion of ANDREW BUCHANAN, leave is granted him to put a Petition entered agreed at the last Court by mistake brought by him against WILLIAM DULING on the Dockett

- Ordered that the Court be adjourned till the Court in Course

" JOSEPH BLACKWELL "

p. 81 - At a Court held for Fauquier County the 22d day of May 1769

present WILLIAM BLACKWELL, ARMISTEAD CHURCHHILL
WILLIAM EDMONDS JEREMIAH DARNALL
and JOSEPH HUDNALL Gentlemen

- For certain reasons to the Court appearing, JAMES FRAZER is discharged from paying County Levies

- On the motion of CATHERINE McNEIL, it is ordered that ELIZABETH KEIRNS pay her seventy five pounds of tobacco for three days attendance as a witness for her against JOHN CHURCHHILL

- JEFFRY JOHNSON, SENR., Plt. agt. JEFFRY JOHNSON, JUNR. Deft. In Case
This day came the Plt. by his Attorney and came also MOSES JOHNSON and became Special Bail and Pledge for the Deft. in this suit, and the said Deft. defends the force & injury when, &c., and pleads non assumpsit and the trial of the issue is refered untill the next Court

- On the motion of SAMUEL CONYERS, an Injunction is granted him to stay the Execution of Judgment obtained against him by the Church Wardens of Hamilton Parish as Security for ELIZABETH FRYAR on his giveing Bond and security at the next Court

- WILLIAM UNDERWOOD, Gent., produced a Licence from the persons appointed to examine Attornies and haveing first taken the usual Oaths to his Majesties person & Government and subscribed the Test, had the Oath of an Attorney administered to him

- A Bill of Sale from THOMAS MADDOX to JOHN MOFFETT was proved by JAMES NEAVILL and THOMAS SMITH, witnesses thereto, ordered to be recorded

- WILLIAM JENNINGS is appointed Surveyor of the Road in the room of HARMAN KAMPER and it is ordered that he with the Tithes belonging to the said Road do clear and keep the same in repair according to Law

- On the motion of JAMES FREEMAN, a Licence is granted him to kee

p. 82 Fauquier County Court 22d of May 1769

ORDINARY at his House in this County for one year and from thence untill the next Court to be held for this County, he haveing executed and acknowledged Bond as the Law directs

- DAVIS HOLDER is appointed Surveyor of the Road in the room of JOHN BELL and it is ordered that he with the Tithes belonging to the said Road do clear and keep the same in repair according to Law

- Present. JOHN MOFFETT, Gent.

- CHARLES MARTIN is appointed Surveyor of the Road in the room of JOHN COLVIN and it is ordered that he with the Tithes belonging to the said Road do clear and keep the same in repair according to Law

- A Report by the Jury on the acre of land petitioned for by GEORGE NEAVILL was returned in these words, to wit -

"In Obedience to an Order of the Worshipfull Court of Fauquier County dated February Court 1768, we the Jury being summoned and sworn and met on the premises according to the said Order, have proceeded to value the said acre of Land therein mentioned after the same was laid of by the Surveyor of the said County and do on our Oaths value the said acre of Land to twenty shillings current money and do intimate the damage the said CHURCHHILL may sustain by the flowing of the back water occasioned by the said NEAVILLs erecting a Mill on the Land proposed to twenty shillings p acre for all the lands overflowed thereby. Given under our hands and seals this 10th day of April 1769." THOMAS MARSHALL, Sheriff

JAMES SCOTT	JOHN CHILTON	WM. RANSDELL
PARNACH GEORGE	THOS: KEITH	CHARLES MARTIN
JOHN BALY	SIMON MORGAN	WM. NORRISS
BENJA: ROBINSON	WM. KIRK	JOHN HUDNALL

which report with a Plott of the said acre is ordered to be recorded, and the acre of Land condemned accordingly, & the said NEAVILL came into Court and tendered the valuation money

- MAXIMILLIAN BERRYMAN, THOMAS HELMS, JOSEPH DUNCAN, PETER CORNWELL, WILLIAM RUSSELL, HENRY MARTIN, JAMES BAILY

p. Fauquier County Court 22d of May 1769

83 HENRY JONES, EDMUND BASY, WILLIAM BARKER, JOHN DUNCAN, THOMAS SMITH, SIMON MORGAN, JOSEPH HITT and JOHN SYAS were sworn a Grand Jury of Inquest for the body of this County and haveing received their charge withdrew to consider of their Presentments, and after some time returned into Court and brought their Presentments in these words, to wit.

"We the Grand Jury of our Lord the King for the body of the County aforesaid, do upon Oath present -

"We present GEORGE KERNARD of Hamilton Parish for profane swearing at the Parish aforesaid within two months last to the knowledge of two of us;

"We also present JOHN DUNCAN, JUNR. for profane swearing at the same Parish within two months by the Information of WILLIAM STAMPS;

"We also present JOHN STAMPS of the same Parish for profane swearing at the same Parish within two months by the Information of WILLIAM STAMPS;

"We also present JOHN RYLY of the same Parish for profane swearing at the said Parish within two months by information of WILLIAM STAMPS,

"We also present THOMAS ELLIOTT, JUNR. for profane swearing at the Parish aforesaid within two months to the knowledge of two of us;

"We present the Surveyor of the Road from MARS BRIDGE to Mr. COVINGTONs for not keeping the same in repair within six months last past to the knowledge of two of us;

And haveing nothing farther to Present, were discharged. Ordered that the several persons presented by the Grand Jury be summoned to appear at the next Court to answer the same respectively

- The Tithables belonging to HENRY PEYTON are discharged from clearing the Main Road

- ORIGINAL YOUNG & JOHN BLACKWELL, Plts. agt. THOMAS STONE, Deft.
On a Petition

Judgment is granted the Plts. against the said Deft. for their costs by them in this behalf expended

p. Fauquier County Court 22d of May 1769
84 - The persons appointed to view the Road from ELK RUN CHURCH to STAFFORD County Line returned their report in these words, to wit;

"We the Subscribers being sworn and appointed by an Order of Fauquier Court to view the way from ELK RUN CHURCH to the County Line of STAFFORD and find it convenient to have a Road but through the Lands of JOHN JAMES, BRERETON JONES, HENRY SMITH and the Lands of Doctor SAVIDGE. Given under our hands this 22d of May 1769.
BRERETON JONES, JOHN NELSON, DANIEL HARRILD"
And the Road is established according to the said Report

- RHODAM TULLOS is appointed Surveyor of the Road from ELK RUN CHURCH to STAFFORD County Line and it is ordered that he with the Tithes that shall be appointed by WILLIAM EUSTACE and JOHN JAMES do clear and keep the same in repair according to Law

- Ordered that RICHARD COVINGTON, BRERETON JONES, JOHN JAMES & THOMAS CONWAY or any three of them being first sworn do view the most convenient way from COVINGTONs to JOHN EDGEs wehre the New Road goes and report the conveniences and inconveniences thereof to the Court

- On the motion of SAMUEL RUST, it is ordered that a Dedimus issue to take the Deposition of ALEXANDER FARROW and JAMES OBANNON, witnesses for him at the suit of MILDRED OBANNON

- WILLIM ALLAN is appointed Surveyor of the Road in the room of CHARLES MORGAN and it is ordered that he with the Tithes belonging to the said Road do clear and keep the same in repair according to Law

- WILLIAM ALLASON, Plt. agt. JOHN HURMANS, Deft. In Debt

This day came the Plt. by his Attorney and came also ALEXANDER McPHERSON and became Special Bail and Pledge for the Deft. in this suit, and the said Deft. defends the force and Injury when, &c.

p. Fauquier County Court 22d of May 1769
85 and pleads paiment, and the Trial of the issue is refered untill the next Court, and then to plead. WILLIAM BLACKWELL, Gent., objected to the sufficiency of the Bail in this suit

- JOSEPH HOPPER is appointed Surveyor of the Road in the room of THOMAS MATTHEWS and it is ordered that he with the Tithes belonging to the said Road do clear and keep the same in repair according to Law

- TILLMAN WEAVER is appointed Surveyor of the Road in the room of PHILIP HUFFMAN and it is ordered that he with the Tithes belonging to the said Road do clear and keep the same in repair according to Law

- THOMAS HUDNALL, Plt. agt. THOMAS OXFORD, Deft. In Case

This day came as well the Plt. by his Attorney as the Deft. in his proper person and the said Deft. acknowledged the Plts. action against him for eighteen pounds, thirteen shillings & four pence. Therefore it is considered by the Court that the Plt. recover against the said Deft. the aforesaid eighteen pounds, thirteen shillings & four pence and his costs by him in this behalf expended, And the said Deft. in mercy, &c.

- JOHN SHUMATE, Plt. agt. GAVIN LAWSON, Deft. In Case

This day came the parties by their Attornies and thereupon came also a Jury, to wit, HENRY PEYTON, JAMES NELSON, JOHN JETT, JAMES NEAVILL, WILLIAM PARKER, JOSEPH LAVELL, FRANCIS PAYNE, THOMAS OXFORD, JAMES BLACKWELL, GARNER BURGESS, RICHARD COVINGTON & SAMUEL BLACKWELL, who being elected tried and sworn the truth to speak upon the issue joyned, upon their Oaths do say that the said

Deft. did assume upon himself in manner and form and the Plt. against him hath declared and they do assess the Plts. damages by means of the Defts. breach of that assumption to six pounds, twelve shillings and nine pence half

p. 86 Fauquier County Court 22d of May 1769

penny besides his costs. Therefore it is considered by the Court that the Plt. recover against the said Deft. his damages aforesaid in form aforesaid assessed and his costs by him in this behalf expended, and the said Deft. in mercy, &c.

- ORIGINAL YOUNG & JOHN BLACKWELL, Plts. agt. JOHN STONE, Deft. On a Petition

Judgment is granted the Plt. against the said Defts. for three pounds, one shilling and eight pence and their costs by them in this behalf expended, But this Judgment is to be discharged by the paiment of one pound, ten shillings and ten pence with Interest thereon to be computed after the rate of five per centum per annum from the twenty second day of August 1768 till paid & the costs

- Ordered that the Church Wardens of Hamilton Parish bind SARAH BRONAUNT to ELIZABETH YOUNG according to Law

- On the motion of WILLIAM MORGAN, it is ordered that JOHN SHUMATE pay him two hundred pounds of tobacco for eight days attendance as a witness for him against GAVIN LAWSON

- The same Order for BUSHROD DOGGETT;

- The same Order of HENRY MAUZEY;

- The same Order for JOHN NELLSON

- On the motion of WILLIAM KNOX, it is ordered that JOHN SHUMATE pay him three hundred and eight pounds of tobacco for two days attendance and twice comeing forty three miles and returning, as a witness for him against JOHN SHUMATE

- Present JAMES SCOTT, Gent.

- DAVID DALYELL, GEORGE OSWALD & CO., Plts. agt. EDWARD WILLBURNE, Deft. In Case

This day came the Plt. by his Attorney and came also ANTHONY

p. 87 Fauquier County Court 22d of May 1769

LATHAM and became Special Bail and Pledge for the Deft. in this suit, and the said Deft. by his Attorney prays and has leave to imparl specially to the Plts. Declaration untill the next Court and then to plead

- For certain reasons to the Court appearing, JOHN CATLETT is discharged from paying County Levies

- JOSEPH LAVEL is appointed Surveyor of the Road in the room of BENJAMIN SETTLE and it is ordered that he with the Tithes belonging to the said Road do clear and keep the same in repair according to Law

- Ordered that the Court be ajourned till tomorrow morning ten of the Clock

WILLIAM BLACKWELL

- At a Court held for Fauquier County the 23d day of May 1769

Present JOSEPH BLACKWELL, WILLIAM BLACKWELL, ARMISTEAD CHURCHHILL, WILLIAM EDMONDS & JOSEPH HUDNALL Gent.

- CHARLES CHINN is appointed Surveyor of the Road from LOUDOUN County Line to JOHN KINCHELOEs and it is ordered that he with the Tithes that shall be appointed by JOHN MOFFETT, Gent., do clear and keep the same in repair according to Law

- JOHN KINCHELOE is appointed Surveyor of the Road from his House to the Upper Church and it is ordered that he with the Tithes that shall be appointed by JOHN MOFETT, Gent., do clear and keep the sam ein repair according to Law

- WILLIAM EUSTACE, Gent., is appointed to take the List of Tithables this year in the same Precinct where WILLIAM GRANT, Gent., took them last year

- JEREMIAH DARNALL in the room of ARMISTEAD CHURCHHILL;

- JOHN MOFFETT in the room of JAMES SCOTT;

- The Attachment obtained by JOHN WOODSIDE against the Estate of ALEXANDER WOODSIDE is dismist

p. Fauquier County Court 23d of May 1769
88 - Present. JAMES SCOTT, Gent.

- WILLIAM DOBBIE, Plt. agt. ALEXANDER WOODSIDE, Deft. On an Attachment
This day came the Plt. by his Attorney and the Sherif haveing returned that he had levied the Attachment on the same goods as is mentioned on JOHN WOODSIDEs Attachment and the said Deft. failing to apear and replevy the attached effects, tho called, it is considered by the Court that the Plt. recover against the said Deft. fourteen pounds Virginia currency and his costs by him in this behalf expended and the said Deft. in mercy &c., But this Judgment is to be discharged by the paiment of seven pounds and the costs; And ordered that the Sherif sell the attached effects and return an account of the sales to the Court

- Messieurs GLASSFORD & HENDERSON, Plts. agt. ALEXANDER WOODSIDES, Deft. On an Attachment
It appearing to the Court that the Attachment and Bond are not agreeable to the Act of Assembly. It is ordered that this Attachment be dismissed. Memorandum; That at the Trial of this Attachment, the Plts. filed the following Bill of Exceptions -
Messrs. GLASSFORD & HENDERSON by JOHN RIDDELL, their Factor vs. ALEXANEER WOODSIDES, Memorandum, that on the Tryall of this Attachment, ANDREW BUCHANAN Attorney moved to quash the same for the Bonds not being executed by JOHN RIDDELL himself and also WILLIAM UNDERWOOD, Attorney, moved to quash the same for the word Court being left out in the Attachment. Whereupon CUTHBERT BULLITT, Attorney for the Plts., called on Mr. BUCHANAN to know who he appeared for who said for

p. Fauquier County Court 23d of May 1769
89 JOHN WOODSIDES, and as a Friend to the Court, the said UNDERWOOD also saying he appeared as a Friend to the Court, the ( ) of these three Gentlemen's opinions were asked by the Court, the Plts. by their Attorney then moved to mend the Attachment by the Justice who granted the same & was present, adding these words for (further proceedings thereupon to be had at the next Court), but the Court being against the amendment dismissed the same to which the said Plts. excepted & prayed that their exceptions might be saved to them & ensealed and enrolled &c., & it is done but after the Court had given their opinion and the Plts. prayed an appeal, the said BUCHANAN beged to retract his appearance for WOODSIDES

JOS. BLACKWELL, A. CHURCHHILL, W. EDMONDS

from which Judgment the Plts. prayed an appeal to the Eleventh day of the next General Court which is granted them on their giveing Bond and Security at the next Court

- Present JOHN MOFFETT)
- Absent. JOSEPH BLACKWELL) Gent.

- Messieurs GLASSFORD & HENDERSON, Plts. agt. JOSHUA KING, Deft., In Debt

This day came the Plts. by their Attorney and came also JOHN BLACKWELL and WILLIAM BLACKWELL and became Special Bail and Pledge for the Deft. in this suit, and the said Deft. acknowledged the Plts. action against him. Therefore it is considered by the Court that the Plts. recover against the said Deft. thirty two pounds, fourteen shillings & two pence, the Debt in the Declaration mentioned, and their costs by them in this behalf expended, And the said Deft. in mercy, &c. But this Judgment is to be discharged by the paiment of sixteen pounds, seven shillings and a penny with Interest thereon to be computed after the rate of five per centum per annum from the 20th day of May 1768 till paid and the costs. Execution stayed till November

p. Fauquier County Court 23d of May 1769

90 - On the motion of WILLIAM NEWTON, it is ordered that JOHN BALLARD pay him one hundred and fifty pounds of tobacco for one days attendance, comeing forty three miles and returning, as a witness for him agaisnt JOSEPH BLACKWELL & RICHARD LEWIS

- JOHN WRIGHT and ARMISTEAD CHURCHHILL, Church Wardens of Hamilton Parish who sue for the use of the said Parish, Plts. agt. MARY MARR, Deft. In Debt

This day came the Plts. by their Attorney and the Sherif haveing returned on the Attachment awarded against the said Defts. Estate that he had attached a parcell of Thread, and the said Deft. failing to appear and replevy the attached effects, tho called, It is considered by the Court that the Plts. recover against the said Deft. five hundred pounds of tobacco and cask or fifty shillings current money, the Debt in the Declaration mentioned and their costs by them in this behalf expended, and the said Deft. in mercy &c., And it is ordered that the Sherif sell the attached effects and return an account of the sales to the Court

- WILLIAM EDMONDS and FRANCIS BELL, Assignees of WILLIAM BLACKWELL, late Sherif of Fauquier, Plts. agt. ELIAS EDMONDS & WILLIAM ELLZEY, Defts. In Debt

Discontinued. The Plts. not further prosecuting

- A Lease between RICHARD HENRY LEE of the one part and JOHN HATHAWAY of the other part and a Receit thereon endorsed were proved by the Oaths of JOSEPH BLACKWELL, JOSEPH BLACKWELL, JUNR. and RANDOLPH SPISER witnesses thereto, and ordered to be recorded

p. Fauquier County Court 23d. of May 1769

91 - EDMUND PENDLETON & PETER LYONS, Gent., Surviving Admors. of JOHN ROBINSON, Esqr., deced., Plts. agt. JOHN CHURCHHILL, Deft. In Debt

This day came the Plts. by their Attorney and came also ARMISTEAD CHURCHHILL, Gent., and became Special Bail and Pledge for the Deft. in this suit, and the said Deft. prays Oyer of the Writing Obligatory and he hath it, &c.

- JOHN BALLARD, Plt. agt. JOSEPH BLACKWELL & RICHARD LEWIS, Defts. In Debt

This day came the parties by their Attornies and by the Defts. consent the new Trial granted them in this suit is waived, Therefore it is considered by the Court that the Plt. recover against the said Defts. two pounds, eight shillings and six pence, the damages by the Jury in this Cause found in manner and form as by them assessed and his costs by him in this behalf expended, and the said Defts. in mercy, &c.

- ANDREW COCKRANE, WILLIAM CUNNINGHAME, & CO., Plts. agt. JOSEPH HUDNALL, Deft. In Case

This day came the Plts. by their Attorney and came also JOSEPH HUDNALL & became Special Bail and Pledge for the Deft. in this suit, and the said Deft. prays and has leave to imparl specially to the Plts. Declaration untill the next Court and then to plead

- DANIEL NEWLAND, Plt. agt. GEORGE TURBEVILLE KENNER, Deft. In Case

This suit is agreed, and it is ordered that the Deft. pay to the Plt. his costs by him in this behalf expended

- JAMES SOMERVILL, Merchant, Plt. agt. JOSEPH LAVELL, Deft. In Debt

This day came the Plt. by his Attorney and the said Deft. altho solemn-

p. Fauquier County Court 23d of May 1769

92 ly called came not but made default; Therefore it is considered by the Court that the Order of the last Court against the said Deft. and JOHN BLACKWELL, his Security, be confirmed and that the Plt. recover against the said Deft. and his said Security sixty nine pounds, seventeen shillings and ten pence, the Debt in the Declaration mentioned, and his costs by him in this behalf expended; And the said Deft. in mercy, &c., But this Judgment is to be discharged by the paiment of thirty four pounds, eighteen shillings and eleven pence with Interest thereon to be computed after the rate of five per centum per annum from the fourth day of September 1768 till paid and the costs

- Messieurs DICK & STURGES, Plts. agt. WILLIAM KENTON, Deft. In Debt

This day came the Plts. by their Attorney and the Sherif haveing returned on the Attachment awarded against the said Defts. Estate that he had attached one Spoon, and the said Deft. not appearing to replevy the same, tho called, It is considered by the Court that the Plts. recover against the said Deft. Sixteen pounds, the Debt in the Declaration mentioned, and their costs by them in this behalf expended, and the said Deft. in mercy &c., But this Judgment is to be discharged by the paiment of seven pounds, nine shillings and eight pence with Interest thereon to be computed after the rate of five per centum per annum from the third day of September 1766 till paid & the costs;

And it is ordered that the Sherif sell the attached effects and return and account of the sales to the Court

- RICHARD LINGHAM HALL, Plt. agt. JOSHUA LAMPTON, Deft. In Debt

This day came the Plt. by his Attorney and came also WILLIAM

p. Fauquier County Court 23d of May 1769

93 BLACKWELL and became Special Bail and Pledge for the Deft. in this suit, and the said Deft. prays Oyer of the Writing Obligatory and he hath it, &c.

- JAMES McCLANAHAM, Plt. agt. JEREMIAH RUST, Deft. In Case

This suit abates, the Sherif haveing returned that the Deft. is no Inhabitant of this County

- HANCOCK LEE, Assignee of MARTIN PICKETT & CO., Plt. agt.
JOHN & WILLIAM CONYERS, Defts. In Debt

This day came the Plt. by his Attorney and came also JAMES BAILY, and became Special Bail and Pledge for the Defts. in this suit, and the said Defts. pray Oyer of the Writing Obligatory and to them it is granted &c.

- SAMUEL THORNBERRY, Plt. agt. JOHN MORGAN, Deft. On a Petition

Judgment is granted the Plt. against the said Deft. for three pounds and his costs by him in this behalf expended

- On the motion of RICHARD BRYAN, it is ordered that SAMUEL THORNBERRY pay him one hundred pounds of tobacco for four days attendance as a witness for him against JOHN MORGAN

- On the motion of JOSHUA SHUMATE, it is ordered that JOHN SHUMATE pay him one hundred and twenty five pounds of tobacco for five days attendance as a witness for him against GAVIN LAWSON

- The Attachment obtained by THOMAS LAWSON & JOHN LEE, Exors. &c. of ALLAN MACRAE, deced., against the Estate of ALEXANDER WOODSIDE is dismissed

- Ordered that the Court be adjourned till tomorrow morning ten of the Clock

WILLIAM BLACKWELL

p. 94 At a Court continued and held for Fauquier County the 24th day of May 1769

Present WILLIAM BLACKWELL, WILLIAM EDMONDS
JOSEPH HUDNALL JAMES SCOTT
& JOHN MOFFETT Gent.

- On the motion of MATTHEW ADAMS, it is ordered that BURGESS BALL pay him seventy five pounds of tobacco for three days attendance as a witness for JOHN ANDERSON at the suit of the said BALL, the Cause being continued at his costs

- The same Order for JACOB ADAMS

- JEMIMA MINOR, Plt. agt. WILLIAM KEIRNS, Deft. In Trespass
This suit is dismist, and it is ordered that the Plt. pay to the Deft. his costs by him in this behalf expended

- Absent. WILLIAM EDMONDS,)
- Present JOSEPH BLACKWELL) Gent.

- Aminadab Seekright, Plt. agt. JOHN MAUZEY, JUNR. Deft. In Ejectment for one Plantation and Messuage and three hundred acres of Land with the appurtenances situate lying and being in the Parish of Hamailton in the County of Fauquier of the demise of WILLIAM MOUNTJOY

This day came the parties by their Attorneys and thereupon the matters of Law arriseing on the Special Verdict found by the Jury in this Cause being argued and by the Court fully understood and mature deliberation had threon, it seem that the Law is with the Deft. Therefore it is considered by the Court that the Plt. take nothing by his Bill but for his false clamour be in mercy, &c., And that the Deft. go thereof without day and recover against the Lessor of the Plt.

p. 95 Fauquier County Court 24th of May 1769

his costs by him in this behalf expended

From which Judgment, the Lessor of the Plt. prayed an appeal to the eleventh day of the next General Court which is granted him, he haveing executed and acknowledged Bond as the Law directs

- The Attachment obtained by JAMES ARNOLD against the Estate of THOMAS GARNER is dismissed

- The Attachment obtained by JAMES ARNOLD and THOMAS POPE against the Estate of THOMAS GARNER is dismissed

- JOHN WADDELL, Plt. agt. HENRY TAYLOR, Deft. In Case
Discontinued, being agreed by the parties

- HENRY TAYLOR and MARY his Wife, Plts. agt. JOHN WADDELL, Deft. In Case
This suit is dismist and it is ordered that the Plts. pay to the Deft. his costs by him in this behalf expended

- Present. ARMISTEAD CHURCHHILL & JEREMIAH DERNALL, Gent.

- JAMES ADKINS, Plt. agt. JOHN SMITH & JOHN SMITH, JUNR. Defts.
In Trespass, Assault and Battery

This day came the parties by their Attorneys and thereupon came also a Jury, to wit, JOHN McCORMACK, NICHOLAS SPRINGS, WILLIAM FEILDER, WILLIAM SUTTON, JAMES WRIGHT, FRANCIS BRONAUGH, JAMES BAILY, JOSEPH WILLIAMS, WILLIAM CONYERS, JOHN CONYERS, JAMES ARNOLD & THOMAS POPE, who being elected tried and sworn the truth to speak upon the issue joined upon their Oaths do say that the said Defts. are Guilty in manner and form as the Plt. against them hath declared and they do assess the Plts. damages by occasion thereof to five pounds besides his costs; Therefore it is considered

p. Fauquier County Court 24th of May 1769
96 by the Court that the Plt. recover against the said Defts. his damages aforesaid in form aforesaid assessed and his costs by him in this behalf expended, and the said Defts. in mercy, &c.

- On the motion of RICHARD COVINGTON it is ordered that JAMES ADKINS pay him two hundred and fifty pounds of tobacco for ten days attendance as a witness for him against JOHN SMITH & JOHN SMITH, JUNR.

- On the motion of WINNIFRED COVINGTON, it is ordered that JAMES ADKINS pay her two hundred pounds of tobacco for eight days attendance as a witness for him against JOHN SMITH & JOHN SMITH, JUNR.

- On the motion of FRANCIS PAYNE, it is ordered that JOHN SMITH & JOHN SMITH, JUNR. pay him two hundred pounds of tobacco for eight days attendance as a witness for them at the suit of JAMES ADKINS

- On the motion of PETER WAGONER, JUNR., it is ordered that JOHN JETT pay him one hundred and ninety five pounds of tobacco for three days attendance, comeing forty miles and returning, as a witness for PETER WAGONER against him the Petiton being continued at his cost

- JOHN SHUMATE, Plt. agt. ALEXANDER WOODSIDES, Deft. On a Petition
Judgment is granted the Plt. against the said Deft. for two pounds current monty and his costs by him in this behalf expended

- HENRY MOORE, Plt. agt. JOHN KEITH, Deft. On a Petition
Judgment is granted the Plt. against the said Deft. for one

p. Fauquier County Court 24th of May 1769
97 pound, nineteen shillings and his costs by him in this behalf expended

- JOHN HERMANS, Plt. agt. JOHN STONE, Deft. On a Petition
Judgment is granted the Plt. against the said Deft. for one pound, ten shillings and nine pence and his costs by him in this behalf expended

- On the motion of JAMES WRIGHT, it is ordered that JOHN SHUMATE pay him two hundred pounds of tobacco for eight days attendance as a witness for him against ALEXANDER WOODSIDE

- RICHARD VOWLES, Plt. agt. WILLIAM DOUGLASS, Deft. On a Petition
This Petition abates, the Sherif haveing returned that the Deft. is no Inhabitant of this County

- RICHARD VOWLES, Plt. agt. JOSEPH DOUGLASS, Deft. On a Petition
This Petition abates, the Sherif haveing returned that the Deft. is no Inhabitant of this County

- CUTHBERT COMBS, Plt. agt. GEORGE KENNER, Deft. On a Petition
Discontinued, being agreed by the parties

- JAMES BUCHANAN, Plt. agt. GEORGE TURBEVILLE KENNER, Deft. On a Petition
Judgment is granted the Plt. against the said Deft. for three pounds, eight shillings

and his costs by him in this behalf expended, But this Judgment is to be discharged by the paiment of one pound, fourteen shillings with Interest thereon to be computed after the rate of five percentum per annum from the twenty second day of June 1768 till paid & the costs

p. Fauquier County Court 24th of May 1769
98 - JOSEPH STRICKLER & JACOB BONAHAM, Plts. agt. HUGH BRENT, Deft. On a Petition

By consent of the parties, all matters in difference relative to this Petition are refered to CUTHBERT BULLITT and his Award to be made the Courts Judgment

- JOSEPH GARNER, an Infant by CHARLES GARNER, his next Friend, Plt. agt BLAND BALLARD, Deft. On a Petition

Discontinued, being agreed by the parties

- ROGER DIXON, Plt. agt. HENRY JONES, Deft. On a Petition

Judgment is granted the Plt. against the said Deft. for two pounds, eight shillings with Interest thereon to be computed after the rate of five per centum per annum from the seventeenth day of March 1767 till paid and his costs by him in this behalf expended

- ANDREW BUCHANAN, Assignee of MARTIN PICKETT & CO., Plt. agt. WILLIAM DULING, SENR., Deft. On a Petition

Judgment is granted the Plt. against the said Deft. for three pounds, thirteen shillings and a penny with Interest thereon to be computed after the rate of five per centum per annum from the second day of March 1767 till paid and the costs by him in this behalf expended

- WILLIAM CONYERS, Plt. agt. WILLIAM SUTTON, Deft. On a Petition

Judgment is granted the Plt. against the said Deft. for one pound, eighteen shillings and nine pence and his costs by him in this behalf expended

p. Fauquier County Court 24th of May 1769
99. - JAMES SCOTT, JUNR. Plt. agt. THOMAS BAUGGESS, Deft. On a Petition

Judgment is granted the Plt. against the said Deft. for fourteen shillings and his costs by him in this behalf expended

- On the motion of JAMES BAILY, it is ordered that WILLIAM CONYERS pay him one hundred and twenty five pounds of tobacco for five days attendance as a witness for him against WILLIAM SUTTON

- ORIGINAL YOUNG, Plt. agt. JOHN MARKHAM, Deft. On a Petition

Judgment is gratned the Plt. against the said Deft. for three pounds, five shillings and tw pence and his costs by him in this behalf expended. But this Judgment is to be discharged by the paiment of one pound, twelve shillings and seven pence with Interest thereon to be computed after the rate of five per centum per annum from the twenty fourth day of November 1767 till paid & the costs

- ORIGINAL YOUNG & JOHN BLACKWELL, Plts. agt. WILLIAM CORDER & WILLIAM CORDER SENR., Defts. On a Petition

Judgment is granted the Plts. against the said Defts. for four pounds, fourteen shillings and their costs by them in this behalf expended, But this Judgment is to be discharged by the paiment of two pounds, seven shillings with Interest thereon to be computed after the rate of five per centum per annum from the second day of June 1768 till paid and the costs

- The Same, Plts. agt. WILLIAM SMITH, Deft. On a Petition

Judgment is granted the Plts. against the said Deft. for three pounds, thirteen shillings and their costs by them in this behalf expended, But this Judgment is to be discharged by the paiment of one pound, eleven shillings with Interest

p. Fauquier County Court 24th of May 1769
100 thereon to be computed after the rate of five per centum per annum from the twenty fifth day of July 1768 till paid and the costs

- ORIGINAL YOUNG & JOHN BLACKWELL, Plts. agt. MORRIS JACOBS, Deft. On a Petition

Judgment is gratned the Plts. against the said Deft. for three pounds, one shilling and ten pence and their costs by them in this behalf expended; But this Judgment is to be discharged by the paiment of one pound ten shillings and eleven pence with Interest thereon to be computed after the rate of five per centum per annum from the tenth day of September 1763 till paid & the costs

- THOMAS OBANNON, Plt. agt. JOSEPH WILLIAMS, Deft. On a Petition

This Petition is agreed, and it is ordered that the Deft. pay to the Plt. his costs by him in this behalf expended

- On the motion of NICHOLAS SPRINGS, it is ordered that JOHN JETT pay him seventy five pounds of tobacco for three days attendance as a witness for PETER WAGONER against him, the Petition being continued at his costs

- HANCOCK LEE, Assignee of MARTIN PICKETT & CO., Plt. agt. JANE SMITH, Deft. On a Petition

Judgment is granted the Plt. against the said Deft. for one pound, six shillings and two pence with Interest thereon to be computed after the rate of five per centum per annum from the second day of March 1767 till paid and his costs by him in this behalf expended

- CUTHBERT BULLITT, Plt. agt. EDWARD WILLBURNE, Deft. On a Petition

Judgment is granted the Plt. against the said Deft for two hundred & sixty five pounds of tobacco and his costs by him in this behalf expended

p. Fauquier County Court 24th of May 1769
101 - HANCOCK LEE, Assignee of MARTIN PICKETT & CO., Plt. agt. THOMAS WILLIAMS, Deft. On a Petition

Judgment is granted the Plt. against the said Deft. for four pounds and a penny with Interest thereon to be computed after the rate of five per centum per annum from the fifteenth day of April 1768 till paid, and his costs by him in this behalf expended

- Ordered that the Court be adjourned till the Court in Course

" ARMISTEAD CHURCHHILL "

- At a Court held for Fauquier County the 26th day of June 1769

Present THOMAS HARRISON ARMISTEAD CHURCHHILL
WILLIAM EDMONDS & JOSEPH HUDNALL Gent.

- An Indenture of Feofment between RICHARD HACKLY and ELIZABETH his Wife of the one part and THOMAS GRINNAN of the other part and a Memorandum of Livery of Seisen and a Receit thereon endorsed were proved by the Oaths of DAVID PARTLOW, JAMES HACKLY, AMBROSE ARNOLD & MORRIS JACOBS, witnesses thereto, & ordered to be recorded

- A Bond from RICHARD HACKLY to THOMAS GRINNAN was proved by the Oath of JAMES HACKLY, a witness thereto, and ordered to be recorded

- An Inventory and Appraisment of the Estate of ABRAHAM DODSON, deced., was returned and ordered to be recorded

- On the motion of LYDIA WATTS, who made Oath and executed and acknowledged Bond as the Law directs, Certificate is granted her for obtaining Letters of Administration of the Estate of THOMAS WATTS, deced.

- Ordered that ROBERT ASHBY, JOHN SUTHARD, WILLIAM HARRISON and HEZEKIAH TURNER or any three of them being first sworn do appraise the Estate of THOMAS WATTS, deced., and return the appraisment to the Court

p. Fauquier County Court 26th of June 1769

102 MAXIMILLIAN BERRYMAN is appointed Surveyor of the Road in the room of CHARLES MORGAN, and it is ordered that he with the Tithes belonging to the said Road do clear and keep the same in repair according to Law

- WILLIAM HARRISON is appointed Surveyor of the Road from the GOOSE CREEK to BARTONS TRACT and it is ordered that he with the Tithes belonging thereto do clear and keep the same in repair according to Law

- MICHAEL DERMONT is appointed Surveyor of the Road from his House to GOOSE CREEK and it is ordered that he with the Tithes belonging to the said Road do clear and keep the same in repair according to Law

- An Indenture of Feofment between JOHN CRUMP and BETTY his Wife, THOMAS HARRISON & CUTHBERT HARRISON of the one part and LINAUGH HELM of the other part and Memorandum of the Livery of Seisen and Receit thereon endorsed were proved by the Oaths of WILLIAM BLACKWELL, WILLIAM BLACKWELL JUNR. and JOHN KERR, witnesses thereto to be the act and deed of JOHN CRUMP, THOMAS HARRISON and CUTHBERT HARRISON and the same were also acknowledged by BETTY CRUMP (she being first privily examined as the Law directs) to be his act and deed and ordered to be recorded

- An Indenture of Feofment between DANIEL NEWLAND of the one part and WILLIAM SMITH of the other part and Memorandum of Livery of Seisen and Receit thereon endorsed were acknowledged by the said DANIEL & ordered to be recorded

- An Indenture of Feofment between DANIEL NEWLAND of the one part and STEPHEN PRITCHARD of the other part with Memorandum of Livery of Seisen & Receit thereon endorsed were acknowledged by the said DANIEL & ordered to be recorded

- ZACHARIAH LEWIS, Captain, took the usual Oaths to his Majesties person and Government and subscribed the Test

p. Fauquier County Court 26th of June 1769

103 - On the motion of HENRY ELLISON by his Attorney, Judgment is granted him against THOMAS BRONAUGH & FRANCIS BRONAUGH, his Security, for fifty one pounds, twelve shillings and one penny current money and one hundred and sixty kfour pounds of nett tobacco with Interest thereon to be computed after the rate of five per centum per annum from the seventeenth day of October 1768 till paid (it being the amount of a Replevy Bond taken by the Sherif of this County by virtue of a Fierifacias to him directed) and his costs by him in this behalf expended, and the said THOMAS BRONAUGH and FRANCIS BRONAUGH, his Security, in mercy, &c., it appearing that the Deft. had legal notice of this motion

- JEFFRY JOHNSON, Plt. agt. JEFFRY JOHNSON, JUNR., Deft. In Case

Discontinued

- WILLIAM BLACKWELL, Plt. agt. JOHN KNOX, Exor. &c. of PETER HEDGEMAN, Deft. In Case

This suit abates by the Defts. death

- JAMES CRAP, Plt. agt. THOMAS SKINKER, Deft. In Case

Judgment is granted the Plt. against the said Deft. for his costs by him in this behalf expended and the said Deft. in mercy, &c.

- ELIZABETH KIERNS, Plt. agt. JOHN CHURCHHILL, Deft. In Case

This suit is agreed, and it is ordered that the Deft. pay to the Plt. her costs by her in this behalf expended

p. Fauquier County Court 26th of June 1769
104 - HUMPHREY BROOKE, Plt. agt. ANTHONY MORGAN, Deft. On an Attachment
Discontinued

- JOHN HACKNEY, Plt. agt. THOMAS CONNOR, Deft. In Case
This day came the Plt. by his Attorney and came also ROBERT ASHBY and became Special Bail and Pledge for the Deft. in this suit, and the said Deft. prays and has leave to imparl specially to the Plts. Declaration untill the next Court and then to plead

- An Indenture of Bargain and Sale between WILLIAM CHURCHHILL, JOHN CHURCHHILL and ARMISTEAD CHURCHHILL, Exors. of the Last Will and Testament of ARMISTEAD CHURCHHILL, deced., of the one part and WILLIAM BRENT of the other part and Receit thereon endorsed were proved by the Oaths of WILLIAM JONES, CHURCHHILL JONES and PHILIP ALLANSWORTH, witnesses thereto and ordered to be recorded

- Indentures of Lease and Release between JAMES GRINSTEAD & ELIZABETH his Wife of the one part and WILLIAM DULING of the other part and Receit thereon endorsed were proved by the Oaths of WILLIAM CARR and ORIGINAL YOUNG, witnesses thereto

- WILLIAM CARR, Plt. agt. ANDREW MARTIN, Deft. On an Attachment
Discontinued

- JAMES HATHAWAY, Plt. agt. PHILIP THOMAS, Deft. On an Attachment
Discontinued

p. Fauquier County Court 26th of June 1769
105 - HUMPHREY BROOKE, Plt. agt. ALEXANDER FARROR, Deft. On an Attachment
Discontinued

- JOHN BELL, Plt. agt. WILLIAM WRIGHT, Deft. On an Attachment
This Attachment abates by the Plts. death

- VINCENT GARNER, Plt. agt. JOHN GARNER, Deft. On an Attachment
Discontinued

- Messieurs GLASSFORD & HENDERSON, Plts. agt. WILLIAM WATTS, Deft. In Case
Discontinued, being agreed by the parties

- JOHN COMBS, Plt. agt. JOHN CUMMINS, Deft. On an Attachment
Judgment is granted the Plt. against the said Deft. for his costs by him in this behalf expended and the said Deft. in mercy, &c.

- ELIZABETH RENNOLDS, Admrx. of JOHN RENNOLDS, deced., Plt. agt.
FRANCIS MOORE, Deft. On an Attachment
This day came the Plt. by her Attorney and the Sherif haveing returned that he had attached a parcell of tobacco in the custody of SAMUEL MOORE, and the said SAMUEL MOORE, a Garnishee, being sworn declares that he hath sufficient effects in his hands to satisfy the Plts. debt and costs, and the said Deft. not appearing to replevy the same, tho called, It is considered by

p. Fauquier County Court 26th of June 1769
106 the Court that the Plt. recover against the said Deft. five pounds current money and his costs by him in this behalf expended and the said Deft. in mercy, &c.. And it is ordered that the effects in the Garnishees hands be condemned to satisfy this Judgment

- JAMES WINN, Plt. agt. WILLIAM FIELD, Deft. In Debt
This day came the Plt. by his Attorney and the said Deft. in his proper person and the said Deft. acknowledged the Plts. action against him for six pounds, one shilling and six pence, the Debt in the Declaration mentioned, Therefore it is considered by the Court

that the Plt. recover against the said Deft. the said six pounds, one shilling and six pence and his costs by him in this behalf expended, and the said Deft. in mercy, &c.

- Messieurs DAVID DALYELL, GEORGE OSWALD & CO., Plts. agt. JOHN POPE, Deft. On an Attachment

This day came the Plts. by their Attorney and ORIGINAL YOUNG, a Garnishee, being sworn declares that he has a Negro of the Defts. which he hired for three dollars and that he hath expended six shillings and twenty pounds of tobacco for the Defts. use and the said Deft. failing to appear and replevy the same, tho called, it is considered by the Court that the Plts. recover against the said Deft. eighteen pounds, fifteen shillings and nine pence half penny with Interest on seventeen pounds, sixteen shillings and a penny half penny, part thereof, to be computed after the rate of five per centum per annum from the Fourth day of January 1769 till paid and their costs by them in this behalf expended and the said Deft. in mercy, &c.

And it is ordered that the Sherif sell the Negroe in the Garnishees hands and return an account of the sale to the Court

p. Fauquier County Court 26th of June 1769

107 - JOHN BARNES, Plt. agt. THOMAS SLAUGHTER, Deft. In Case

By consent of the parties all matters in difference relative to this suit are refered to BENJAMIN ROBERTS and HENRY FIELDS, JUNR., and their Award or the Award of such person as they shall chuse for Umpire is case they disagree to be the Judgment of the Court

- JOHN BARNES, Plt. agt. REUBEN PAYNE, Deft. On an Attachment

This day came the Plt. by his Attorney and THOMAS GRUBS, a Garnishee, being sworn declares he owed the Deft. thirty five pounds at the time he was summoned as a Garnishee but has since paid it for the Defts. use, And the said Deft. not appearing, tho called, it is considered by the Court that the Plt. recover against the said Deft. twelve pounds, four shillings and six pence and his costs by him in this behalf expended, and the said Deft. in mercy, &c., And it is ordered that the money which was in the Garnishees hands at the time he was summoned be condemned to satisfy this Judgment

- CUTHBERT BULLITT, Plt. agt. REUBEN PAYNE, Deft. On an Attachment

This day came the Plt. in his proper person and THOMAS GRUBS, a Garnishee, being sworn declares that he owed the Deft. thirty five pounds at the time he was summoned a Garnishee but has since paid it for the Defts. use; And the said Deft. not appearing, tho called, It is considered by the Court that the Plt. recover against the said Deft. two pounds, thirteen shillings and ninepence and his costs by him in this behalf expended and the said Deft. in mercy, &c., And it is ordered that the money which was in the hands of the Garnishee at the time he was summoned be condemned towards satisfying this Judgment

p. Fauquier County Court 26th of June 1769

108 - On the motion of JOHN BARNES, it is ordered that WILLIAM FOOTE pay him two hundred and thirty seven pounds of tobacco for three days attendance and three time comeing eighteen miles and returning as a witness for him against REUBEN PAYNE

- On the motion of JOHN BARNES, it is ordered that EDWARD TURNER pay him fifty pounds of tobacco for two days attendance as a witness for him against STEPHEN McCORMACK

- On the motion of WILLIAM SLAUGHTER, it is ordered that THOMAS SLAUGHTER pay him two hundred and thirty seven pounds of tobacco for three days attendance and three times coming eighteen miles and returning as a witness for him at the suit of JOHN BARNES

- On the motion of GEORGE SLAUGHTER, it is ordered tht THOMAS SLAUGHTER pay him one hundred and seventy pounds of tobacco for two days attendance and twice comeing twenty miles and returning as a witness for him at the suit of JOHN BARNES

- On the motion of JOSEPH ALLAN, it is ordered that THOMAS SLAUGHTER pay him seventy five pounds of tobacco for three days attendance as a witness for him at the suit of JOHN BARNES

- On the motion of NATHANIEL REDMAN, it is ordered that JOHN BARNES pay him three hundred pounds of tobacco for three days attendance and three times comeing twenty five miles and returning as a witness for him against THOMAS SLAUGHTER, Gent.

- Present WILLIAM BLACKWELL, Gent.

- JOHN JETT, Plt. agt. WILLIAM ROBERTSON, Deft. On a Petition

Judgment is granted the Plt. against the said Deft. for five pounds current money and his costs by him in this behalf expended

- WILLIAM FIELD, Plt. agt. REUBIN PAYNE, Deft. On an Attachment

Discontinued

p. Fauquier County Court 26th of June 1769

109 - JOSEPH STRICKLIN and JACOB BONHAM, Plts. agt. WILLIAM PARKER, Deft. On a Petition

Judgment is granted the Plts. against the said Deft. for nine shillings and their costs by them in this behalf expended

- On the motion of JOHN FLETCHER, it is ordered that JOHN BARNES pay him seventy five pounds of tobacco for three days attendance as a witness for him against THOMAS SLAUGHTER

- On the motion of JOHN GRIMSLY, it is ordered that JOHN BARNES pay him seventy pounds of tobacco for one days attendance and comeing fifteen miles and returning as a witness for him against THOMAS SLAUGHTER

- JOHN BAILY, Special Bail for HENRY BOATMAN at the suit of WILLIAM BOGLE & COLLIN DUNLOP, Surviving Partners of PATRICK & WILLIAM BOGLEs and COLLIN DUNLOP of Glasgow, Merchants, surrendered him up in discharge of his recognizance and THOMAS MARSHALL and ELIAS EDMONDS came into Court and undertook and became Special Bail and Pledge for the Deft. in this suit

- ALEXANDER MOREHEAD is appointed Surveyor of the Road from the Forks of the Road below ELK RUN CHURCH to JOHN ASHBYs and it is ordered that he with the Tithes that shall be appointed by JEREMIAH DARNALL, Gent, do clear and keep the same in repair according to Law

- TILLMAN WEAVER is appointed Surveyor of the Road from JOHN ASHBYs to LICKING RUN and it is ordered that he with the Tithes that shall be appointed by JEREMIAH DARNALL, Gent., do clear and keep the same in repair according to Law

- On the motion of ORIGINAL YOUNG, it is ordered that JOSEPH STRICKLIN & JACOB BONHAM pay him fifty pounds of tobacco for two days attendance as a witness for them against WILLIAM PARKER

- PHILIP THOMAS, Plt. agt. THOMAS OXFORD, Deft. On a Petition

This Petition is dismist, and it is ordered that the Plt. pay to the Deft. his costs by him in this behalf expended

p. Fauquier County Court 26th of June 1769

110 - On the motion of GEORGE ROBERTS, it is ordered that THOMAS OXFORD pay him eighty five pounds of tobacco for one days attendance and comeing twenty miles and returning as a witness for him at the suit of PHILIP THOMAS

- The same Order for JOHN MORGAN

- Ordered that JOSEPH LAVELL, THOMAS BRONAUGH, JAMES ARNOLD and GEORGE CRUMP or any three of them being first sworn do view the most convenient way from KENDALLS BRANCH into the Main Road near VINCENT GARNERs and report thereof to the Court

- On the motion of JOHN McCORMACK, it is ordered that a Dedimus issue to take the Deposition of CUTHBERT McMILLIAN an infirm witness for him at the suit of JOHN SNELLING

- JAMES JOHNSTON, Assee of WILLIAM NEWTON, Plt. agt. JAMES BROWN, Deft. In Debt

This day came the Plt. by his Attorney and came also GERARD McCARTY and became Special Bail and Pledge for the Deft. in this suit, and the said Deft. prays Oyer of the Writing Obligatory and he hath it &c.

- Ordered that THOMAS BROOKS, THOMAS MATTHEWS, RHODAM TULLOS & JOSHUA TULLOS or any three of them being first sworn do view the most convenient way from COVINGTONs to JOHN EDGEs and report thereof to the Court

- Ordered that the Court be adjourned till tomorrow morning nine of the Clock

" WILLIAM BLACKWELL "

p. - At a Court continued and held for Fauquier County the 27th day of June 1769

111 Present THOMAS HARRISON, WILLIAM BLACKWELL, WILLIAM EDMONDS, JOSEPH BLACKWELL, WILLIAM EUSTACE, JAMES SCOTT & JOSEPH HUDNALL Gent.

- On the motion of JOHN WOODSIDE, it is ordered that GAVIN LAWSON pay him one hundred and fifty pounds of tobacco for six days attendance as a witness for him at the suit of JOHN SHUMATE

- CHARLES RECTOR, Plt. agt. GEORGE RUSSELL, Deft. In Case

Discontinued, being agreed by the parties

- GEORGE RUSSELL, Plt. agt. CHARLES RECTOR, Deft. In Trover

Discontineud, being agreed by the parties

- GEORGE RUSSELL, Plt. agt. HENRY RECTOR, Deft. In Trespass, Assault & Battery

This suit is agreed and it is ordered that the Deft. pay to the Plt. his costs by him in this behalf expended

- JOHN KEEBLE, Plt. agt. JOHN VICE, Deft. On an Attachment

This day came the parties by their Attornies and on hearing, it is considered by the Court that the Plt. recover against the said Deft. one pound, eight shillings and three pence and his costs by him in this behalf expended, and the said Deft. in mercy, &c. And JOHN GRIGSBY, a Garnishee, being summoned and not appearing

p. Fauquier County Court 27th of June 1769

112 to declare what effect he hath in his hands belonging to the Deft., it is ordered that an Attachment issue against him returnable to the next Court

- On the motion of WILLIAM LOVEL, it is ordered that JOHN VICE pay him fifty pounds of tobacco for two days attendance as a witness for him at the suit of JOHN KEEBLE

- The same Order for THOMAS OBANNON

- On the motion of JOHN KEEBLE, JUNR., it is ordered that JOHN KEEBLE pay him fifty pounds of tobacco for two days attendance as a witness for him against JOHN VICE

- The same Order for MOSES CONYERS

- WILLIAM SINCLAIR, Plt. agt. EDWARD WILLBURNE, Deft. On an Attachment Discontinued

- Messieurs COCKRANE & COMPANY, Plts. agt. JOHN POPE, Deft. On an Attachment This day came the Plt. by his Attorney and the Sherif haveing returned that he had attached one Rule and the said Deft. failing to appear & replevy the same, tho called, it is considered by the Court that the Plts. recover against the said Deft. thirteen pounds, fifteen shillings current money, and their costs by them in this behalf expended, and the said Deft. in mercy, &c., But this Judgment is to be discharged by the paiment of six pounds, seventeen shillings and six pence with Interest thereon to be computed after the rate of five per centum per annum from the sixth day of September 1768 till paid and the costs; And it is ordered that the Sherif sell the attached effects and return an account of the sales to the Court

p. Fauquier County Court 27th of June 1769

113 - JOHN NEILSON, Plt. agt. ALEXANDER WOODSIDE, Deft. On an Attachment This day came the Plt. by his Attorney and the Sherif haveing returned that he had levied the Attachment on the same goods as mentioned on JOHN WOODSIDEs Attachment and the said Deft. failing to appear and replevy the attached effects, tho called, it is considered by the Court that the Plt. recover against the said Deft. seven pounds, eighteen shillings and eleven pence and his costs by him in this behalf expended, and the said Deft. in mercy, &c., And it is ordered that the Sherif pay the Plt. the amount of this Judgment out of the money arriseing from the sale of the goods condemned by DOBBIEs Attachment against the said Deft.

- Present. JEREMIAH DARNALL, Gent.

- The Attachment obtained by JOHN NEILSON, JUNR. against the Estate of THOMAS GARNER is dismissed

- MARTIN PICKETT, Plt. agt. THOMAS ELLIOTT, Deft. On an Attachment This day came the Plt. by his Attorney and the Sherif haveing returned that he had attached four Cows and one Calf, five Yearlings, two Ewes & Lambs, one Desk, one Table, three Feather Beds and Furniture, two Chests, one Table, three Chairs, two Potts, one dozen Plaits, one hand Iron, one Wheel, one do., one Looking Glass, one Desk, five Spoons, one Slait, two Tubs, two Piggans, one Hogshead, three small Tubs, one Chest, one Frying Pan, one Ladle, one Flesh Fork, two Maires, a parcell of Wheat & Rye, and the Deft. failing to appear and replevy the attached effects, tho called,, it is considered by the Court that the Plt. recover against the said Deft. thirty two pounds, ten shillings and his costs by him in this behalf expended, and the said Deft. in mercy, And it is ordered that the Sherif sell the attached effects and return an account of the sale to the Court

p. Fauquier County Court 27th of June 1769

114 - JOSEPH HUDNALL, Gent., Plt. agt. BENJAMIN TURNER, Deft. On an Attachment This day came the Plt. by his Attorney and the Sherif haveing returned that he had attached one Pewter Plaite, and the Deft. failing to appear and replevy the same, tho called, it is considered by the Court that the Plt. recover against the said Deft. two pounds, eleven shillings and three pence and his costs by him in this behalf expended and the said Deft. in mercy, &c., And it is ordered that the Sherif sell the attached effects and return an account of the sales to the Court

- JOHN SINCLAIR, Plt. agt. ALEXANDER WOODSIDES, Deft. On an Attachment

This day came the Plt. by his Attorney and the Court being of opinion that the Plt. could not support this Attachment as the money therein mentioned would not become due untill the tenth day of June after the date of the Attachment, ordered that the same be dismissed;

From which Judgment the Plt. prayed an appeal to the eleventh day of the next General Court which is granted him, he haveing executed and acknowledged Bon as the Law directs

- Messieurs, ARCHIBALD HENDERSON & JOHN GLASSFORD, Merchants of Glasgow, Plts. agt. ALEXANDER WOODSIDE, Deft. On an Attachment

This day came the Plts. by their Attorney and the Court being of opinion that the proceedings in this Attachment are illegal and irregular, it is ordered that the same be dismissed, From which Judgment the Attorney for the Plts. prayed an appeal to the eleventh day of the next General Court which is granted them, Bond and Security being given as the Law directs

p. <u>Fauquier County Court 27th of June 1769</u>

115 - JOSEPH MARTIN, Plt. agt. JOSEPH REEDER, Deft. In Debt

This day came the Plt. by his Attorney and came also JOSEPH REEDER and became Special Bail and Pledge for the Deft. in this suit, and the said Deft. prays Oyer of the Writing Obligatory and to him it is granted, &c.

- Messieurs GLASSFORD & HENDERSON, Plts. agt. ALEXANDER WOODSIDE, On an Attachment

Discontinued

- JAMES ARNOLD, Plt. agt. THOMAS GARNER, Deft. On an Attachment

This day came the Plt. by his Attorney and the Sherif haveing returned that he had attached one small grey Horse, and the said Deft. not appearing to replevy the same, tho called, it is considered by the Court that the Plt. recover against the said Deft. five pounds current money and his costs by him in this behalf expended, and the said Deft. in mercy, &c., And it is ordered that the Sherif sell the attached effects and return an account of the sales to the Court

- The Attachment obtained by THOMAS POPE & JAMES ARNOLD against the Estate of THOMAS GARNER id dismissed

- SAMUEL RUST is appointed Surveyor of the Road in the room of WILLIAM ASBURY and it is ordered that he with the Tithes belonging thereto do clear and keep the same in repair according to Law

- On the motion of MATTHEW ADAMS, it is ordered that JOHN ANDERSON pay him fifty pounds of tobacco for two days attendance as a witness for him against BURGESS BALL, the suit, the suit being continued at his costs

- The same Order for JACOB ADAMS

p. <u>Fauquier County Court 27th of June 1769</u>

116 - On the motion of JOHN JONES, it is ordered that THOMAS SLAUGHTER pay him fifty pounds of tobacco for two days attendance as a witness for him at the suit of JOHN BARNES

- SAMUEL CLAYTON, JUNR., RICHARD POLLARD and WILLIAM WILLIAMS, Exors. &c. of AMBROSE KEMP, deced., Plts. agt. WILLIAM PINKARD, Deft. In Case

This day came the Plts. by their Attorney and came also FRANCIS BRONAUGH and became Special Bail and Pledge for the Deft. in this suit, and the said Deft. prays and has leave to imparl specially to the Plts. Declaration untill the next Court and then to plead

- THOMAS RENOE, Plt. agt. THOMAS GARNER, JUNIOR, Deft. In Case
Yhis day came the parties by their Attornies and thereupon came also a Jury, to wit, JAMES WINN, GEORGE GLASSCOCK, GEORGE BENNITT, SANFORD CARROL, WILLIAM ROBERTSON, WILLIAM CORDER, JOHN NEILSON, JOHN JAMES, JOSEPH ALLAN, JOHN RUSSELL, JOHN HATHAWAY & JOSEPH HUDNALL, who being elected tried and sworn the truth to speak upon the issue joined, upon their Oaths do say that the said Deft. did assume upon himself in manner and form as the Plt. against him hath declared and they do assess the Plts. damages by means of the Deft. breach of that assumption to seventeen pounds, thirteen shillings and eight pence besides his costs. Therefore it is considered by the Court that the Plt. recover against the said Deft. his damages aforesaid in form aforesaid assessed and his costs by him in this behalf expended, and the said Deft. in mercy, &c.

- GARRETT RAISONER, Plt. agt. WILLIAM SLAUGHTER, Deft. In Case
This suit is dismist and it is ordered that the Plt. pay to the Deft. his

p. Fauquier County Court 27th of June 1769
117 costs by him in this behalf expended

- On the motion of WILLIAM BLACKWELL, it is ordered that THOMAS RENOE pay him four hundred pounds of tobacco for sixteen days attendance as a witness for him against THOMAS GARNER, JUNIOR

- WILLIAM KITTSON, Plt. agt. FRANCIS JAMES, Deft. In Trespass, Assault and Battery
This day came the parties by their Attornies and thereupon came also a Jury, to wit, JAMES WITHERS, CHARLES MOREHEAD, JOSEPH STRICKLAND, JOHN HOPPER, JACOB ADAMS, JOHN SINCLAIR, FRANCIS BRONAUGH, JOHN SHUMATE, NICHOLAS SPRINGS, JOHN WOODSIDES, JAMES WINN & THOMAS SHUMATE, who being elected tried and sworn the truth to speak upon the issue joined, upon their Oaths do say that the said Deft. is Not Guilty in manner and form as the Plt. against him hath declared as by pleading he hath alledged; Therefore it is considered by the Court that the Plt. take nothing by his Bill but for his false clamour be in mercy, &c., And that the Deft. go thereof without day and recover against the Plt. his costs by him in this behalf expended

- On the motion of JEREMIAH DARNALL, Gent., it is ordered that THOMAS GARNER pay him seventy five pounds of tobacco for three days attendance as a witness for him againt THOMAS GARNER, JUNR.

- On the motion of JEREMIAH DARNALL, Gent., it is ordered that ELIZABETH KIERNS pay him seventy five pounds of tobacco for three days attendance as a witness for hier against JOHN CHURCHHILL

- On the motion of JOSEPH HUDNALL, it is ordered that WILLIAM KITTSON pay him two hundred pounds of tobacco for eight days attendance as a witness for him against FRANCIS JAMES

- Ordered that the Court be adjourned till tomorrow morning eight of the Clock

" THOMAS HARRISON "

p. - At a Court continued and held for Fauquier County the 28th day of June 1769
118 Present THOMAS HARRISON WILLIAM BLACKWELL
WILLIAM EUSTACE WILLIAM EDMONDS Gent.

- EUPHEMIA DAVIS, Plt. agt. PHILIP DAVIS, Deft. In Chancery
Ordered that GABRIEL JONES be made a Defendant in this suit and that a Subpaena in Chancery issue against him

- JAMES DUNCANSON, Assignee of GEORGE WITHERAL, Plt. agt. ELI THOMPSON and DANIEL GRINNAN, Defts. In Debt

The Deft., ELI, being arrested and not appearing, on the motion of the Plt. by his Attorney, it is ordered that Judgment be entered for the Plt. against him & WILLIAM McCLANAHAM, his Security, for the Debt in the Declaration mentioned unless, &c.

And this suit abates against the Deft., DANIEL, the Sherif haveing returned that he is no Inhabitant of this County

- JOHN HUDNALL, Plt. agt. JOHN CATLETT, Deft. In Debt

This day came the Plt. by his Attorney and the Sherif haveing returned on the Attachment awarded against the said Defts. Estate that he had attached one Spoon, and the Deft. failing to appear & replevy the same, tho called, it is considered by the Court that the Plt. recover against the said Deft. twelve pounds current money, the Debt in the Declaration mentioned, & his costs by him in this behalf expended, And the said Deft. in mercy, &c., And it is ordered that the Sherif sell the attached effects and return an account of the sales to the Court

p. Fauquier County Court 28th of June 1769

119 - SYLVESTER WELCH, Assee. of JOHN CREEL, Plt. agt. JOHN POPE WILLIAMS, Deft. In Debt

This day came the Plt. by his Attorney and the Sherif haveing returned on the Attachment awarded against the Defts. Estate that he had attached one Hog, and the said Deft. failing to appear and replevy the same, tho called, it is considered by the Court that the Plt. recover against the said Deft. one hundred and forty pounds current money, the Debt in the Declaration menmtioned, and his costs by him in this behalf expended, and the said Deft. in mercy, &c., But this Judgment is to be discharged by the paiment of twenty seven pounds, three shillings and six pence with Interest thereon to be computed after the rate of five per centum per annum from the twenty fourth day of February 1768 till paid and the costs

- JOHN WALLIS, Plt. agt. JAMES GARNER, Deft. In Case

This day came the Plt. by his Attorney and came also WILLIAM BLACKWELL and became Special Bail and Pledge for the Deft. in this suit, and the said Deft., altho solemnly called, doth not come nor say any thing in bar or preclusion of the Plts. action against him, whereby the Plt. remains against the said Deft. therein undefended; Therefore it is considered by the Court that Judgment be entered for the Plt. against the said Deft. for what damages shall appear the Plt. hath sustained by an Enquiry to be made at the next Court

- ORIGINAL YOUNG & JOHN BLACKWELL, Plts. agt. THOMAS WILLIAMS, Deft. In Debt

This day came the Plts. by their Attorney and the Sherif haveing returned

p. Fauquier County Court 28th of June 1769

120 on the Attachment awarded against the said Defts. Estate that he had attached one Snuff Box, and the Deft. not appearing to replevy the same, tho, called, it is considered by the Court that the Plt. recover against the said Deft. seven pounds, eight shillings and four pence current money, the Debt in the Declaration mentioned, and his costs by him in this behalf expended, and the said Deft. in mercy, &c. But this Judgment is to be discharged by the paiment of three pounds, fourteen shillings and two pence with Interest thereon to be computed after the rate of five per centum per annum from the twenty second day of August 1768 till paid and the costs; And it is ordered that the Sherif sell the attached effects and return an account of the sales to the Court

- ROGER DIXON, Assee. of NATHANIEL PENDLETON, Plt. agt. DANIEL BROWN & FRANCIS BROWN, Defts. In Debt

The Deft., DANIEL, not appearing, on the motion of the Plt. by his Attorney, it is ordered that an Attachment issue against his Estate for one hundred and forty nine pounds, eleven shillings & costs returnable to the next Court; and this suit abates against the Deft., FRANCIS, the Sherif haveing returned that he is no Inhabitant of this County

- WILLIAM EDMONDS, MOSES LUNSFORD, GEORGE PAYNE, JOHN EDMONDS, JOHN PINKARD & ROBERT PINKARD, Assignees of WILLIAM BLACKWELL, late Sherif of Fauquier County for the use of the said WILLIAM EDMONDS, FRANCIS BELL & Others, Plts. agt. ELIAS EDMONDS & WILLIAM ELLZEY, Defts. In Debt

This day came the Plts. by their Attorney and came also THOMAS KEITH and became Special Bail and Pledge for the Deft. ELIAS, in this suit, and the Deft. prays Oyer of the Writing Obligatory &

p. Fauquier County Court 28th of June 1769

121 he hath it, &c., and this suit abates against the Deft., WILLIAM, the Sherif haveing returned that he is no Inhabitant of this County

- ROBERT BRENT, Plt. agt. FRANCIS PAYNE, Deft. On a Petition

Judgment is granted the Plt. against the said Deft. for two pounds, seven shillings and eleven pence and his costs by him in this behalf expended. Execution stayed till November

- WILLIAM ALLASON, Plt. agt. JAMES OLDHAM, Deft. On a Petition

Judgment is granted the Plt. against the said Deft. for three pounds and his costs by him in this behalf expended. Execution stayed till October

- NEIL JAMESON & COMPANY, Plts. agt. JOHN CHURCHHILL, Deft. On a Petition

Judgment is granted the Plt. against the said Deft. for two pounds, eight shillings and their costs by them in this behalf expended

- PETER WAGONER, Plt. agt. JOHN JETT, Deft. On a Petition

Judgment is granted the Plt. against the said Deft. for two pounds, twelve shillings and his costs by him in this behalf expended

- PATRICK CARY, Plt. agt. JOSEPH WILLIAMS, Deft. On a Petition

Discontinued

- On the motion of CHARLES MOREHEAD, it is ordered that ELIAS EDMONDS pay him seventy five pounds of tobacco for three days attendance as a witness for ROBERT SANFORD against him, the Petition being continued at his cost

p. Fauquier County Court 28th of June 1769

122 - GREGORY SMITH, Exor. &c. of ROBERT ARMISTEAD, Plt. agt. WILLIAM HUTCHISON, Deft. On a Petition

Judgment is granted the Plt. against the said Deft. for three pounds current money and his costs by him in this behalf expended

- GREGORY SMITH, Exor. &c. of ROBERT ARMISTEAD, deced., Plt. agt. JOHN BLACK, Deft. On a Petition

Discontinued

- WILLIAM & JOSEPH DELANEYs, Plts. agt. ANDREW BARBEE, Deft. In Case

This suit is dismist and it is ordered that the Plts. pay to the Deft. his costs by him in this behalf expended

- The Same, Plts. agt. JOHN SMITH, Deft. In Case

This suit is dismist and it is ordered that the Plts. pay to the Deft. his costs by him in this behalf expended

- JAMES GALLANT, Assignee of WILLIAM BLACKWELL, late Sherif of Fauquier County, Plt. agt. DAVID BARTON & GEORGE BENNITT, Defts. In Debt

This day came the Plt. by his Attorney and thereupon a Jury, to wit, CHARLES MOREHEAD, NICHOLAS SPRINGS, FRANCIS PAYNE, FRANCIS ATWELL, WILLIAM JONES, WILLIAM KITTSON, FRANCIS JAMES, JOHN RUSSELL, VALENTINE HEART, JOHN HATHAWAY, GEORGE SULLIVAN and MINOR WIN, who being sworn well and truly to Enquire of damages in this suit, upon their Oaths do say that the Plt. hath sustained damages by means of the Defts. breach of the condition of the Bond in the Declaration mentioned

p. Fauquier County Court 28th of June 1769

123 to twenty two pounds, fifteen shillings and three pence besides his costs; Therefore it is considered by the Court that the Plt. recover against the said Defts. and JOHN BARTON & JAMES FOLEY, their Securities, his damages aforesaid in form aforesaid assessed and his costs by him in this behalf expended and the said Deft. in mercy &c.

- THOMAS GARNER, JUNR., Plt. agt. CHARLES MORGAN, Deft. In Case

This suit abates by the Defts. death

- NICHOLAS GEORGE, Plt. agt. THOMAS BULLITT, Deft. In Debt

This day came the parties by their Attorneys and the said Deft. relinquishing his former plea acknowledged the Plts. action against him; Therefore it is considered by the Court that the Plt. recover against the said Deft. twelve pounds current money, the Debt in the Declaration mentioned, and his costs by him in this behalf expended, and the said Deft. in mercy, &c., But this Judgment is to be discharged by the paiment of six pounds with Interest thereon to be computed after the rate of five per centum per annum from August 1766 till paid and the costs

- DAVID DALYELL, GEORGE OSWALD & COMPANY, Merchants in Glasgow, Plts. agt. MARY ISHAM KEITH, Deft. In Debt

This day came the parties by their Attornies and the said Deft. relinquishing her former plea acknowledged the Plts. action against her; Therefore it is considered by the Court that the Plts. recover against the said Deft. forty five pounds, two shillings & four pence current money, the Debt in the Declaration mentioned, and their costs by them in this behalf

p. Fauquier County Court 28th of June 1769

124 expended and the said Deft. in mercy, &c., But this Judgment is to be discharged by the paiment of twenty two pounds, eleven shillings and two pence with Interest thereon to be computed after the rate of five per centum per annum from the first day of November 1768 till paid and the costs

- JEFFRY JOHNSON, Plt. agt. THOMAS EDWARDS, Deft. In Debt

This day came the parties by their Attornies and the said Deft. relinquishing his former plea acknowledged the Plts. action against him; Therefore it is considered by the Court that the Plt. recover against the said Deft. forty seven punds, five shillings & four pence current money, the Debt in the Declaration mentioned, and the said Deft. in mercy &c., But this Judgment is to be discharged by the paiment of twenty three punds, twelve shillings and eight pence with Interest thereon to be computed after the rate of five per centum per annum fromthe first day of September 1767 till paid and the costs

- JOHN ROUSAU, Plt. agt. JAMES WINN, Deft. In Case

This day came the parties by their Attornies and the said Deft. relinquishing his former plea acknowledged the Plts. action against him for eight pounds, five shillings and seven pence current money, the Debt in the Declaration mentioned; Therefore it is considered by the Court that the Plt. recover against the said Deft. the said eight pounds, five shillings and seven pence and his costs by him in this behalf expended, And the said Deft. in mercy, &c.

- GEORGE WILLSON, Plt. agt. JAMES WINN, Deft. In Debt

This day came the parties by their Attornies and the said

p. Fauquier County Court 28th of June 1769

125 Deft. relinquishing his former plea acknowledged the Plts. action against him; Therefore it is considered by the Court that the Plt. recover against the said Deft. thirty eight pounds, six shillings current money, the Debt in the Declaration mentioned and his costs by him in this behalf expended; And the said Deft. in mercy, &c., But this Judgment is to be discharged by the paiment of nineteen pounds, three shillings with Interest thereon to be computed after the rate of five percentum per annum from the twenty eighth day of July 1767 till paid and the costs

- ELIZABETH FALLIN, Assignee of THOMAS MARSHALL, Sherif, Plt. agt. JAMES CUMMINGS, WILLIAM REDDING & JOSEPH WILLIAMS, Defts. In Debt

This day came the Plt. by her Attorney and thereupon a Jury, to wit, CHARLES MOREHEAD, NICHOLAS SPRINGS, FRANCIS PAYNE, FRANCIS ATWELL, WILLIAM JONES, WILLIAM KITTSON, FRANCIS JAMES, JOHN RUSSELL, VALENTINE HEART, JOHN HATHAWAY, GEORGE SULLIVAN and MINOR WINN, who being sworn well and truly to Enquire of the damages in this suit, upon their Oaths do say that the Plt. hath sustained damages by means of the Defts. breach of the condition of the Bond in the Declaration mentioned to four pounds, eight shilligns and ten pence besides his costs. Therefore it is considered by the Court that the Plt. recover against the said Deft. his damages aforesaid in form aforesaid assessed and her costs by her in this behalf expended and the said Deft. in mercy, &c., And it is ordered that the money attached by the Sherif be condemned towards satisfying this Judgment and that he sell the attached effects and return an account of the sales to the Court

- WILLIAM ALLASON, Plt. agt. JOHN HARMANS, Deft. In Debt

This day came the parties by their Attornies and the said Deft. relinquishing his former plea acknowledged the Plts. action against him. Therefore

p. Fauquier County Court 28th of June 1769

126 it is considered by the Court that the Plt. recover against the said Deft. twenty eight pounds, sixteen shillings and eight pence current money, the Debt in the Declaration mentioned, and his costs by him in this behalf expended; And the said Deft. in mercy, &c., But this Judgment is to be discharged by the paiment of fourteen pounds, eight shillings & four pence with Interest thereon to be computed after the rate of five percentum per annum from the twenty fifth day of July 1768 till paid and the costs

- On the motion of NICHOLAS SPRINGS, it is ordered that PETER WAGONER pay him seventy five pounds of tobacco for three days attendance as a witness for him against JOHN JETT

- ANTHONY GARRETT, who as well for our Lord the King as for himself sues Plt. agt. JOHN HAILY, Deft. In Debt

Dismist

- JAMES OLDHAM who sues as well for our Lord the King as himself, Plt. agt. JOHN HAILY, Deft. In Debt

Dismist

- PETER CARTER and ELIZABETH his Wife, Plts. agt. FORTUNATUS & WILLIAM LEGG, Defts. In Debt

The Deft., WILLIAM, being arrested and not appearing, on the motion of the Plts. by their Attorney, it is ordered that Judgment be entered fro the Plts. against the said Deft., WILLIAM, and EDWARD DICKINSON, his Security, for the Debt in the Declaration mentioned unless, &c. And this suit abates against the Deft., FORTUNATUS, the Sherif haveing returned that he is no Inhabitant of this County

- THOMAS JETT, Assignee of ANDREW MONROE, Plt. agt. MARY SMITH, Deft. In Debt

Abates by the Defts. death

p. 127 Fauquier County Court 28th of June 1769

- THOMAS SMITH, Plt. agt. BENJAMIN PIPER, Deft. In Case

This suit is agreed and it is ordered that the Plt. pay to the Deft. his costs by him in this behalf expended

- PRESLY THORNTON and FRANCIS THORNTON, Exors. of FRANCIS THORNTON, deced., Plts. agt. THOMAS WATTS, Deft. In Case

This suit abates by the Defts. death

- AMBROSE KEMP, Plt. agt. WILLIAM PINKARD, Deft. In Case

This suit abates by the Plts. death

- PEGGY EDGAR, Plt. agt. JOHN WOODSIDES, Deft. In Case

This suit abates by the Plts. marriage

- WILLIAM DULANY, Plt. agt. JOHN KNOX, Deft. In Case

This suit abates by the Defts. death

- ORIGINAL YOUNG, Plt. agt. EDWARD LAWRENCE, Deft. In Trespass, Assault & Battery

EDWARD LAWRENCE is appointed Guardian to the Deft. to defend him in this suit, and the said Deft. by his Guardian comes and defends the force and injury when, &c., and pleads Not Guilty with leave, and the Trial of the issue is refered to the next Court

- On the motion of JOHN RUSSELL, it is ordered that FRANCIS JAMES pay him four hundred and fifty pounds of tobacco for eighteen days attendance as

p. 128 Fauquier County Court 28th of June 1769

a witness for him at the suit of WILLIAM KITTSON

- Present. ARMISTEAD CHURCHHILL, Gent.

- On the motion of GAVIN LAWSON, an Injunction is granted him to stay the Execution of a Judgment obtained at the last Court by JOHN SHUMATE against him untill the matter can be heard in Equity on a Bill for that purpose this day filed, Bond and security being given as the Law directs

- Ordered that the Court be adjourned till the Court in Course

" THOMAS HARRISON "

p. 129 - At a Court held for Fauquier County the 28th day of August 1769 for the Examination of JOHN HOLLIS for Felony

Present ARMISTEAD CHURCHHILL, WILLIAM EDMONDS, JEREMIAH DARNALL, JAMES SCOTT & JOSEPH HUDNALL Gent.

- The said JOHN HOLLIS who was committed to the Goal of thsi County and charged with the Felonious breaking and entering the House of ALEXANDER McKINTON and stealing a Silver Watch, the property of the said ALEXANDER McKINTON. It appearing to the Court that the said Offence is as committed in the County of LOUDOUN and the Court being of the opinion that the said HOLLIS ought to be there tried for the said offence, It is ordered that he be remanded to Goal in order to be sent to the said County of LOUDOUN for examination

ARMISTEAD CHURCHHILL

(Fauquier County Minute Book, 1768-1773, will be continued in another book beginning on page 130 with the Court held for Fauquier County the 28th day of October 1769.)

 (Keith, contd.)

Heritage Books by Ruth and Sam Sparacio:

Abstracts of Account Books of Edward Dixon, Merchant of Port Royal, Virginia, Volume I: 1743–1747

Abstracts of Account Books of Edward Dixon, Merchant of Port Royal, Virginia, Volume II

Albemarle County, Virginia Deed and Will Book Abstracts, 1748–1752

Albemarle County, Virginia Deed Book Abstracts, 1758–1761

Albemarle County, Virginia Deed Book Abstracts, 1761–1764

Albemarle County, Virginia Deed Book Abstracts, 1764–1768

Albemarle County, Virginia Deed Book Abstracts, 1768–1770

Albemarle County, Virginia Deed Book Abstracts, 1776–1778

Albemarle County, Virginia Deed Book Abstracts, 1778–1780

Albemarle County, Virginia Deed Book Abstracts, 1780–1783

Albemarle County, Virginia Deed Book Abstracts, 1787–1790

Albemarle County, Virginia Deed Book Abstracts, 1790–1791

Albemarle County, Virginia Deed Book Abstracts, 1791–1793

Augusta County, Virginia Land Tax Books, 1782–1788

Augusta County, Virginia Land Tax Books, 1788–1790

Amherst County, Virginia Land Tax Books, 1789–1791

Caroline County, Virginia Appeals and Land Causes, 1787–1794

Caroline County, Virginia Committee of Safety and Early Surveys, 1729–1762 and 1774–1775

Caroline County, Virginia Land Tax Book Alterations, 1782–1789

Caroline County, Virginia Land Tax Book Alterations, 1792–1795

Caroline County, Virginia Land Tax Book Alterations, 1795–1798

Caroline County, Virginia Order Book Abstracts, 1765

Caroline County, Virginia Order Book Abstracts, 1767–1768

Caroline County, Virginia Order Book Abstracts, 1768–1770

Caroline County, Virginia Order Book Abstracts, 1770–1771

Caroline County, Virginia Order Book, 1764

Caroline County, Virginia Order Book, 1765–1767

Caroline County, Virginia Order Book, 1771–1772

Caroline County, Virginia Order Book, 1772–1773

Caroline County, Virginia Order Book, 1773

Caroline County, Virginia Order Book, 1773–1774

Caroline County, Virginia Order Book, 1774–1778

Caroline County, Virginia Order Book, 1778–1781

Caroline County, Virginia Order Book, 1781–1783

Caroline County, Virginia Order Book, 1783–1784

Caroline County, Virginia Order Book, 1784–1785

Caroline County, Virginia Order Book, 1785–1786

Caroline County, Virginia Order Book, 1786–1787

Caroline County, Virginia Order Book, 1787, Part 1

Caroline County, Virginia Order Book, 1787, Part 2

Caroline County, Virginia Order Book, 1787–1788

Caroline County, Virginia Order Book, 1788

Culpeper County, Virginia Deed Book Abstracts, 1795–1796

Culpeper County, Virginia Land Tax Book, 1782–1786

Culpeper County, Virginia Land Tax Book, 1787–1789

Culpeper County, Virginia Minute Book, 1763–1764

Digest of Family Relationships, 1650–1692, from Virginia County Court Records

Digest of Family Relationships, 1720–1750, from Virginia County Court Records

Digest of Family Relationships, 1750–1763, from Virginia County Court Records

Digest of Family Relationships, 1764–1775, from Virginia County Court Records

Essex County, Virginia Deed and Will Abstracts, 1695–1697

Essex County, Virginia Deed and Will Abstracts, 1697–1699

Essex County, Virginia Deed and Will Abstracts, 1699–1701

Essex County, Virginia Deed and Will Abstracts, 1701–1703

Essex County, Virginia Deed and Will Abstracts, 1745–1749

Essex County, Virginia Deed and Will Book, 1692–1693

Essex County, Virginia Deed and Will Book, 1693–1694

Essex County, Virginia Deed and Will Book, 1694–1695

Essex County, Virginia Deed and Will Book, 1701–1704

Essex County, Virginia Deed, 1753–1754 and Will Book 1750

Essex County, Virginia Deed Abstracts, 1721–1724

Essex County, Virginia Deed Book, 1724–1728

Essex County, Virginia Deed Book, 1728–1733

Essex County, Virginia Deed Book, 1733–1738

Essex County, Virginia Deed Book, 1738–1742

Essex County, Virginia Deed Book, 1742–1745

Essex County, Virginia Deed Book, 1749–1751

Essex County, Virginia Deed Book, 1751–1753

Essex County, Virginia Land Trials Abstracts, 1711–1716 and 1715–1741

Essex County, Virginia Order Book Abstracts, 1695–1699

Essex County, Virginia Order Book Abstracts, 1699–1702

Essex County, Virginia Order Book Abstracts, 1716–1723, Part 1

Essex County, Virginia Order Book Abstracts, 1716–1723, Part 2

Essex County, Virginia Order Book Abstracts, 1716–1723, Part 3

Essex County, Virginia Order Book Abstracts, 1716–1723, Part 4

Essex County, Virginia Order Book Abstracts, 1723–1725, Part 1

Essex County, Virginia Order Book Abstracts, 1723–1725, Part 2

Essex County, Virginia Order Book Abstracts, 1725–1729, Part 1

Essex County, Virginia Order Book Abstracts, 1727–1729

Essex County, Virginia Order Book, 1695–1699

Essex County, Virginia Will Abstracts, 1730–1735

Essex County, Virginia Will Abstracts, 1735–1743

Essex County, Virginia Will Abstracts, 1745–1748

Fairfax County, Virginia Deed Abstracts, 1799–1800 and 1803–1804

Fairfax County, Virginia Deed Abstracts, 1804–1805

Fairfax County, Virginia Deed Book Abstracts, 1799

Fairfax County, Virginia Deed Book, 1798–1799

Fairfax County, Virginia Land Causes, 1788–1824

Fauquier County, Virginia Minute Book Abstracts, 1759–1761

Fauquier County, Virginia Minute Book Abstracts, 1761–1762

Fauquier County, Virginia Minute Book Abstracts, 1766–1767

Fauquier County, Virginia Minute Book Abstracts, 1767–1769

Fauquier County, Virginia Minute Book Abstracts, 1769–1771

Hanover County, Virginia Land Tax Book, 1782–1788

Hanover County, Virginia Land Tax Book, 1789–1793

Hanover County, Virginia Land Tax Book, 1793–1796

King George County, Virginia Order Book Abstracts, 1721–1723

King George County, Virginia Deed Book Abstracts, 1721–1735

King George County, Virginia Deed Book Abstracts, 1735–1752

King George County, Virginia Deed Book Abstracts, 1753–1773

King George County, Virginia Deed Book Abstracts, 1773–1783

King George County, Virginia Will Book Abstracts, 1752–1780

King William County, Virginia Record Book, 1702–1705

King William County, Virginia Record Book, 1705–1721

King William County, Virginia Record Book, 1722 and 1785–1786

Lancaster County, Virginia Deed and Will Book, 1652–1657

Lancaster County, Virginia Deed and Will Book, 1654–1661

Lancaster County, Virginia Deed and Will Book, 1661–1702 (1661–1666 and 1699–1702)

Lancaster County, Virginia Deed Book Abstracts, 1701–1706

Lancaster County, Virginia Deed Book, 1710–1714

Lancaster County, Virginia Order Book Abstracts, 1656–1661

Lancaster County, Virginia Order Book Abstracts, 1662–1666

Lancaster County, Virginia Order Book Abstracts, 1666–1669

Lancaster County, Virginia Order Book Abstracts, 1670–1674

Lancaster County, Virginia Order Book Abstracts, 1674–1678

Lancaster County, Virginia Order Book Abstracts, 1678–1681

Lancaster County, Virginia Order Book Abstracts, 1682–1687

Lancaster County, Virginia Order Book Abstracts, 1729–1732

Lancaster County, Virginia Order Book Abstracts, 1736–1739

Lancaster County, Virginia Order Book Abstracts, 1739–1742

Lancaster County, Virginia Order Book, 1687–1691

Lancaster County, Virginia Order Book, 1691–1695

Lancaster County, Virginia Order Book, 1695–1699

Lancaster County, Virginia Order Book, 1699–1701

Lancaster County, Virginia Order Book, 1701–1703

Lancaster County, Virginia Order Book, 1703–1706

Lancaster County, Virginia Order Book, 1732–1736

Lancaster County, Virginia Will Book, 1675–1689

Loudoun County, Virginia Order Book, 1763–1764

Loudoun County, Virginia Order Book, 1764

Louisa County, Virginia Deed Book, 1744–1746

Louisa County, Virginia Order Book, 1742–1744

Madison County, Virginia Deed Book Abstracts, 1793–1804

Madison County, Virginia Deed Book, 1793–1813, and Marriage Bonds, 1793–1800

Middlesex County, Virginia Deed Book, 1679–1688

Middlesex County, Virginia Deed Book, 1688–1694

Middlesex County, Virginia Deed Book, 1694–1703

Middlesex County, Virginia Deed Book, 1703–1709

Middlesex County, Virginia Deed Book, 1709–1720

Middlesex County, Virginia Order Book Abstracts, 1686–1690

Middlesex County, Virginia Order Book Abstracts, 1697–1700

Middlesex County, Virginia Record Book, 1721–1813

Northumberland County, Virginia Deed and Will Book, 1650–1655

Northumberland County, Virginia Deed and Will Book, 1655–1658

Northumberland County, Virginia Deed and Will Book, 1658–1662

Northumberland County, Virginia Deed and Will Book, 1662–1666

Northumberland County, Virginia Deed and Will Book, 1666–1670

Northumberland County, Virginia Deed and Will Book, 1670–1672 and 1706–1711

Northumberland County, Virginia Deed and Will Book, 1711–1712

Northumberland County, Virginia Order Book, 1652–1657

Northumberland County, Virginia Order Book, 1657–1661

Northumberland County, Virginia Order Book, 1665–1669

Northumberland County, Virginia Order Book, 1669–1673

Northumberland County, Virginia Order Book, 1680–1683

Northumberland County, Virginia Order Book, 1683–1686

Northumberland County, Virginia Order Book, 1699–1700

Northumberland County, Virginia Order Book, 1700–1702

Northumberland County, Virginia Order Book, 1702–1704

Orange County, Virginia, Chancery Suits, 1831–1845

Orange County, Virginia Deeds, 1743–1759

Orange County, Virginia Deed Book Abstracts, 1759–1778

Orange County, Virginia Deed Book Abstracts, 1778–1786

Orange County, Virginia Deed Book Abstracts, 1795–1797

Orange County, Virginia Deed Book Abstracts, 1797–1799

Orange County, Virginia Deed Book Abstracts, 1799–1800

Orange County, Virginia Deed Book Abstracts, 1800–1802

Orange County, Virginia Deed Book Abstracts, 1786–1791, Deed Book 19

Orange County, Virginia Deed Book Abstracts, 1791–1795, Deed Book 20

Orange County, Virginia Land Tax Book, 1782–1790

Orange County, Virginia Land Tax Book, 1791–1795

Orange County, Virginia Order Book Abstracts, 1747–1748

Orange County, Virginia Order Book Abstracts, 1748–1749

Orange County, Virginia Order Book Abstracts, 1749–1752

Orange County, Virginia Order Book Abstracts, 1752–1753

Orange County, Virginia Order Book Abstracts, 1753–1754

Orange County, Virginia Order Book Abstracts, 1755–1756

Orange County, Virginia Order Book Abstracts, 1756–1757

Orange County, Virginia Order Book Abstracts, 1757–1759

Orange County, Virginia Order Book Abstracts, 1759–1762

Orange County, Virginia Order Book Abstracts, 1762–1763

Orange County, Virginia Will Abstracts, 1778–1821

Orange County, Virginia Will Abstracts, 1821–1838

Orange County, Virginia, Will Digest, 1734–1838

Pamunkey Neighbors of Orange County, Virginia (Transcriptions from the original files of County Courts in Virginia, Kentucky and Missouri of wills, deeds, order books & marriages as well as some family lines...)

A Supplement to Pamunkey Neighbors of Orange County, Virginia, Volumes 1 and 2
Ruth and Sam Sparacio, Luretta and Eldon Corkill

Petersburg City, Virginia Hustings Court Deed Book Abstracts, 1784–1787

Petersburg City, Virginia Hustings Court Deed Book Abstracts, 1787–1790

Petersburg City, Virginia Hustings Court Deed Book Abstracts, 1790–1793

Prince William County, Virginia Deed Book Abstracts, 1749–1752

Prince William County, Virginia Order Book Abstracts, 1752–1753

Prince William County, Virginia Order Book Abstracts, 1753–1757

(Old) Rappahannock County, Virginia Deed and Will Book Abstracts, 1656–1662

(Old) Rappahannock County, Virginia Deed and Will Book Abstracts, 1662–1665

(Old) Rappahannock County, Virginia Deed and Will Book Abstracts, 1663–1668

(Old) Rappahannock County, Virginia Deed and Will Book Abstracts, 1665–1677

(Old) Rappahannock County, Virginia Deed and Will Book Abstracts, 1668–1670

(Old) Rappahannock County, Virginia Deed and Will Book Abstracts, 1670–1672

(Old) Rappahannock County, Virginia Deed and Will Book Abstracts, 1672–1673/4

(Old) Rappahannock County, Virginia Deed and Will Book Abstracts, 1673/4–1676

(Old) Rappahannock County, Virginia Deed and Will Book Abstracts, 1677–1678/9

(Old) Rappahannock County, Virginia Deed and Will Book Abstracts, 1678/9–1682

(Old) Rappahannock County, Virginia Deed and Will Book Abstracts, 1682–1686

(Old) Rappahannock County, Virginia Deed and Will Book Abstracts, 1686–1688

(Old) Rappahannock County, Virginia Deed and Will Book Abstracts, 1688–1692

(Old) Rappahannock County, Virginia Order Book Abstracts, 1683–1685

(Old) Rappahannock County, Virginia Order Book Abstracts, 1689–1692

(Old) Rappahannock County, Virginia Will Book Abstracts, 1682–1687

Richmond County, Virginia Deed Book Abstracts, 1692–1695

Richmond County, Virginia Deed Book Abstracts, 1695–1701

Richmond County, Virginia Deed Book Abstracts, 1701–1704

Richmond County, Virginia Deed Book Abstracts, 1705–1708

Richmond County, Virginia Deed Book Abstracts, 1708–1711

Richmond County, Virginia Deed Book Abstracts, 1711–1714

Richmond County, Virginia Deed Book Abstracts, 1715–1718

Richmond County, Virginia Deed Book Abstracts, 1718–1719

Richmond County, Virginia Deed Book Abstracts, 1719–1721

Richmond County, Virginia Deed Book Abstracts, 1721–1725

Richmond County, Virginia Order Book Abstracts, 1694–1697

Richmond County, Virginia Order Book Abstracts, 1697–1699

Richmond County, Virginia Order Book Abstracts, 1699–1701

Richmond County, Virginia Order Book Abstracts, 1714–1715

Richmond County, Virginia Order Book Abstracts, 1719–1721

Richmond County, Virginia Order Book Abstracts, 1721–1725

Richmond County, Virginia Order Book, 1692–1694

Richmond County, Virginia Order Book, 1702–1704

Richmond County, Virginia Order Book, 1717–1718

Richmond County, Virginia Order Book, 1718–1719

Spotsylvania County, Virginia Deed Book, 1722–1725

Spotsylvania County, Virginia Deed Book, 1725–1728

Spotsylvania County, Virginia Deed Book: 1730–1731

Spotsylvania County, Virginia Order Book Abstracts, 1742–1744

Spotsylvania County, Virginia Order Book Abstracts, 1744–1746

Stafford County, Virginia Deed and Will Book, 1686–1689

Stafford County, Virginia Deed and Will Book, 1689–1693

Stafford County, Virginia Deed and Will Book, 1699–1709

Stafford County, Virginia Deed and Will Book, 1780–1786, and Scheme Book Orders, 1790–1793

Stafford County, Virginia Deed Book, 1722–1728 and 1755–1765

Stafford County, Virginia Order Book, 1664–1668 and 1689–1690

Stafford County, Virginia Order Book, 1691–1692

Stafford County, Virginia Order Book, 1692–1693

Stafford County, Virginia Will Book, 1729–1748

Stafford County, Virginia Will Book, 1748–1767

Westmoreland County, Virginia Deed and Will Abstracts, 1723–1726

Westmoreland County, Virginia Deed and Will Abstracts, 1726–1729

Westmoreland County, Virginia Deed and Will Abstracts, 1729–1732

Westmoreland County, Virginia Deed and Will Abstracts, 1732–1734

Westmoreland County, Virginia Deed and Will Abstracts, 1734–1736

Westmoreland County, Virginia Deed and Will Abstracts, 1736–1740

Westmoreland County, Virginia Deed and Will Abstracts, 1740–1742

Westmoreland County, Virginia Deed and Will Abstracts, 1742–1745

Westmoreland County, Virginia Deed and Will Abstracts, 1745–1747

Westmoreland County, Virginia Deed and Will Abstracts, 1747–1748

Westmoreland County, Virginia Deed and Will Abstracts, 1749–1751

Westmoreland County, Virginia Deed and Will Abstracts, 1751–1754

Westmoreland County, Virginia Deed and Will Abstracts, 1754–1756

Westmoreland County, Virginia Order Book, 1705–1707

Westmoreland County, Virginia Order Book, 1707–1709

Westmoreland County, Virginia Order Book, 1709–1712

www.ingramcontent.com/pod-product-compliance
Lightning Source LLC
Chambersburg PA
CBHW080336270326
41927CB00014B/3246
* 9 7 8 1 6 8 0 3 4 4 8 7 5 *